Shoot Like a Pro!

DIGITAL PHOTOGRAPHY TECHNIQUES

About the Author

Photographer Julie Adair King is the author of several popular books about digital photography and photo editing. Her most recent titles include *Digital Photography For Dummies, Photo Retouching and Restoration For Dummies, Easy Web Graphics,* and *Adobe PhotoDeluxe For Dummies.* A graduate of Purdue University, King established her own company, Julie King Creative, in 1988, in Indianapolis, Indiana.

Shoot Like a Pro!

DIGITAL PHOTOGRAPHY TECHNIQUES

Julie Adair King

McGraw-Hill/Osborne

New York   Chicago   San Francisco   Lisbon   London   Madrid   Mexico City
Milan   New Delhi   San Juan   Seoul   Singapore   Sydney   Toronto

The McGraw·Hill Companies

McGraw-Hill/Osborne
2100 Powell Street, 10 Floor
Emeryville, California 94608
U.S.A.

To arrange bulk purchase discounts for sales promotions, premiums, or fund-raisers, please contact
McGraw-Hill/Osborne at the above address. For information on translations or book distributors
outside the U.S.A., please see the International Contact Information page immediately following the
index of this book.

Shoot Like a Pro! Digital Photography Techniques

1234567890 QPD QPD 019876543

ISBN 0-07-222949-7

Publisher
Brandon A. Nordin

Vice President &
Associate Publisher
Scott Rogers

Executive Acquisitions Editor
Jane K. Brownlow

Senior Project Editor
LeeAnn Pickrell

Acquisitions Coordinator
Tana Allen

Technical Editor
Alfred DeBat

Copy Editor
Lisa Theobald

Proofreader
Marian Selig

Indexer
Karin Arrigoni

Illustrators
Lyssa Wald, Kathleen Edwards,
Melinda Lytle, Will Voss

Series Designer
Jean Butterfield

Cover Design
Pattie Lee, Jeff Weeks

Cover Photograph
© Albert Normandin/Masterfile

This book was composed with Corel VENTURA™ Publisher.

Contents at a Glance

Contents

I Gearing Up for Great Pictures

II   Discovering the Secrets of the Pros

3   Taking Memorable Portraits 47

III Printing and Sharing Your Photos

IV Appendixes

Acknowledgments

I am deeply indebted to many people who helped make this book a reality, starting with Jane Brownlow, Tana Allen, LeeAnn Pickrell, Lisa Theobald, Dodie Shoemaker, Jean Butterfield, Lyssa Wald, and everyone else at McGraw-Hill/Osborne who lent their talents to the project. I also want to express my thanks to my wonderful agent, Danielle Jatlow, for everything she does on my behalf, and to Will Voss for bringing his design skills to the color insert.

In addition, I was blessed to have photography guru Alfred DeBat on board as technical editor. Al, your generosity in sharing your knowledge is truly appreciated.

I'm also grateful to all the companies that provided information and product loans for this book, especially the following:

ACDSystems   Adobe Systems   Bogen Photo/Manfrotto
Canon USA   Cokin   Epson America
Fuji Photo Film   Hewlett-Packard   Lowel
Minolta   Monaco Systems   nik multimedia
Nikon   Olympus America   Tiffen

Last, but absolutely not least, a huge thank you to the people who let me photograph them for this book: Terry and Mary Beth Ingram; Barbara and Dale King; Lana, Lisa, and Newton Kinney; Betsy Kranz; and Laura and Brandon Wright. I love you all for being such good sports—not to mention the immeasurable other ways you make my world a little brighter.

Introduction

As someone who writes photography books, I often get calls from friends and colleagues who are unhappy with their current cameras and want me to recommend something that "takes better pictures." Nine times out of ten, further discussion reveals that a new camera isn't the answer. All most people need to turn out terrific photos is simply a little technical guidance and some help with their photographic technique.

To get good results from a digital camera, you need to understand traditional photography controls, such as exposure and focus options. That's only half the story, however. You also have to master digital-only features such as white balance, resolution, and image file formats.

Professional photographers go to school for years to study these subjects and refine their craft. Just because you have neither the time nor the inclination to get a degree in photography doesn't mean that you, too, can't take professional-looking pictures, however. With this book, you can get stellar results from your digital camera without setting foot inside a classroom.

Shoot Like a Pro! Digital Photography Techniques condenses the most important lessons of photography school into one, easy-to-digest package. You'll not only get the information you need to decipher the jargon associated with digital photography, but also learn techniques that enable you to take full advantage of all the creative controls your camera offers.

Each chapter shows you secrets that the pros use every day to get perfect pictures, no matter how challenging the subject. Whatever you want to do with your digital camera, from taking product shots for your business to capturing a family celebration, this book will help *you* look like a pro.

Better Photography: It's Easier (and Cheaper) Than You Think

If you're just beginning to explore photography or if you're new to the digital side of things—or both—you may be intimidated by all the new lingo that you encounter. Thumb through the color insert in this book, for example, and you'll probably see at least a few terms that are completely foreign to you.

Unfortunately, both the photography and computer industries are infatuated with technical jargon. Bring the two together, and you get twice the technospeak. As a result, concepts that are actually quite simple seem incredibly complex. Rest assured that you don't need photography or computer experience to successfully use the techniques featured in this book. I'll give you all the background information you need to understand each concept.

Nor do you need expensive, studio-level equipment. Some techniques that I discuss do involve features that aren't found on low-cost, entry-level digital cameras—things like manual exposure control, for example. Don't fret if your camera doesn't offer all the bells and whistles; I'll show you ways to achieve similar results with even a basic, fully automatic camera.

As for the techniques themselves, I've concentrated on tricks that make a big impact without being complicated. In fact, most people are surprised to find out just how *easily* they can improve their pictures by incorporating these techniques into their shooting routine. I think you will be, too.

Pixels to Portraits to Panoramas: All You Need to Know

This book emphasizes simple, practical ways to get pro-quality results with your digital camera. Among other things, you'll find out how to

- Take better advantage of all the options on your digital camera—from resolution to ISO to exposure metering mode.

- Shoot flattering formal portraits and memorable family snapshots.

- Take dynamic product shots for your company's ads or web site.

- Exploit your camera's macro-focusing capabilities to capture the intricate details of a subject.

- Create seamless wide-format panoramas and 360-degree virtual reality images.

- Manipulate colors using traditional and digital filters.

- Solve common photo problems, such as eliminating reflections in glass objects, wiping out red-eye, and working in dim lighting.

- Produce stunning, long-lasting prints of your favorite pictures.

- Prepare image files for use on the web or in a multimedia presentation.

Along the way, I'll introduce you to camera accessories that can enhance your photography as well as computer hardware and software that make photo retouching and file management a breeze. Most of these products are very affordable—you may even be able to find a no-cost solution just by looking around your home or office.

A few products, such as tripod heads for shooting panoramas and special macro flash units, *are* on the expensive side. But if you specialize in the type of projects that call for these accessories, you'll find that they'll quickly pay for themselves by saving you time and frustration.

Margin Icons, Featured Software, and Other Details

To help you quickly locate the information that's of most interest to you, this book uses little graphics—known as *icons* in tech talk. Here's your icon decoder ring:

- **Pro Tip**   This icon highlights a trick that professionals use to achieve a particular creative goal more easily.

- **Cost-cutter**   Look to paragraphs marked with this icon for tips on ways to stretch your photography budget.

- **Cool Tools**   This label points you toward camera features and accessories that I find especially useful, fun, or both.

- **Troubleshooter**   Information marked with this icon has two purposes: to help you avoid problems in the future and to help you get out of jams that you didn't see coming.

- **Technical Aside**   This icon flags background details that give you a better understanding of a technical issue or term.

- **How To**   Sections that carry the How-To logo walk you step-by-step through a digital-darkroom process, such as removing red-eye and setting the print dimensions for a picture.

Speaking of the How-To sections, you'll notice that they all feature one particular software product, Adobe Photoshop Elements 2.0. I selected this software because it's reasonably priced (under $100), offers all the tools most digital photographers need, and is available for both Macintosh and Windows-based computers. Moreover, you can download a trial copy from the Adobe web site (*www.adobe.com*) for free.

If you use Photoshop Elements 1.0 or Adobe Photoshop, you'll find that most instructions mesh with your software exactly. You can easily adapt the steps in the How-To sections to other programs as well.

One final bit of instruction about the instructions: This book uses a vertical line to indicate a chain of menu commands. For example, when you see the instruction "Choose File | Print," click File on the menu bar (at the top of the program window) to open the File menu. Then click the Print command on that menu.

Experiment, Be Patient, and Enjoy!

As I mentioned earlier, you may feel a little overwhelmed when you first start exploring this book. Instead of trying to absorb everything all at once, try incorporating one new technique each time you use your camera. The best way to improve your photography technique is bit by bit, just as you would learn any other skill. To make the learning process more fun, practice with subjects you enjoy, whether that's the great outdoors, a family member or pet, or downtown streets.

Remember that with your digital camera, experimentation is free. If you don't like the outcome of a shot, just delete the image and try again. Before long, you won't be pressing that Delete button nearly so much. And for every picture that doesn't turn out, you'll take ten that make you stop and say, "Wow, that's a *great* picture!"

PART I

Gearing Up for
Great Pictures

Getting the Right Gear

You've probably heard the axiom, "It's a poor carpenter who blames his tools." The same can be said for photographers. If a picture turns out poorly, the fault rarely lies with the camera, contrary to what those of us who pursue photography for a living would like to have you believe. In skilled hands, a cheap point-and-shoot camera can turn out images that are every bit as captivating as those that come from a studio camera costing thousands of dollars.

That said, having equipment that's geared to the type of photography you want to do makes a big difference in how easily you can capture a scene. If you need to shoot employee portraits for your company's annual report, for example, a camera that accepts an external flash will cut down on the number of pictures that you have to redo (or retouch) because of red-eye problems. And if you're passionate about wildlife photography, working with a powerful zoom lens will enable you to get close-up shots of skittish creatures without actually having to *be* up close.

This chapter introduces you to some products that can save you time, expand your creative options, and generally help you get better results. In case your budget is limited—and whose isn't?—I've bypassed ultra-expensive, high-end studio tools and instead focused on products that enhance your photography at affordable prices.

How Much Camera Do You Need?

My goal in writing this book is to show you how to get better results from any digital camera, even an entry-level, fully automatic model. For every technique that features an option found only on more advanced cameras, I try to present a workaround that you can use if you own a simpler model.

There's no denying, though, that cameras that offer advanced photographic options enable you to fine-tune focus, exposure, and color with more precision than a basic-features camera. The good news is that if you feel limited by your current equipment, there's never been a better time to upgrade.

For less than $500, you can get a camera with all the features a photographic control freak could want, with the exception of the ability to use interchangeable lenses. For that, you need a digital SLR (single-lens reflex) camera, just as you do for film photography, and you'll have to pay $1000 and up for the camera body, plus more for the lenses. If you're in the market for a digital SLR, enjoy! If not, rest assured that lower priced point-and- shoot models offer the same advanced imaging features found on an SLR, just without the lens flexibility.

Before you start shopping, you may want to review Chapter 2, which discusses critical digital-camera options and the best settings to use for a variety of photographic projects. Having that background will give you a better idea of which features you want your new camera to have and which ones you can live without.

I also want to bring to your attention a few issues that don't occur to most people when they're shopping but play a big role in their long-term satisfaction with a camera. The next few sections discuss these important and often overlooked factors.

SEE ALSO   *Although I've done my best to keep the technical jargon to a minimum, you may encounter some unfamiliar terms as you read this chapter. The glossary at the back of the book provides a quick decoder if you need help; upcoming chapters explain the important stuff in more detail.*

Manual Exposure Controls

When you take a picture, three camera components affect exposure:

- **Aperture**   The *aperture* is an iris in the lens that can be adjusted in size to control how much light enters through the lens. Aperture size is represented by *f-numbers* and written with the letter *f* followed by a slash and the f-number—for example, f/2.8. The higher the f-number, the *smaller* the aperture size. The aperture settings themselves are referred to as *f-stops*.

- **Shutter speed**   The *shutter* is like a window shade behind the camera lens. When you take a picture, the shutter opens briefly to allow light to enter through the lens and strike the camera's image sensor. *Shutter speed* refers to how long the shutter remains open. The slower the shutter speed, the more light the sensor soaks up.

- **ISO rating**   ISO ratings are used to indicate the light sensitivity of the image sensor. The higher the ISO number, the greater the light sensitivity and the less light is required to expose the image.

If you're used to working with autoexposure cameras, you may not be aware that being able to set aperture and shutter speed manually gives you creative control over more than just how light or dark your picture appears. Aperture affects depth of field, which is the range of distance in the picture that's in sharp focus. Shutter speed determines whether a moving subject appears frozen in time or blurred.

Advanced cameras offer you the option of working in either autoexposure (AE) mode, in which the camera chooses the aperture size and shutter speed, or in manual mode, in which you make these decisions. As an alternative, many cameras offer semiautomatic modes called *aperture-priority autoexposure* and *shutter-priority exposure*. In these modes, you set one control (aperture or shutter speed) and the camera selects the other.

Although you can sometimes persuade the autoexposure mechanism to select a particular f-stop or shutter speed—upcoming chapters share the tricks you use to do so—working with a camera that offers the option of manual exposure control makes it easier for you to implement your creative decisions. At the least, your next camera should offer one of the semi-automatic modes.

Focal Length: With Digital, It's Different

When you compose a picture, your creative choices are in part controlled by the *focal length* of the camera's lens. Focal length, which is measured in millimeters, is the distance between the optical center of the lens and the element that records the image—in a film camera, the negative; in a digital camera, the image sensor.

Focal length affects the angle of view and the size at which your subjects appear. At a short focal length, you can capture a wide area, but objects appear smaller and farther away. At a long focal length, the opposite is true—you can capture a narrow area, and objects appear larger and closer. As an example, see Figure 1.1. I took both pictures from the same position, but I doubled the focal length for the second image.

FIGURE 1.1   A short focal length captures a wide view of a scene (left); a long focal length makes subjects appear larger and closer (right).

Experienced photographers pay close attention to focal length when camera shopping because of the impact of this feature. Many people, though, aren't aware that you can't evaluate digital camera focal lengths on the same scale you use for a traditional camera lens.

To explain this fully requires a lengthy lesson in camera optics, but here's the short story: The size of the recording element affects what the camera sees at a particular focal length, and image sensors are much smaller than film negatives. To capture the same image as a film camera, a digital camera needs a focal length about one-sixth as long.

Further complicating the matter, digital camera manufacturers use a variety of sensor sizes, so there's no reliable formula for translating traditional focal lengths to digital. Instead, the digital industry has adopted the practice of stating camera focal lengths as 35mm film equivalents.

Camera specs may read something like this: "Focal length: 7.5mm, equivalent to 50mm with 35mm film." In photographic magazines, the abbreviation *efl* (for equivalent focal length) is sometimes used—50mm (efl), for example. Other resources, including this book, use the abbreviation *equiv.* However it's stated, this information tells you that the digital camera lens produces the same image you would get with a 50mm lens if you were shooting 35mm film—the most widely used negative size in film photography.

To sum up, if you're accustomed to judging lenses based on focal length, just ignore the digital focal lengths and look for the 35mm equivalency numbers. If you're new to the whole focal length thing, the following list offers a few guidelines:

- A lens with a focal length equivalency of less than 35mm is considered a wide-angle lens. Wide-angle lenses enable you to cram a large area into the frame at close distance. They're perfect for shooting groups of people in a living room, for example, and for landscape photography.

- A focal length equivalency of 50mm produces the most natural view, recording a subject at approximately the same size and distance as your eyes see it.

- A focal length equivalency of 85mm and up is considered a telephoto lens. These lenses are designed to help you capture a close-up view of a distant subject.

- A zoom lens enables you to shift between a range of focal lengths—equivalent to 28–105mm, for example. But this applies only to optical zoom lenses, not the digital zoom function found on most cameras. (See Chapter 5 for more information about optical versus digital zooms.)

PRO TIP

If you're moving from a film SLR camera to a digital SLR, you can use your film lenses on your digital camera, assuming that they're compatible with the lens mount on your digital model. (For example, Nikon digital SLRs accept lenses that work with certain models of Nikon film cameras.) Because of the size differences between digital camera image sensors and film negatives, though, the lenses will have a longer apparent focal length when mounted on your digital camera. Telephoto lenses bring you even closer to your subject, which is happy news if you've been wanting more distance power. But you lose ground at the wide-angle end of the spectrum, which may not be to your liking.

Manual Focusing Mechanisms

All digital cameras offer autofocus, but advanced models also offer manual focusing. When you work in manual mode, you typically set focus by dialing in the subject-to-camera distance—such as 11 inches, 2 feet and so on. Only a few cameras, including the Fujifilm FinePix model shown in Figure 1.2, offer the traditional SLR manual focusing design, in which you twist a ring on the lens barrel to adjust focus.

I find the traditional design much easier, because I'm lousy at estimating distance. More mathematically oriented photographers may prefer the numerical approach to setting focus, though. Mind you, most autofocusing systems are very adept, so this issue isn't a major deal for most people. But if you like to take the focusing reins yourself, try both systems before you buy.

FIGURE 1.2 This Fujifilm FinePix model offers a traditional manual focusing ring on the lens barrel.

Control Accessibility

One thing that really drives me crazy is working with a camera that's loaded with photographic controls but buries those options in internal menus. You have to turn on the monitor, scroll through batches of menus to find the control you're after, and then press multiple buttons to make your selection. By the time you work your way through all those menus, you've missed the opportunity to take the shot.

If you plan on taking full advantage of the advanced options you're buying, look for a model that allows you to control important functions via external buttons or dials. A camera that's covered with doodads may look frighteningly complicated at first glance but is actually much easier to use than a menu-driven model.

Traditional vs. Electronic Viewfinder

Some digital cameras do not offer a viewfinder, forcing you to use the camera's monitor to frame your shots. I don't recommend these cameras for serious photography work for several reasons. First, because you have to hold the camera away from your face to take the picture, you increase the chance for camera shake, which leads to blurred images. Second, the displays on most monitors tend to wash out in bright sunlight, making outdoor photography a challenge. Finally, your camera eats batteries faster when the monitor is turned on all the time.

Most cameras that do have viewfinders use the traditional type—the same kind that's been used for decades. But some models offer electronic viewfinders instead. When you look through an electronic viewfinder, you see whatever the lens is looking at plus all the information normally displayed on the LCD monitor. In other words, an electronic viewfinder is like a mini monitor, but brighter, clearer, and without the bright-light washout problems.

Some folks love this new viewfinder option, and some folks hate it. I've got one foot in each camp. Electronic viewfinders are nice in that they display more information than a normal viewfinder—typically, you see all the same icons and other data that would appear on the monitor if you were using it to frame the shot. What I don't like about electronic viewfinders is that you can't see anything through them when the camera is turned off. So you can't experiment with framing without switching on the camera. In addition, electronic viewfinders consume battery power, which is always at a premium with digital cameras. I leave you to judge whether the pros outweigh the cons for the type of photography you like to do.

CooL TooLs

If you want to use your LCD monitor in bright light, whether it's to frame a shot or review photos you've already taken, attaching an LCD *hood* to the camera makes seeing the picture easier. The hood acts like a window awning, reducing the amount of light that hits the monitor. Shown here is one such device, sold by Hoodman (*www.hoodmanusa.com*). This particular hood, which sells for $50, comes with a detachable eyepiece that magnifies the display as well as a clear monitor shield that protects the display from scratches. Simpler shades without the eyepiece and shield sell for about $20.

Filter and Converter Compatibility

As you expand your photography knowledge, you may want to take advantage of creative filters, such as the warming and polarizing filters explored in Chapter 8. In addition, you may want to extend your camera's field of vision by attaching wide-angle, fisheye, or telephoto converters. These converters give you some of the lens flexibility that you enjoy with SLR cameras.

Until recently, few filters or converters were available in sizes to fit digital camera lenses. But now that digital has caught on, manufacturers have begun to address this need. Figure 1.3 shows an assortment of filters from two major players in the filter market, Tiffen (*www.tiffen.com*) and Cokin (*www.cokin.com*).

To attach most filters and converter lenses, you simply screw them onto the end of your camera's lens barrel. Of course, your lens barrel must have a threaded ring that accepts such add-ons. Many digital cameras don't offer threaded lens barrels, unfortunately.

You may be able to buy an adapter that slips over the lens, giving you the threaded-ring functionality. Adapters aren't available for all cameras, though,

FIGURE 1.3   Accessory filters expand your creative options.

and they can be expensive. In some cases, you can't use third-party adapters so you have to buy the manufacturer's proprietary (and more costly) products.

Cokin offers another filter alternative, shown in the middle of Figure 1.3. First you attach a filter holder to the bottom of the camera, screwing it into the tripod mount. Then you slip the filter into slots on the holder's two vertical arms. This solution can work great for some cameras, but make sure that the holder works with your lens barrel size and tripod-mount position before you buy.

>> TROUBLESHO⊕TER

Be careful to remove filters and converter lenses before you power down the camera! If you don't, the filter or converter can crack the lens housing when the lens barrel retracts into the camera body.

Technical Aside
What's a Filter Factor?

Most lens filters reduce the amount of light that enters the camera lens. To let photographers know how much light reduction to expect, manufacturers provide a guide number, known as *filter factor,* for every filter.

Filter factors are stated in X numbers—1X, 2X, 4X, and so on. The number indicates how many times more light you need to produce the same exposure you would get without the filter. A factor of 1X means that no light reduction occurs; 2X means that you need twice as much light; 4X means that you need four times as much light.

When cameras required photographers to set exposure manually, filter factors were vital. With most autoexposure cameras, the camera makes the necessary adjustments for you. However, this automatic adjustment occurs only on autoexposure cameras that offer through-the-lens (TTL) light metering. With TTL metering, the autoexposure mechanism analyzes the light that's actually coming through the lens.

Some inexpensive autoexposure cameras take the light reading from a window that's separate from the lens, which means that the camera won't know when you attach a light-reducing filter. If you're using this type of camera, you can ramp up exposure by using the *EV (exposure value) compensation control,* discussed in the next chapter. (Don't worry; the control sounds complicated, but it isn't.) You can preview and review your shots in the camera monitor to check exposure.

Tripod Mount

To get razor-sharp shots at night and in other situations that call for a slow shutter speed, you need to mount your camera on a tripod. Almost all digital cameras except the cheap plastic ones have the necessary screw threads for attaching the camera to a tripod. But some manufacturers are more thoughtful about this feature than others.

If the battery chamber or memory card slot is on the bottom of the camera, you may not be able to swap out either component without removing the camera from the tripod. Très annoying—especially if you run out of battery power or memory after you just spent a long time framing the perfect shot.

Lighting Solutions

One of the most important things you can do to enhance your photography is to learn to assess and control lighting. Lighting is critical to a properly exposed photo, of course, but good photographers also use light to set a mood, emphasize important aspects of a scene, and play down distracting or unattractive elements.

When you're shooting outdoors in the daytime, too much light is sometimes a problem. Chapter 6 discusses some ways to deal with this situation. More often, though, you need to bring more light to a scene. You can use a number of lighting tools to do so, from your camera's built-in flash to powerful, studio-style lights. The following sections introduce you to these lighting solutions.

CooL TooLs

To get a basic education in lighting, fire up your web browser and click over to *www.webphotoschool.com*. This online learning center offers several free lighting lessons. For $60, you can get a year's access to dozens of additional lessons; a one-month membership is just $20.

Built-in Flash

The small flash unit on your camera is supposed to allow you to take pictures in a darkened room or at night. But the light from a built-in flash is so narrowly focused that it doesn't serve well as a sole light source. Pictures taken with a built-in flash usually show a small, bright blast of light, with rapid falloff to shadows around the perimeter of the shot. See Page 24 of the color insert for an example of this effect. Built-in flash usually causes red-eye in indoor and nighttime portrait pictures, too.

Ironically, a built-in flash is most useful for shooting outdoors in daylight. Strong sun can produce shadows on a subject, and the small pop of light produced by a built-in flash is the perfect way to eliminate those shadows. Page 12 of the color insert offers an example of this technique.

Reflectors

A *reflector* is a thin, flat panel that has a light-reflecting surface. It acts like a mirror of sorts, reflecting any light that strikes it. The left image in Figure 1.4 shows an assortment of portable fabric reflectors from Photoflex (*www.photoflex.com*).

(Photo courtesy Photoflex Inc.)

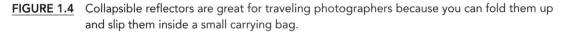

FIGURE 1.4   Collapsible reflectors are great for traveling photographers because you can fold them up and slip them inside a small carrying bag.

Reflectors come in handy for eliminating shadows in a scene. For example, in the portrait series featured on pages 8 and 9 of the color insert, I positioned my subject next to a window. I wanted the daylight shining through that window to serve as the main light source. But because the light was coming from a single direction, one half of the face was in the shadows. I positioned a reflector opposite the window to bounce light back onto the shadowed side of the face. (See Chapter 3 for more information about portrait lighting.)

You don't need to buy a commercially-made reflector to use this technique—a piece of white cardboard will do. Those foil-covered windshield shades that you use to keep your car cool in summer also make good reflectors. These solutions are a little cumbersome for traveling photographers, however, which is why I prefer collapsible commercial reflectors like those shown in Figure 1.4. You can fold up these reflectors and slip them inside a small carrying case, as shown on the right side of the figure.

Prices for commercial reflectors start at about $15 for a small, 12-inch reflector. In addition to Photoflex, other companies that sell popular reflector lines include Visual Departures (*www.visualdepartures.com*) and Westcott (*www.fjwestcott.com*).

Reflectors come in different colors, and each color produces a slightly different lighting effect:

- **White**   Produces neutral reflected light—that is, the reflector doesn't change the color of the light source. (Light color is discussed in detail in Chapter 8.)

- **Silver**   Produces slightly cooler (bluer) reflected light. Silver reflectors also create a bit stronger, more sparkly light than white reflectors.

- **Gold**   Produces slightly warmer, more golden reflected light, making it a terrific choice for portrait lighting.

Usually, commercial reflectors are dual-sided affairs, each side covered with a different material. For most projects, a white/gold combo is a good fit.

> **PRO TIP**
>
> *When you go reflector shopping, you'll also find black, silk, and translucent reflectors, which actually are light reducers instead of light reflectors. You can place a black reflector between a subject and the sun to create instant shade, for example. Silk and translucent reflectors act as light diffusers, creating a softer, less focused light.*

Auxiliary Flash Units

If you do a lot of indoor or nighttime photography, you may want to invest in an auxiliary flash. Figure 1.5 shows such a flash unit.

External flash units offer several advantages over your camera's built-in flash:

- You can angle the flash head, which lets you control the direction of the light. For example, you can aim the head toward the ceiling, so that the light bounces off the ceiling and down onto the subject. This creates a diffused light source and softer shadows than a flash aimed directly at the subject.

FIGURE 1.5   An external flash unit features a movable head that you can swivel to adjust the direction of the light.

- The light is stronger and more broadly focused than what you get from a built-in flash, so a larger area of the scene is illuminated.

- External flash units typically enable you to adjust the strength of the flash. Some digital cameras also offer this function for built-in flashes, but you usually have to buy at the higher end of the price spectrum to get this feature.

You can connect an external flash to your digital camera in a couple of ways. Most so-called *prosumer* cameras—that is, the high-end models with advanced photographic bells and whistles—offer a *hot shoe*. A hot shoe is a little flash connection bracket on the top of the camera, as shown in the left image in Figure 1.6. You simply slide the base of the flash unit into the bracket.

Hot shoe

FIGURE 1.6　Cameras at the higher end of the consumer price spectrum include a hot shoe or socket for attaching an external flash.

In medium-priced cameras, you may instead find a flash-cord socket that enables you to attach a *handle-mount* flash, like the one shown on the right side of Figure 1.6. You use a cord supplied with the flash to connect flash and camera. You can then either hold the flash in one hand and the camera in the other, or you can attach both to a bracket, as shown in the figure. (In photography jargon, handle-mount flash units are called *potato mashers* because of their resemblance to that kitchen tool.)

What if your camera offers neither hot shoe nor flash socket? You can still enjoy the flexibility of external flash power by using a *slave flash*. A slave flash works in conjunction with your camera's built-in flash. When your camera flash fires, the slave flash "sees" that burst of light and triggers its own light in response.

External flashes range in price from $50 to hundreds of dollars. At the high end of the spectrum, you get sophisticated flash controls, such as the ability to adjust precisely the timing and power of the flash output. Some advanced flash units, like the $190 Minolta model shown in Figure 1.5, work either attached to the camera or as a wireless remote flash, which gives you great flexibility in positioning the flash.

Although working with external flashes isn't complicated, buying one can be. You need to be sure that the flash you buy can communicate with your camera so that the flash fires at the appropriate time. In addition, your camera's autoexposure mechanism may or may not be able to adjust exposure properly to account for the varying flash power of the external unit. Typically, you get the maximum coordination between flash and camera when you buy the camera manufacturer's flash equipment. Unfortunately, those units are usually pricier than third-party units.

If you're in the market for an external flash, I suggest you take your camera to your local camera store for advice. Tell the staff what type of photography you plan to do so that they can steer you to the proper equipment. This guidance is especially important if you're buying a slave flash. Some slave units are engineered to operate as a secondary light to a shoe-mounted flash and don't respond properly to a built-in flash.

Also check out your camera manufacturer's web site for recommendations. For third-party flash equipment, check out Digi-Slave (*www.srelectronics.com*), Sunpak (*www.sunpak.com*), and Metz (*www.bogenphoto.com*).

For close-up photography, you may want to invest in a special macro flash unit. Chapter 5 discusses this type of flash.

"Hot" Lights

Although auxiliary flash units expand your lighting power tremendously, getting good results requires a good deal of experimentation because you can't see in advance where the light from the flash will fall and how brightly it will shine. High-end studio flash units come with modeling lights, which are little setup lights that show the photographer the approximate intensity and direction of the flash. But these flash units are expensive, complicated to use, and don't work with many digital cameras. For that reason, I recommend that you investigate so-called *hot lights* if your photography requires precision lighting. Hot lights provide constant illumination, just like the lamp on your bedside table, but they use powerful bulbs—anywhere from 250 to 1000 watts—to produce a stronger light. With hot lights, you can see exactly how your subject will be lit and adjust the position or angle of the lights accordingly before you press the shutter button.

Figure 1.7 shows one popular style of hot light, the Tota-Light from Lowel (*www.lowel.com*). Tota-Lights feature swinging metal panels—called *barn doors* in the lighting biz—that you can adjust to control the spread of the light. You can attach an umbrella, as shown in the right picture in the figure, to diffuse the light. (You can also use a translucent reflector or screen to soften the light.)

(Photos courtesy Lowel-Light Manufacturing, Inc.)

FIGURE 1.7   Some hot lights come with barn doors that allow you to adjust the spread of the light; attaching a white, translucent umbrella creates a more diffused light, which creates softer shadows.

Another common hot-light design resembles the shop lights you buy in the hardware store—a bulb surrounded by an aluminum reflector, sometimes called a *can*. In fact, many people take the budget approach and just use those shop lights as illumination. For casual projects, that's perfectly fine, by the way. But don't make the mistake of putting super-wattage photo bulbs into hardware-store cans.

If you do, you may find yourself calling the fire department's emergency number.

Here are a few other bits of advice about buying and using hot lights:

- You can get more equipment for less money if you buy a lighting kit instead of purchasing each component separately. For example, an individual Tota-light like the one shown in Figure 1.7 retails for about $110; a 10-foot expandable stand to hold and position the light, about $60; and an umbrella, $25. But you can buy a kit with two lights, two stands, and two umbrellas for about $325. All the equipment in the kit may not come from the same manufacturer, but the pieces should work together just the same.

- Light bulbs—officially called *lamps*—range in price from a few bucks to $30. The cheap bulbs can cost more in the long run, though, because they have a much shorter life span than the expensive variety.

- Hot lights got their nickname for good reason. You can easily burn yourself just by standing too close to the bulb for a long period of time. Ditto for subjects placed too close to the light.

- If you're using a light with the barn door design, follow the manufacturer's guidelines about positioning the doors. When the doors aren't open wide enough, smoke ensues (not, unfortunately, hilarity).

- Hot lights require a lot of power. So plug each light into a different electrical circuit to avoid blowing fuses. Also, try not to run your dishwasher, washing machine, or other large appliances while you're working. They can create fluctuations in the electricity flow, which slightly affects the color and intensity of your light's output.

- Finally, never touch the glass surface of a hot-light bulb with your bare fingers. The oil from your skin can transfer to the bulb surface, and when you next turn on the light, the oil may cause the glass to explode. For this reason, some hot lights come with protective screens that you place over the bulb.

Hot lights come in a confusing variety of designs; selecting the correct bulbs is even more perplexing. To make sure that you buy equipment that's appropriate for the type of subjects that you shoot, consult with the experts at your local camera store.

>> TROUBLESHOOTER

The auto white balance function on some digital cameras can't deal properly with some hot lights. Preview the scene on your camera's monitor, and if colors look off, switch to manual white balance. Normally, the Incandescent or Tungsten setting works best. See Chapter 8 for more information on adjusting white balance.

Setting Up the Digital Darkroom

When photography pundits use the term *digital darkroom,* they're referring to computer hardware and software tools that you use to edit and print your digital pictures. The name is a bit of a misnomer, if you ask me—one of the best things about going digital is that you no longer *have* to stumble about in a darkened room to develop and print your film negatives.

At any rate, being able to retouch, enhance, and print my own photos is one of the things I like best about digital photography. But you, like many people, may decide to opt out of this part of the game, preferring to have pictures printed at a retail lab. Or you may buy a home photo printer that can output images directly from your memory card. Even so, you'll need a computer and software to store, organize, and manage your image files as well as to share them over the Internet.

How sophisticated a system you need depends on the type of post-capture work you want to do. The rest of this chapter offers some guidance on choosing hardware and software to help you put together a digital darkroom that fits your needs.

SEE ALSO

For information about printers and printing, see Chapter 9.

Computer Central: Is Your System Fit for Duty?

As the heart of the digital darkroom, your computer can make your photo projects either fun and easy or a downright drag. Photo editing puts a big demand on a computer, especially if you're working with high-resolution images. If your system is lacking in processor power, RAM (memory), or hard drive storage space, it will carry out your editing commands at a snail's pace, or perhaps not at all.

The next five sections tell you what you need to know about these critical computer components along with a few others: monitor, video card, memory-card reader, and long-term image-storage device.

Processor and RAM

On a PC, I recommend a Pentium II processor or better; on a Macintosh system, a G3 processor or better. If your system is of recent vintage—say, no more than three years old—it likely meets this specification.

No matter how fast your processor, though, you need to feed it lots of computer memory, called RAM, for your photo software to run smoothly. You need at least 64MB (megabytes) if you work with low-resolution files, and twice that if you want to edit high-res images. For even faster performance, add as much memory as your system accepts. (Also check the RAM requirements for the software you want to use; some programs require 96MB or more.)

> **PRO TIP**
>
> *Many people ask whether a Windows or Macintosh machine is better for photo editing. The art community has long had a fondness for Macs, and a Macintosh is a fine machine. However, because the majority of consumers dance to the Windows tune, many software manufacturers don't offer Macintosh versions of their programs. So you'll be able to choose from a wider spectrum of software if you go Windows. Don't get me wrong—you can find good programs for the Mac, too—just not as many.*

Hard Drive Storage Space

The hard drive is your computer's filing cabinet, where you store all your programs and files. As with RAM, the amount of hard drive space you need depends on the size of the image files you want to store.

However, you need to keep a chunk of the hard drive empty at all times. Your system uses this free drive space for temporary data storage while you're working in a photo editor or other program. I suggest that you keep at least 500MB free for this purpose.

>> TROUBLESHOOTER

If your photo program displays an error message saying that your *scratch disk* is full, it means you don't have enough free hard drive space. To give your computer the hard-drive breathing room it needs, go through your files and dump those you no longer need.

Video Card and Monitor

Your video card determines how many colors your monitor can display as well as what screen resolution settings you can use. Screen resolution affects the size at which your pictures display, as discussed in Chapter 10, but even the poorest excuse for a video card is likely adequate in this regard.

For photo editing, a more critical issue is whether the card offers so-called *true color* display—also called 24-bit color—which gives you the ability to display about 16.7 million colors. Your digital camera captures all those colors, so you should be able to view them on your monitor.

As for the monitor itself, size doesn't matter, although your eyes will certainly appreciate a 17-inch or larger screen more than a puny 15-incher. What is important is the type of monitor you use. The new flat-panel LCD monitors look cool and eat up less desk space, but they're not the best choice for doing intensive retouching and color-critical photo projects because image colors, contrast, and brightness appear different depending on your angle of view. Traditional CRT (cathode-ray tube) monitors produce a more even, reliable display.

Memory-Card Reader

Your digital camera box no doubt included a cable that lets you connect the camera to your computer in order to transfer picture files from the camera's memory to the computer's hard drive (or other storage device). But transferring picture files this way sometimes involves some extra steps, or requires that you use the camera manufacturer's proprietary transfer software, or both. In addition, you have to keep the camera turned on during the file transfer, which consumes battery power.

A better transfer solution is to attach a memory-card reader to your computer. When you're ready to transfer pictures, you insert your camera memory card and then drag and

FIGURE 1.8 Memory card readers simplify the process of transferring picture files to your computer; this SanDisk reader accepts six types of memory cards.

drop files from the card to the computer's hard drive, just as you do when you're moving files from a floppy disk or CD to the hard drive. (And you no longer have to spend an hour trying to remember where you left the camera cable the last time you used it.)

Readers that accept a single type of memory card cost less than $30; for a bit more, you can get a model that accepts a variety of cards. Figure 1.8 shows one multiformat reader, the 6-in-1 ImageMate from SanDisk. This product sells for about $40.

✂ COST CUTTER

A printer that can print directly from camera memory cards can double as a card reader. While the printer is connected to the computer, the system sees the printer's memory-card slot as another hard drive.

Archival Storage Device

Never use your computer's hard drive for long-term picture storage. Hard drives can die, taking your picture files with them to the great electronics beyond. In addition, you run the risk that you or others who use your computer will accidentally delete important picture files.

At present, CD-ROM offers the best option for archival image storage. CD burners are cheap, as are blank CDs, and you can buy external models so you don't even have to crack open your computer case to add one to your system. Be sure to copy your image files to CD-R discs, which can't be erased, and not the rewritable CD-RW discs. And for long-term security of your image files, use brand-name CDs, not the el-cheapo brands sold in outlet stores.

DVD recorders are another storage possibility. However, prices are higher than CD technology, and the industry hasn't yet agreed on a common DVD format, which means that a DVD you create on your system may not play on another computer or DVD drive. Having lived through the deaths of Betamax video tapes and the LaserDisc, I'm not keen on joining the early-adopter ranks when it comes to recording devices.

CooL TooLs

(*Photo Courtesy Wacom Technology Corp.*)

Using a mouse for photo editing is a cumbersome way to go. A graphics tablet, which enables you to swap out your mouse for a pen stylus, gives you far better control over your editing tools and also is easier on the wrist. Shown here is a model from Wacom, the leading tablet manufacturer. Called the Graphire 2, this tablet sells for about $70 and comes with a cordless mouse as well as a stylus.

Software

A high-powered computer does you absolutely no good unless you have the appropriate software. Every serious digital photographer needs a photo editing program and an image organizer. The next two sections look at these tools.

PRO TIP

Not all programs mentioned here or elsewhere in the book are available for both Windows and Macintosh computers. So if you're interested in a particular product, visit the manufacturer's web site to check the system requirements.

Photo Editing Programs

Even if you don't plan on doing much photo editing, you need a photo editor to prepare pictures for printing or e-mailing. If that's all you want to do, you can get by with a bare-bones program—in fact, your camera or printer probably shipped with a tool for performing these basic operations. Many photo organizers (discussed next) also include simple editing tools.

For more involved retouching work or creative photo artistry, you need software that's a little more sophisticated. In this book, I feature Adobe Photoshop Elements, which sells for about $90. (Watch the sale ads, and you often can find the program for substantially less.) For the novice photo editor, Elements offers on-screen assistance with common editing tasks, as shown in Figure 1.9. But the program also offers a surprisingly robust assortment of advanced editing tools.

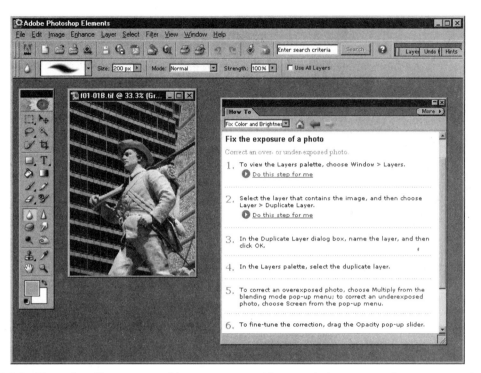

FIGURE 1.9 Photoshop Elements provides on-screen guidance to help you complete common photo editing projects.

You can download a trial copy of Photoshop Elements at the Adobe web site (*www.adobe.com*). In the same price range, also check out Ulead PhotoImpact ($90, *www.ulead.com*) and Jasc Paint Shop Pro ($100, *www.jasc.com*).

For professional-level tools, you have two choices: Adobe Photoshop, which will set you back about $600, and Corel PHOTO-PAINT, which is sold together with CorelDRAW (in a package called Corel Graphics Suite) for about $430 (*www.corel.com*). Among other things, the extra money buys you more advanced exposure and color tools, plus some features that are important for folks who prepare photos for output on a commercial printing press.

If you make a living from digital imaging, as I do, these features are important—as is a good book or class to help you learn to take full advantage of the program. But I certainly wouldn't recommend that you invest this much in any photo editor until you're sure that you really enjoy this aspect of digital imaging—even then, most people find that programs like Photoshop Elements, PhotoImpact, and Paint Shop Pro provide all the tools they need.

Image Organizers

An image organizer enables you to sort, manage, and catalog your image files. This type of program is essential for keeping track of your pictures, especially if you're a prolific photographer.

Some photo editing programs have a built-in file browser, as do some versions of the Windows and Macintosh operating systems. You may also find a basic image-management tool on the software CD that came with your camera. You can do simple organizing tasks with these tools, but after you accumulate more than 100 or so files, you'll want something more advanced.

Two of my favorite programs in this category are ACDSee, from ACDSystems ($50, *www.acdsystems.com*) and ThumbsPlus, from Cerious Software ($80, *www.thumbsplus .com*). Both give you a wealth of tools for the money. You can browse thumbnails of your pictures, organize your files, catalog images by subject matter, print contact sheets (pages of thumbnails), and even do some basic editing.

In addition, these programs allow you to view file *metadata.* Metadata is extra information that's stored with the image file when you take a picture. This data includes the type of camera, the exposure settings, focal length, time, date, and more. Cameras store this data in a standard format called EXIF, which stands for Exchangeable Image File Format, so that you can view it in any organizer that can speak the EXIF language. Figure 1.10 gives you a look at the EXIF viewer in ACDSee.

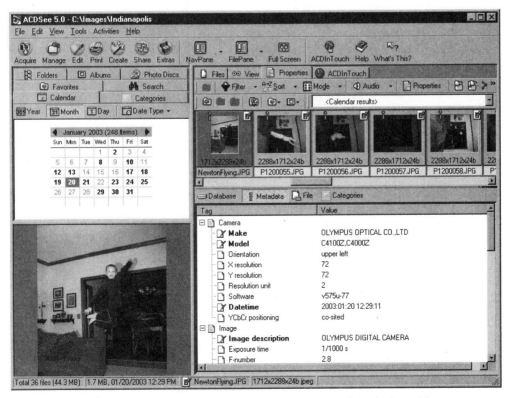

FIGURE 1.10   Image organizers such as ACDSee include an EXIF reader, which enables you to see the camera settings that you used when you took a picture.

ACDSee and ThumbsPlus aren't the only good organizers, of course. Ulead PhotoExplorer ($30, *www.Ulead.com*) and Adobe Photoshop Album ($50, *www.adobe.com*) are two other contenders that come to mind, and you can find dozens more by doing an online search on "image-management software." Many companies, including all those mentioned here, offer free, downloadable trial versions at their web sites, so you can work with each one and see which you like best.

Exploring Creative Controls

If you've ever tuned in to the Food Network on TV, you may have caught an episode of *Iron Chef,* a Japanese-language import in which two famous chefs do culinary battle. The participants are challenged to combine a random assortment of ingredients into a gourmet feast for a panel of celebrity taste-testers. As the contestants chop, sauté, and sauce, commentators describe the action in dramatic, play-by-play fashion.

The dishes, which include such delicacies as octopus risotto and eel à la mode, don't always appeal to my American palette as much as they seem to enchant the celebrity judges, but the show is good, campy fun nonetheless. Even better, it provides the perfect analogy to describe this chapter, thus lending credence to my claim that when I'm watching TV, I'm *not* wasting time but in fact *working.*

You see, the first thing that the Iron Chef competitors do is assess the ingredients they've been given to see what goodies they may be able to prepare. Similarly, your first step as a photographer should be to evaluate your subject, the setting, and your camera's capabilities. You then can figure out how to bring those components together to create a tasty visual treat.

Later chapters detail techniques related to specific subjects and surroundings. This chapter provides an overview of all the major digital camera controls, explaining the creative impact of each option and offering my recommendation about which settings to use in various shooting scenarios. As you read, you may want to have your camera manual handy so that you can confirm whether your camera offers a particular option, and if so, how you activate that feature.

Image Resolution

The *resolution* control determines the number of pixels that your camera uses to produce a picture. Your camera likely offers three or more resolution settings, each delivering a different pixel count.

You may see your options presented in terms of *pixel dimensions*, such as 2288×1712, with the horizontal pixel count listed first, followed by the number of vertical pixels. However, some manufacturers refer to the *total* number of pixels when labeling resolution options, using the term *megapixel* to mean one million pixels. For example, if you multiply 2288×1712 pixels, you get roughly 3.9 million pixels, or 3.9 megapixels (which the folks in the camera marketing department round up to 4 megapixels).

Creative Impact

If you're an experienced film photographer, you know that the larger the film negative, the more you can enlarge the photo without losing sharpness and detail. You can make a similar connection between pixel count and print size. The more pixels you capture, the larger you can print your photo without a noticeable loss of quality, as illustrated by Figures 2.1 and 2.2.

3 megapixels, 1.3MB

1 megapixel, 620K

FIGURE 2.1   At snapshot size, the 3-megapixel tulip (left) doesn't look much different from the 1-megapixel version (right).

3 megapixel   1 megapixel

FIGURE 2.2   When the print size is doubled, the 3-megapixel image (left) offers significantly higher quality than the 1-megapixel photo (right).

I shot both tulip pictures with the same camera. For the left images in both figures, I used the camera's 3-megapixel setting. For the right images, I reduced the camera resolution to 1 megapixel.

When printed at snapshot size, as in Figure 2.1, both images are perfectly acceptable, although small details such as the dewdrops appear slightly sharper in the 3-megapixel version. But in Figure 2.2, which shows a portion of both pictures as they would appear if the original were enlarged to 5×7 inches, the 1-megapixel file doesn't hold up. A dearth of pixels leads to a stair-stepped appearance along diagonal and curved lines, and subtle details are lost. The result is a picture that appears jagged in some areas and blurry in others.

On the down side, more pixels means larger file sizes, so you can fit fewer pictures in a given amount of camera memory. In addition, larger files take longer to process in a photo-editing program. As a point of comparison, the 1-megapixel tulip in Figure 2.1 has a file size of roughly 620K(kilobytes); the 3-megapixel version, 1300K, which equals 1.3MB (megabytes). Note that file compression, explained next, also has an impact on file size; I shot both images at the same compression setting.

Although good printed output requires a hefty pixel count, the story changes for pictures displayed on a computer monitor, television, or digital projector. For screen images, the number of pixels does *not* affect picture quality, just display size. At maximum, the image pixel dimensions should equal the screen resolution (640×480, 800×600, and so on).

Chapter 10 provides more details about preparing pictures for the web and other on-screen uses.

Recommended Setting

The appropriate resolution setting depends on what you plan to do with your image:

- **For printed photos**   You need 200–300 pixels per each linear inch of your print; the exact number depends upon the printer. Home photo printers, for example, tend to deliver the best results when fed 300 pixels per inch (ppi), while commercial machines used by retail photo labs produce great prints at just 200 ppi. Consult your printer manual or the retail technician to find out the optimum resolution, and do your own testing to see whether you notice any significant difference at a higher or lower ppi.

- **For web photos**   A resolution of 640×480 pixels—sometimes referred to as *VGA resolution*—is usually adequate. That setting gives you enough pixels to fill the entire screen on a monitor that's running at a screen resolution of 640×480. Most people today set their monitors to a resolution of at least 800×600, but keep in mind that the web browser itself eats up some of the available screen space. Also remember that fewer pixels means smaller file sizes and therefore faster download times.

- **For pictures in a multimedia presentation**   Follow the same guidelines as for web photos, matching the pixel dimensions to the display device.

When you're not sure how you plan to use your picture, shoot with print output in mind. If necessary, you can easily eliminate extra pixels in a photo editor. You can add pixels in a photo program, too, but you won't get any noticeable improvement in print quality by doing so. In fact, your prints may look worse than they did before you added pixels. So when in doubt, always opt for too many pixels rather than too few.

Shooting pictures at a decent resolution setting also gives you more flexibility in the editing stage because you can crop and enlarge a portion of the image to good result. This benefit becomes especially important when you're shooting spontaneous events, such as parties, or when you're photographing moving targets. You don't always have the opportunity to achieve the perfect composition, and starting with a high-resolution image enables you to correct the framing later, as shown in Figure 2.3.

Although the children in the original portrait in Figure 2.3 look terrific, the objects on the sofa table behind them are distracting. To create a better image, I opened the picture in my photo editor and cropped the image to the horizontal framing indicated by the black box.

❓ How To

MATCH CAMERA RESOLUTION TO PRINT SIZE

If you know the optimum image resolution (ppi) to send your printer, you can calculate what camera resolution you need to produce a quality print at a specific size. Just multiply print width by the ppi value to determine how may horizontal pixels you need, and multiply print height by the ppi value to determine vertical pixels.

The following table provides a quick reference to the number of pixels needed for quality prints at standard frame sizes, assuming an optimum image resolution of 200 ppi. Note that because the aspect ratio of a digital camera image is 4:3, which is different from that of traditional photo frames, most cameras won't offer a resolution setting that matches these pixel counts exactly. Go with the setting that gets you closest to the larger of the two pixel values. You can then crop the image to the correct frame size in your photo editor. Chapter 3 provides more information about digital camera aspect ratios.

PRINT SIZE	PIXELS*	MEGAPIXELS
3½×5 in.	700×1000	<1
4×6 in.	800×1200	1
5×7 in.	1000×1400	1.5
8×10 in.	1600×2000	3.2
11×14 in.	2200×2800	6

*Assumes a desired image output resolution of 200 ppi

FIGURE 2.3   Starting with a 3-megapixel original enabled me to crop this casual portrait closely to create better composition.

Because I started with a 3-megapixel image, the cropped image contained enough pixels to produce a high-quality 4×6-inch print, a portion of which you see to the right of the original.

Compare the images in Figure 2.3 with those in Figure 2.4, which began life as a 1-megapixel picture. As with the low-resolution tulip featured earlier, the cropped and enlarged low-pixel portrait doesn't look nearly as crisp as its high-resolution cousin.

FIGURE 2.4   A lack of pixels is again to blame for the low quality of this cropped enlargement.

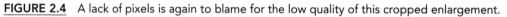

As you ponder the resolution question, consider these additional points:

- If you're working with a very high resolution camera—say, 4 megapixels or more—you don't always need to use its maximum setting. Shooting routine images at the top resolution is a waste of memory and photo-editing time. I mean, how many times do you make prints larger than 8×10?

- Some cameras require more time to send a high-resolution image to the camera's memory than a low-resolution image (due to the larger file size). This issue can prove problematic for action photography, because you can't take another picture until the camera saves the current image. In this situation, you may want to trade off a little picture quality in favor of faster shooting.

- Color photos printed on glossy, high-grade paper reveal resolution problems more than grayscale images printed on uncoated, lower quality paper. Compare the pictures in Figures 2.3 and 2.4 with the color versions on Page 3 of the color insert to see what I mean.

Compression

Compression is a bit of software manipulation done to reduce the file size of a digital image.

When you record an image in the standard digital-camera file format—JPEG—the photo undergoes *lossy compression,* which means that some image data is eliminated in the name of smaller files. You can significantly lower file size by applying lossy compression.

Some cameras also enable you to store pictures in the TIFF format, which applies either no compression or *lossless* compression. Lossless compression tosses only redundant data and therefore doesn't shrink file size much.

On most cameras, the compression option is labeled *Picture Quality* or something similar, and the available settings have vague names, such as High, Fine, Normal, and Basic. The type and amount of compression that these settings apply vary from camera to camera, so look in your manual for details about your model.

Creative Impact

Compression enables you to fit more pictures into your available camera memory. Be aware, however, that the more compression you apply, the more you sacrifice image quality, as illustrated by Figure 2.5. I shot these images with a 6-megapixel camera that offers four compression options (High, Fine, Normal, and Basic). The High option creates an uncompressed TIFF file, and the other three produce JPEG files at compression ratios of approximately 7:1 (that is, the compressed file is about seven times smaller than the original), 15:1, and 39:1.

As is the case with a low-resolution image, a highly compressed image may appear only slightly degraded if printed at a small size and on uncoated paper stock, as in Figure 2.5. But if you enlarge the images or print them on glossy, high-grade stock, the impact of too much compression becomes apparent.

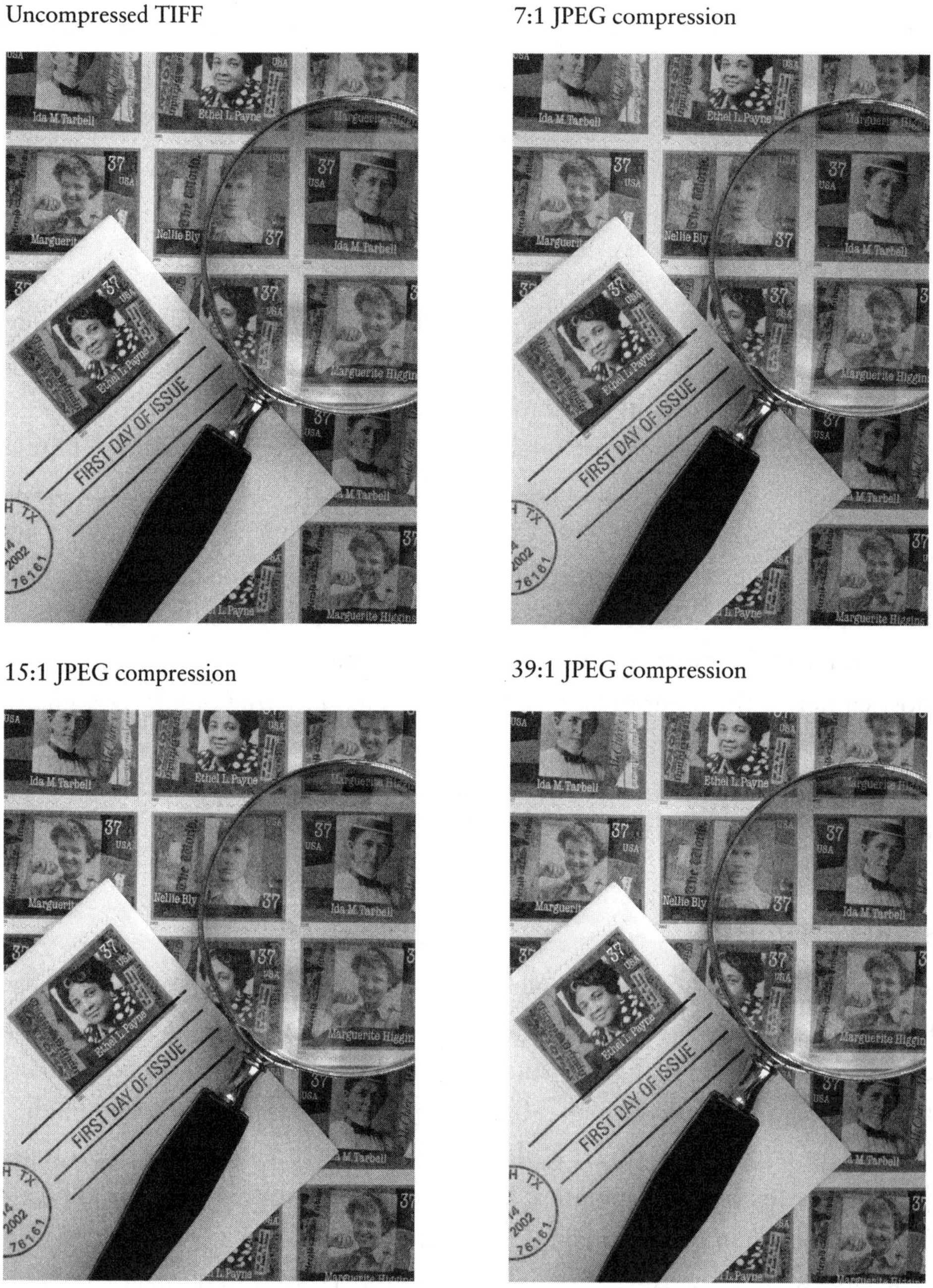

Uncompressed TIFF

7:1 JPEG compression

15:1 JPEG compression

39:1 JPEG compression

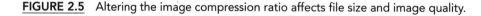

FIGURE 2.5 Altering the image compression ratio affects file size and image quality.

Take a look at Page 4 of the color insert, for example, which shows the color versions of the High (uncompressed) and Basic (39:1 compression ratio) images from Figure 2.5. In the highly-compressed example, subtle color transitions are lost, and areas of high contrast, such as the black text on the white background, are littered with random color flaws, or *artifacts*. (The tiling effect that mars the whole image occurs because the compression algorithm evaluates and reprocesses the image in 8×8-pixel blocks.)

Recommended Setting

Technically speaking, the compression question has an easy answer: For *maximum* quality, use the setting that applies the *least* compression—and stock up on extra memory cards to hold the larger image files you will create.

However, depending on the camera, you may not notice a huge difference in picture quality when you apply moderate JPEG compression, and you can reduce file size dramatically. Take a look at the top pair of images on Page 5 of the color insert, for example. The left image shows the uncompressed TIFF version of the stamp picture, which has a file size of 18MB. The right image shows the same subject captured at a JPEG compression ratio of about 7:1. It's difficult to detect any significant quality loss in the compressed version, and the file size plunges to 2.4MB.

To find out how much compression your pictures can take before they start to fall apart, shoot some test shots at each of the available settings and compare the pictures at different print and screen display sizes. Work with a subject that offers both high-contrast details, such as the lettering in the stamps, and areas of subtle color changes, such as the faces.

Remember, too, that resolution and compression work in tandem to determine picture quality and file size. As you can see from the examples on Page 5 of the color insert, you can achieve similar file sizes—but slightly different image quality.

One final compression caveat: If you're creating photos for the web or some other on-screen use and you plan to make any alterations to the pictures in your photo editor, opt for minimal camera compression. After editing, you'll need to resave your pictures in the web-friendly JPEG format, which applies another round of compression and degrades image quality further.

>> TROUBLESHOOTER

When a shortage of camera memory forces me to choose between a high-resolution, highly compressed image and a moderate-resolution, lightly compressed image, I opt for fewer pixels and less compression. In my experience, compression causes a more noticeable loss of image quality than a shortage of pixels. Note that for prints, the term "moderate resolution" is key—if you drop too low in relation to your desired print size, you'll wind up with a stair-stepping effect that's every bit as ugly as compression artifacts.

Image File Format

A half dozen or so data file formats have been created to store digital images, but only three are widely used in digital cameras:

- **JPEG**   Named for the Joint Photographic Experts Group, the organization that created the format, JPEG is the default format on most cameras.

- **TIFF** Short for Tagged Image File Format, TIFF has been the leading image format for print publications for years but has just recently appeared as an option on mid- to high-resolution cameras.

- **RAW** Typically available only on high-end cameras, this option gives you just what its name implies: a raw, uncooked file. When you select the RAW format, the camera records the image without any of the processing that typically occurs—sharpening and white-balancing, for example.

Few cameras offer all three formats or even a choice other than JPEG. If your camera is limited in this regard, don't be too worried—JPEG is a perfectly acceptable format.

Creative Impact

From a creative standpoint, each of the three image file formats has its pros and cons.

- JPEG applies lossy compression, which shrinks file size but also reduces image quality. (See the earlier section "Compression" for more information.) On the plus side, because JPEG is also an Internet format, you can upload pictures directly from the camera to the web or e-mail.

- TIFF files may also be compressed. But because TIFF uses lossless compression, top picture quality is retained. However, file sizes are much larger than with JPEG, and TIFF images aren't Internet-ready.

- RAW appeals to purists who don't want the camera handling any image processing, even if that processing makes the picture look better (which it usually does). Most photo-editing and cataloging programs can't open RAW files, however, and no web browsers or e-mail programs can handle them, either. So you need to use the camera manufacturer's proprietary software to translate the files to TIFF or JPEG before you can do much of anything with them. In addition, RAW applies no compression at all, so file sizes are large, as with TIFF.

Recommended Setting

Choose JPEG for everyday pictures. As long as you use a light compression setting, you can expect good image quality and reasonable file sizes. And you get the benefit of being able to distribute photos online immediately if needed.

For situations that demand the highest possible image quality, choose TIFF, assuming that you have enough camera memory to store the larger files. You will need to create a copy of the picture in the JPEG format for online sharing, however. (Some cameras can make the copies for you automatically, which is a great time-saver.)

As for RAW, I rarely use it because a) it's a nuisance, and b) I'm not a fanatic about recording "pure" images. The only situation in which I'd consider RAW is when I'm working with a camera that is heavy-handed with image sharpening. For more about that topic, read "Features to Ignore," at the end of this chapter.

CooL TooLs	Many cameras record details about camera settings, such as shutter speed and lens focal length, in a hidden part of a JPEG file. You can view this data—dubbed *EXIF metadata*—in some image-cataloging programs and stand-alone EXIF viewers. See Chapter 1 for more information.

Exposure Modes

Digital cameras, like point-and-shoot film cameras and some film single-lens reflex (SLR) cameras, offer *programmed autoexposure—AE* for short. In this mode, the camera automatically chooses the proper combination of aperture (f-stop) and shutter speed needed to produce a good exposure. (See Chapter 1 if you're new to these terms.)

In addition to programmed AE, advanced cameras typically provide two variations on the theme:

- **Aperture-priority AE**   Chooses the shutter speed automatically after you set the aperture.

- **Shutter-priority AE**   Sets the aperture automatically based on your selected shutter speed.

Your camera may also offer a manual exposure setting that gives you complete control over both aperture and shutter speed.

>> TROUBLESHO⊕TER

When you use any autoexposure camera, you must press the shutter button in a certain way for the exposure mechanism to work properly. After framing the shot, press the shutter button halfway down and wait for the camera to signal you that it's analyzed the scene—usually, by sounding a beep or displaying a light near the viewfinder. Then press the button the rest of the way down to capture the image.

Creative Impact

Just as a movie director uses lighting to set the mood of a scene, you can use your camera's exposure controls to convey a certain feeling in the image. You can purposely underexpose an image to give the subject an air of mystery, for example.

Beyond the obvious balance of light and dark in a photograph, however, you can alter other aspects of an image by taking control of aperture and shutter speed.

For example, you can adjust *depth of field*, or the range of the picture that's in sharp focus, by changing the aperture. The larger the aperture, the smaller the depth of field. As an example, see Figure 2.6, shown in color at the top of Page 13 in the color insert. Depth-of-field shifts get more noticeable as you zoom in or bring the camera closer to the subject, as illustrated by the lower images in the color insert.

f/2.8   f/11

FIGURE 2.6 A large aperture produces shorter depth of field (left); a small aperture brings a greater area into sharp focus (right).

In addition, when photographing a moving subject, you can use a fast shutter speed to "freeze" action. Alternatively, you can emphasize motion by using a slow shutter, which blurs the subject. For two illustrations, see Secrets #6 and #14 in the color insert.

Chapter 6 provides tips for using shutter speed to create different effects when capturing motion.

Recommended Setting

You can rely on today's programmed AE mechanisms to produce a properly exposed image in most situations—assuming, that is, that you take the two-step approach to pushing the shutter button that I described earlier. However, your idea of "proper exposure" may differ from the camera's choice. If you don't like the shutter speed, aperture, or combination thereof that the camera selects, switch to shutter-priority AE, aperture-priority AE, or manual exposure. You may also be able to get your camera to deliver the exposure you want by changing the EV setting, exposure metering mode, or ISO setting, as explained in the next few sections. And of course, you can always use your camera's built-in flash to add light to the scene, which will also force the exposure mechanism to vary aperture and shutter speed.

>> TROUBLESHOOTER

If all else fails, you can force a change in exposure when using an autoexposure camera by "tricking" the exposure mechanism. To brighten the image, aim the camera at an object that's darker than your subject and press the shutter halfway down to set the exposure. Keep holding the shutter button halfway down and then reframe your subject. When you capture the image, the camera will use the exposure setting that it found appropriate for the darker scene, resulting in a brighter exposure. To produce a darker image, use the opposite approach. Remember, though, that if you're working in autofocus mode (explained later in this chapter, in the section "Focus Modes"), the focus is also set when you press the shutter button halfway down. So be sure that the object you use when setting exposure is the same distance from the camera as your subject, or the focus will be off.

Controlling Autoexposure with EV Compensation

Even when you shoot in full programmed AE mode, you may still have some control over exposure. Most digital cameras offer an *EV compensation* control, which slightly increases or decreases the exposure that the autoexposure mechanism deems appropriate. EV stands for *exposure value,* in case you're interested.

The increments of exposure shift vary from camera to camera; typically you can ramp exposure up or down in one-half or one-third steps (for example, +0.5, +1.0, +1.5). Page 17 of the color insert offers an illustration of how EV compensation affects an image.

Choosing an Autoexposure Metering Mode

Many advanced digital cameras also enable you to control autoexposure by changing the *exposure metering mode.* The metering mode determines the area within the frame that's considered when the camera analyzes the scene and sets the exposure. Standard options include the following:

- **Multi-metering**   Measures the light at multiple locations throughout the frame and tries to choose a setting that correctly exposes everything—a task that's not always possible if the image contains very bright highlights and very dark shadows. This mode also goes by the names matrix metering, pattern metering, and multizone metering.

- **Spot metering**   Sets exposure according to the object that's smack dab in the center of the frame, the surrounding area be darned.

- **Center-weighted metering**   Also gives preference to the center of the frame, but doesn't completely discount the perimeter.

For routine shots, use multi-metering mode. However, if you're shooting a subject in strong backlighting, multi-metering will "see" all that bright light in the background and use an exposure that leaves your subject too dark, as illustrated by the first image on Page 12 of the color insert. To remedy the problem, switch to center-weighted or spot-metering. You may also need to add a flash to illuminate your subject, as was the case for the portrait featured on the color plate.

> **PRO TIP**
>
> *Although the monitor on your camera enables you to see whether you achieved a decent exposure, don't rely on it entirely. The brightness of the monitor can make a too-dark or too-light image appear to be properly exposed. To give yourself an exposure safety net, bracket your shots—that is, take the same picture at several different exposures. When you download your pictures to your computer, you can decide which exposure works the best.*
>
> *When working in autoexposure mode, you can bracket shots easily by using the EV compensation control. For example, shoot one picture at EV 0.0, one at a step down from that, and one at a step up. Your camera may even have an auto-bracketing feature that shoots the series of exposures automatically with one press of the shutter button. (Don't confuse auto-bracketing with the multi-exposure mode found on some cameras, however. Auto-bracketing creates a series of individual images; multi-exposure overlays a series of shots on top of each other, as if you had composited them in a photo-editing program.)*

ISO

Another factor affecting exposure, whether you work in autoexposure or manual exposure, is the ISO setting.

The term *ISO* is a carryover from film photography. It's an international standard (from the International Standards Organization, of course) that describes a film's light sensitivity, often called film *speed*. The higher the film speed, the less light is required to record an image. Consumer film ranges from ISO 100 to ISO 800, with higher numbers indicating faster—more sensitive—film.

On digital cameras, ISO indicates the capabilities of the image sensor relative to film. The default setting on most digital cameras is either 100 or 160; some cameras enable you to dial in a higher ISO.

Creative Impact

When you switch to a higher ISO film, you can get a good exposure at a faster shutter speed or smaller aperture. But you pay with an increase in film *grain,* which can make a photo look like it's covered with fine sand. Similarly, raising ISO on a digital camera can give your image a speckled appearance. Page 2 of the color insert offers a look at this phenomenon.

Recommended Setting

For best picture quality, leave the ISO at its lowest setting. Raise the value *only* if you're working in low lighting or trying to capture very fast action—or both—and you don't have any other way to record the scene.

Flash Modes

Every point-and-shoot digital camera costing more than $100 offers a built-in flash, as do most digital SLR models. You also get a choice of flash modes, which control how and when the flash is fired.

Because the correct flash mode varies depending on your subject, lighting, and the type of photography you want to do—all topics explored in detail in later chapters—I won't go into specific creative options or recommendations here. Instead, here's a mini review of commonly available modes and their uses:

- **Auto flash**   Triggers the flash when the camera thinks it's needed, which is a great feature for casual snapshooting.

- **Fill (or Force) flash**   Fires the flash for every shot. You often need to use this mode for good outdoor portraits, for reasons discussed in Chapter 3.

- **No flash**   Prevents the flash from firing, which is a good thing when you're trying to shoot shiny objects, such as glass or chrome. See Chapter 4 for details.

- **Red-eye flash**   Produces a mini flash that lights in advance of the main flash. The idea is that a subject's pupils will constrict in response to the mini flash, thereby lessening the chance of red-eye, which is caused by the main flash reflecting in said pupils. In a dark room, the feature rarely solves the problem entirely—which is why manufacturers refer to this feature as red-eye *reduction* mode, not red-eye *prevention* mode. Chapter 3 offers more advice about red-eye.

- **Slow-sync flash**   Enables you to use slower shutter speeds than the camera normally allows for flash photography. When you're shooting at night or in a dimly lit room, this mode enables you to capture both subject and background. Without it, the background usually appears dark. See Chapter 6 for details.

If you're working with an accessory flash unit instead of a built-in flash, you may not be able to take advantage of the full range of flash modes on your camera; check the camera and flash manual to determine your options. You may also find that you can adjust the intensity of both the on-board flash and the external flash unit by using a Flash EV control.

Chapter 3 provides more details about working with an external flash; see Chapter 4 for a look at how varying flash intensity can come in handy when doing still-life photography.

Focus Modes

For film photographers making the transition from a 35mm SLR camera to a point-and-shoot digital model, learning to cope with the focusing systems is perhaps the most difficult adjustment.

Few digital cameras offer the manual lens-focusing ring found on traditional SLR lenses—the kind that you simply twist to focus. Instead, autofocus is the norm. When you press the shutter button halfway down, the camera reads the lens-to-subject distance and sets the focus automatically. This process happens in conjunction with the autoexposure reading, explained earlier in this chapter.

Typically, you get both a macro focusing option for shooting close-ups and a standard focusing setting for normal photography. Many cameras also offer manual focus control, but you have to use menus to set a specific focusing distance.

Creative Impact

Although autofocusing can be frustrating at first if you're used to a traditional focusing mechanism, it doesn't really limit your creative options. You just have to learn to use the autofocus system properly.

For example, suppose that you don't want your main subject to be centered in the picture. Not a problem. Frame the image with the subject in the center, press and hold the shutter button halfway down to "lock" the focus distance, reframe the scene, and then press the shutter button the rest of the way down.

You're most likely to be limited in close-up focusing distance. You may need to invest in an accessory macro lens if you want to shoot extreme close-ups. But the same is true for a 35mm camera, so don't blame this one on digital technology. In fact, most digital cameras offer *closer* focusing at the macro setting than a film camera.

Chapter 5 discusses close-up digital photography in detail.

Recommendations

If your camera does offer a manual focusing ring, by all means feel free to enjoy it. But if you don't have that option or you just don't want to mess with manual focusing, you can safely leave the camera in autofocus mode for most shots. Today's autofocus mechanisms are pretty savvy, as long as you use the correct technique. Again: Frame, press the shutter button halfway to lock focus, and then depress the button fully to capture the image.

For even greater focusing flexibility, check your manual to see whether your camera offers a way to alter the subject area that the camera considers when setting the focus. Some cameras offer a spot-focusing mode, for example, that enables you to target only the object that's in the very center of the frame.

If you're shooting close-ups, remember to switch to macro focusing mode. For close-ups where specific focusing is critical, you'll probably want to use manual focusing, even though it's a pain to have to use menus to set the focus distance.

White Balance

White balance is purely a digital animal when it comes to still photography, but this control may be familiar to you if you're experienced with video cameras.

As with a video camera, the white balance control addresses the fact that different light sources—daylight, fluorescent light, incandescent bulbs, and so on—have different color temperatures. (*Color temperature* is a measure of the hue emitted by a particular light source.) White balance enables the camera to compensate for any color cast that may be created by the light source.

Creative Impact

Film photographers must account for changing color temperatures by using different films and color filters. Going digital eliminates that hassle. Your digital camera should offer automatic white balancing, freeing you to concentrate on other issues.

As creative digital photographers have discovered, however, you can use the manual white-balance override found on most cameras to create the same effects as you get from a warming or cooling filter. Nifty! See Page 26 of the color insert for examples.

Recommended Setting

Again, unless you're trying to achieve a special color effect, automatic white balancing works well in most lighting conditions. However, when you're working with multiple light sources that have different color temperatures, you may need to take control of white balancing.

If you're shooting in an office that's lit by both fluorescent overhead lights and window light, the camera may be confused about what white balance to use, for example. Turn on your camera's LCD monitor to preview the shot, and if you notice a weird color cast, white balance is the likely culprit.

Features to Ignore (or Turn Off)

In addition to all the other features discussed in this chapter, your camera probably includes a handful of other options, which I consider to be minor conveniences at best and downright annoyances at worst. Here's my take on the most common of these second-tier players, listed in order of their usefulness.

Creative Scene Modes

Most digital cameras offer some preset shooting modes that automatically dial in the settings that the manufacturer considers best for certain types of photography. Typically, you can select from at least two modes: portrait and landscape. Some cameras go further and offer an action mode for capturing moving subjects and nighttime mode for after-hours shooting.

Because every manufacturer uses slightly different settings for these modes, I can't make a wholesale recommendation about which ones work best. You may want to do some tests to compare the images produced by each mode with the results you get when you take the photographic reins. If you have an image browser or viewer that can read the EXIF metadata that's stored in a JPEG image file, you can see the specific settings that the camera uses in each of the scene modes.

PRO TIP

On cameras that don't provide a way to set aperture or shutter speed manually, you may be able to get the setting you want by changing the scene mode. Switching to action mode usually produces the camera's fastest shutter speed, and choosing nighttime mode usually selects the slowest shutter. Similarly, portrait mode typically forces a larger aperture (lower f-stop), while landscape mode selects a smaller aperture.

Correction and Color Filters

With the exception of images captured in the RAW file format, all digital photos undergo some image processing as they're being stored to the camera memory. Color, sharpness, contrast, and other attributes may be tweaked to produce an image that the manufacturer believes will be the most satisfactory to the camera's target audience.

This image manipulation isn't necessarily a bad thing. In fact, whether you know it or not, your film pictures get similar treatment when you have them developed at a retail photo lab. But some cameras can be overzealous, especially in the area of sharpening. Page 22 of the color insert offers an illustration.

If an image seems a little soft, you can always use your photo editor's sharpening filter to improve things. But correcting an oversharpened image is difficult. So either turn off in-camera sharpening or use the lowest available setting.

As for color effects, including those that convert your photo to a black-and-white picture or add special effects such as a sepia tone, I recommend that you ignore them. For reasons explored in Chapter 8, you get more control over your image if you shoot in regular, full-color mode and do any color manipulations in your photo editor.

Digital Zoom

Digital zoom is nothing like having a true, optical zoom lens. Digital zoom simply enlarges the existing image and crops away the outer edges, just as if you had taken the same steps in a photo editor. The quality of the resulting picture is reduced because you have fewer pixels in your "zoomed" image.

So why do manufacturers offer this feature? Simple. Most people don't understand the difference between digital and optical zoom, and they think they're getting something important when they see "digital zoom" on the camera box. Or they may see only the part of the camera ad that claims "28X total zoom!" and completely miss the fine print, which reveals that the model in fact offers an optical zoom factor of only 3X, with the rest of that 28-times magnification being produced by digital trickery. I've even heard camera salespeople say that a cheaper camera with only a digital zoom is better than a more expensive model with an optical zoom—because the magnification number (that X factor) is higher on the model with the digital zoom.

In the immortal words of the Mad Hatter in Walt Disney's version of *Alice in Wonderland,* "Oh, my goodness! THOSE are the things that UPSET me!" (I've been waiting 20 years to use that line. Sometimes spending hours in front of the television doesn't pay off right away.)

SEE ALSO

In case you think I'm mad as a hatter, check out Page 21 of the color insert, which illustrates what happens when you use digital zoom. Chapter 5 offers more advice about using a zoom lens and other means of getting closer to your subject.

PART II

Discovering the Secrets
of the Pros

Taking Memorable Portraits

Have you ever wondered why portraits taken in the early days of photography rarely feature a smiling subject? One theory—a kind of disgusting one, actually—is that dental hygiene wasn't yet a priority, and thus a toothy grin was not the most attractive choice. A more likely explanation, though, was that recording an image in those days required exposure times of many minutes, during which the subject had to remain absolutely still. Sometimes the sitter's head was even clamped into place to make sure it didn't move! Small wonder, then, that the most relaxed, happy-countenanced subjects appear in so-called casket photos that were taken to memorialize a person shortly after death.

Today's cameras can capture a subject in fractions of a second, and most people possess presentable choppers, thanks to all those grade school lessons about the importance of brushing after meals. Even so, a smiling subject doesn't necessarily translate to a good portrait. Improper lighting, unflattering camera angles, and other creative missteps can make the most beautiful subject look terrible. And let's not forget the number-one plague of indoor and nighttime flash photography: red-eye.

This chapter focuses on techniques and tools that will help you improve your people pictures, whether you're taking family photos for the living-room wall or employee head shots for your company newsletter. The first part of the chapter provides some general advice about using your digital camera for portrait work, and the remaining pages offer some specific tricks that you can use when shooting casual, formal, and outdoor portraits.

SEE ALSO

For tips related to nighttime and action portraits, see Chapter 6.

Basics of Digital Portrait Photography

Shooting a digital portrait involves many of the same concerns as a film portrait—good lighting, complementary clothing and backgrounds, and, of course, a reasonably cooperative subject. But working with a digital camera throws some additional issues into the mix, as the next few sections explain.

Composing for Traditional Frame Sizes

An old rule of video photography says that you should include "head room" around the top and sides of the frame so that if people move during the shot, their faces don't shift out of the picture. In still photography, close framing is perfectly acceptable and can even be dramatic. But eliminating all head room when capturing digital images can lead to a problem if you later want to print and frame the picture.

Digital cameras produce images that have a 4:3 *aspect ratio* (width relative to height), which matches that of a computer monitor or television. A 35mm film negative, on the other hand, produces images with a 3:2 aspect ratio, which is the same as for a 4×6-inch photo frame. A 5×7-inch frame has an aspect ratio of 5:7; an 8×10-inch frame, 4:5.

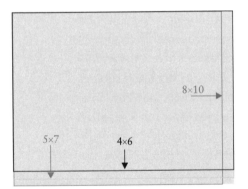

FIGURE 3.1 Pictures from a digital camera have a different aspect ratio than traditional photo frames.

Figure 3.1 illustrates the difference between these various aspect ratios. The light gray background rectangle represents a 4:3 digital image; the outlines represent the 4×6, 5×7, and 8×10 aspect ratios. (For the sake of clarity, everything is oriented with the long edges running horizontally.)

When you enlarge a 35mm film image to a 5×7 or 8×10, the photo lab must either crop the picture or add a white border to account for the difference in aspect ratio between the original and the enlargement. You must make the same decision if you want to mount your digital image in any of the commercially available frame sizes (or mattes), at least until manufacturers get wise and start producing frames with a 4:3 aspect ratio.

As an example, see Figure 3.2. The left image is the digital original; the middle image shows what part of the picture would remain if cropped to the 4×6-inch aspect ratio. At this aspect ratio, part of the toddler's head must be cropped away. Your other option is to reduce the original and add a border, as shown in the right image.

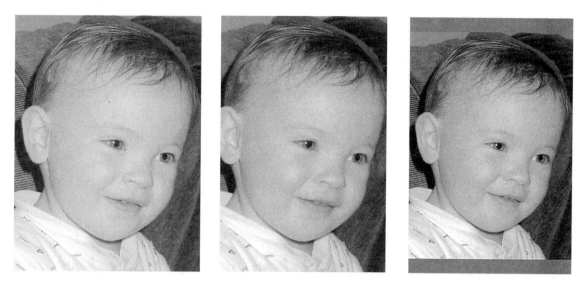

FIGURE 3.2   If you don't leave a little head room (left), you must either crop away a portion of the subject's face (middle) or reduce the image size and add a border (right) if you want to make the picture fit a 4×6-inch photo frame.

The moral of the story: To avoid having to lose part of your subject's face or add an unsightly border, always leave a decent margin of head room when you're shooting digital portraits. The top portrait on Page 6 of the color insert offers an example. This loose framing enables you to crop the photo as needed to fit a variety of frame sizes and aspect ratios.

Of course, another way to solve the problem is to take your digital prints to a framing store and buy a custom-cut matte or frame. But you can save yourself the expense and hassle by simply getting in the habit of allowing adequate head room for all your portraits.

**CooL
 TooLs**   Some digital cameras now offer a special 3:2 format setting in addition to the standard 4:3 format. This option limits you to capturing an area that has a 3:2 aspect ratio, a feature that's especially useful when you're shooting pictures that you know you want to frame.

Choosing Aperture and Shutter Speed

Portrait photography calls for a large aperture, such as f/2.8 or f/3.5, which creates a short depth of field and therefore leaves the background slightly soft in focus. A short depth of field makes the subject more visually prominent because the viewer's eye goes first to whatever is in sharpest focus. In addition, reducing the depth of field makes distracting background objects less noticeable, as discussed in Chapter 2 and illustrated on Page 13 of the color insert.

You can set aperture precisely if your camera offers either manual exposure or aperture-priority autoexposure (AE). Remember that as you enlarge the aperture (by shifting to a lower f-stop number), you need to increase shutter speed to account for the additional light that comes through that larger aperture. In aperture-priority AE, the camera makes the adjustment for you automatically.

≫ TROUBLESHOOTER

If your camera does not offer manual exposure control or aperture-priority AE, you may be able to force a larger aperture by using portrait scene mode (covered next).

Taking Advantage of Portrait Mode

Many digital cameras offer *scene modes,* which automatically select aperture, shutter speed, and other settings that are appropriate for various types of pictures. The two most common scene modes are portrait and landscape.

Each camera manufacturer uses different settings for its scene modes, but portrait mode typically selects the largest available aperture to achieve the shortest possible depth of field. (See the preceding section, "Choosing Aperture and Shutter Speed," for more on this topic.) Depending on the camera, portrait mode may also select a particular focal length, sharpening amount, flash setting, and exposure metering mode.

You can see what settings your camera chooses in portrait mode by shooting some sample pictures and then inspecting the EXIF file data in an image viewer, as explored in Chapter 1. You then can decide whether you can rely on portrait mode or need to take more control. Remember that the settings your camera selects in any scene mode will vary depending on the amount of light; in bright sunlight, for example, the camera will likely choose a smaller aperture than it does in low light.

≫ TROUBLESHOOTER

Using a neutral density filter over your lens reduces the amount of light entering your camera and so enables you to use a wider aperture in bright light. See Chapter 6 for more information.

PRO TIP

Check your camera manual to see whether you can store custom capture settings as your own personal scene modes. This feature gives you the convenience of preset modes without having to give up any creative control.

Finding a Flattering Camera Angle

For most portraits, you should position the camera at the subject's eye level. A high camera angle creates the impression of diminished stature, as if the viewer is towering over the subject. On the flip side, shooting from a very low angle can make subjects appear haughty because they seem to be looking down their noses at the viewer.

In addition, a high or low camera angle may distort your subject's physical proportions, as illustrated by Figure 3.3, which features a selection from my personal photo box of shame. I shot this picture of my nephew from a high angle, which led to a bizarre rendering of his body shape.

Just because your camera is positioned at eye level doesn't mean that you always need to have your subject looking straight into the lens, though. As illustrated by Figure 3.2 and by the left example in Figure 3.4, an upward or downward gaze can be enchanting. However, as you can see when you compare the left and right images in Figure 3.4, a straight-ahead viewpoint creates a greater sense of intimacy because the subject appears to be looking the viewer in the eye.

FIGURE 3.3 Distortion of body proportions can occur when you shoot from an extreme point of view— in this case, from high above the subject.

FIGURE 3.4 Directing your subject's eyes to a position slightly above the camera can help reduce red-eye (left); but a straight-ahead gaze creates a stronger sense of intimacy (right).

Technical Aside
What Causes Red-Eye?

Red-eye is caused by light from a flash reflecting off a subject's retinas, taking on the color of surrounding blood vessels. In some animal eyes, the problem may show up as a green, yellow, or white glare because of a colored membrane that's located behind the retina.

Man or beast, the problem usually occurs only when the flash is positioned close to the camera lens, as it is on point-and-shoot cameras, and in low lighting, when the subject's pupils are dilated (enlarged) to absorb more light. If you have no other choice but to use a flash, you can lessen red-eye by taking advantage of the red-eye reduction flash setting found on most cameras. Before the main flash fires, the camera emits a brief "preflash" light to shrink the pupils a little. Another trick is to tell the subject to look slightly up or down so that reflected light from the retinas doesn't bounce back directly into the lens. Of course, moving farther from your subject also reduces red-eye because less flash light reaches the eyes.

Avoiding Focal Length and Distance Distortions

Extreme camera angles aren't the only cause of subject distortion. You can also warp features if you use a wide-angle lens (short focal length) and position the camera too

close to the subject, as illustrated by the left image in Figure 3.5. This image is doubly awful because I stood so close that I exceeded the camera's minimum focusing distance, leaving the subject distorted *and* blurry. Stepping back from my young friend fixed both problems.

FIGURE 3.5   Using a wide-angle lens and standing too close to the subject caused a blurred image and extreme smushing of facial features (left); putting more distance between subject and camera solved the problem (right).

Even when you can achieve proper focus, however, you may still be in the distortion zone, as shown in Figure 3.6. This time, my niece was the unlucky subject. Her face appears misshapen because I again used the wide-angle setting on my camera's zoom lens and stood only a few feet away. Even my niece's incredible blue eyes, which you can see on Page 6 of the color insert, aren't enough to make this image a winner—the distortion along with the ugly background add up to a picture that's good for illustrating common photography errors, but not much else.

To get a better result, shown in Figure 3.7, I convinced my niece to pose in a spot that would provide a more pleasing backdrop. (My attempts to get her to step in *front* of the bushes instead of climbing in the middle of them weren't successful, but when you're a proud aunt, you don't let little things like that stop you from taking pictures.) I stood about eight or nine feet away and zoomed in to the camera's maximum focal length, which is about three times that used for the previous image.

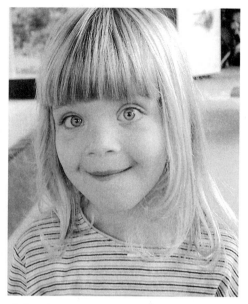

FIGURE 3.6 Even when you're within the camera's minimum focusing distance, you still may be too close to get a distortion-free image with a wide-angle lens.

FIGURE 3.7 This time, I positioned the camera farther from the subject and zoomed to a longer focal length (left). I later cropped the image to fill more of the frame with the face (right).

> **PRO TIP**
>
> *If you want to fill the frame with your subject's head and shoulders, use a focal length equivalent to about 135mm on a 35mm film camera and shoot at a distance of about seven feet to avoid distortion. You need to check your manual to determine how your camera's focal-length range compares to the 35mm film-camera standard. On the camera used for Figures 3.6 and 3.7, the wide-angle setting equates to a focal length of approximately that of a 35mm lens, and the maximum telephoto zoom setting is equal to about 105mm.*

If your camera offers only a fixed focal length, you simply have to keep moving back from your subject until you reach the distortion-free position. Of course, when you do so, you get more background in the picture. If you shoot at a high enough image resolution, you can always crop away the excess background and enlarge the remaining image in your photo editor, as I did to create the right example in Figure 3.7 and Page 6 of the color insert.

Chapter 1 explains how to compare digital camera focal lengths to focal lengths on a 35mm film camera—and why the two technologies work on a different scale. See Chapter 2 for tips on image resolution.

Casual Indoor Portraits

Whenever I walk through my local shopping mall, I pass by one of those quick-portrait places that are so popular in suburbia today. I'm always filled with deepest sympathy for the photographers and their assistants, who more often than not seem trapped in a noisy nightmare. While they work desperately to coax a smile out of a fussy infant, tantrum-throwing toddler, or sarcastic teen, the parent makes their job even harder by scolding the child and giving unsolicited photography advice.

I have tremendous respect for people who can survive that kind of photographic duty on a daily basis, and I certainly don't want to take money out of their deserving pockets. But I also have no doubt that you can produce portraits that are just as satisfactory in your own home, without all the stress to everyone involved. In fact, because your subjects are likely to be more relaxed at home, I dare say that your pictures will be even better than those you bring home from the mall.

The secret to great home portraits is, as with so many things in life, simplicity. You don't need expensive studio lighting or a fancy backdrop that's painted with cartoon characters or a fake beach scene. A chair positioned next to a sunlit window, as shown in Figure 3.8, offers an ideal foundation for an indoor portrait. (If the chair is upholstered, be sure that it isn't covered with a busy fabric that will be distracting in the photo.)

Although window light will serve well as your major light source, it likely will not be entirely sufficient. The following sections discuss a variety of

FIGURE 3.8 Window light provides a good starting point for an indoor portrait.

options for bringing additional light to your photo; some choices produce better results than others, as illustrated by the series of images on Pages 8 and 9 of the color insert and Figures 3.9 through 3.11. (Note that I cropped these images to show just the subject's head and shoulders; as discussed in the preceding section, filling the frame at the subject-to-camera distance shown in Figure 3.8 would have distorted the facial features.)

Using Flash

The easiest way to add light is to switch on your camera's built-in flash. Unfortunately, red-eye problems usually result, as illustrated by the first portrait example on Page 8 of the color insert. I should point out, though, that because your subject's pupils will be constricted somewhat in response to the bright window light, red-eye shouldn't be as severe as it would be if you were using flash in a dark room.

In addition to causing red-eye, a built-in flash is too focused to produce soft, even lighting. Compare the left image in Figure 3.9 with its companion to the right, which I shot using an external flash bounced off the wall behind the subject. (The second image on Page 8 in the color insert shows the external flash example as well.) The face in the second image is much more evenly lit, and as the color version of the picture shows, red-eye is no longer a problem. On the downside, the stronger light produced by the external flash creates a large, harsh shadow that pulls attention away from the subject.

Built-in flash

External bounced flash

FIGURE 3.9 A built-in flash creates uneven lighting (left); an external flash fixes that problem but adds a large, harsh shadow behind the subject's head (right).

>> TROUBLESHO⊕TER

When working with an external flash, you can soften shadows by placing a piece of translucent white plastic or paper over the flash head to diffuse the light. You also can find commercial flash diffusers in your local camera store. Keep in mind that you may need to increase exposure because you will be reducing the amount of direct light hitting the subject. Depending on your camera and flash, you also may be able to adjust the flash output.

Boosting Exposure Through EV Compensation

When you have a fair amount of ambient lighting—in the case of the example portraits, provided via the adjacent window—you may be able to go flashless and get a good exposure by boosting your camera's EV (exposure value) compensation control. Using a positive EV setting produces a brighter exposure than the camera's autoexposure mechanism believes is appropriate. Figure 3.10 shows the exposure produced with the flash disabled and the EV setting at 0.0 (that is, no exposure adjustment) and at +0.7. The first portrait example on Page 9 of the color insert also shows the +0.7 image.

EV 0.0   EV +0.7

FIGURE 3.10   For these images, I turned off the flash and used an EV compensation setting of 0.0 (left) and +0.7 (right).

You may discover, however, that raising the EV setting enough to expose the darkest areas of the face properly overexposes the lighter areas, as it did in the example photo. The window side of the head and hand went almost completely white at the increased exposure.

PRO TIP
If you are working at maximum aperture, as I was for the example portraits, your camera will reduce shutter speed in response to a higher EV compensation setting. Be sure to use a tripod so that you don't blur the image by accidentally moving the camera during the longer exposure.

Adding Reflected Light

If a flash creates harsh shadows or red-eye, and boosting EV compensation blows out highlights, a simple pro trick can save the day. Just use a reflector to bounce window light back onto the shaded side of the face, as shown in Figure 3.11. If you don't have an extra pair of hands around to hold the reflector, you can prop it against a stack of books or a chair.

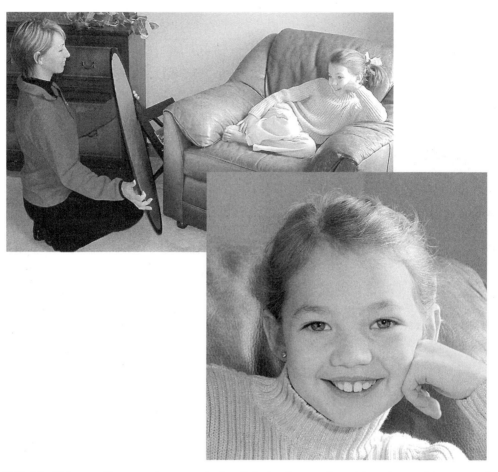

FIGURE 3.11   Using a reflector to bounce window light back onto the subject can enable you to shoot without a flash or increased EV compensation.

✂ COST CUTTER

You don't need a commercially made reflector to create bounced light. A piece of white cardboard will work just fine. If you want a more subtle effect, cover the cardboard with a piece of gold reflective material from the fabric store. Just keep in mind that the smaller the reflector, the more focused the reflected light. I used a 32-inch reflector for the portrait in Figure 3.11 so that both the face and sweater would receive a boost of soft, diffused light. With a smaller size—say, 12 inches— you could concentrate the added light on the face alone.

In the example portrait, the reflector reduced deep shadows on the face without creating heavy shadowing behind the head. And because the scene no longer contained a large expanse of dark areas, the camera didn't crank up the exposure so much that the brightly lit side of the face was overexposed, as it did in the no-flash examples in Figure 3.10.

In the reflector image, the bright side of the picture is only slightly "hot," creating a subtle glow that tells the viewer that the subject is by a window even though the window isn't visible.

>> TROUBLESHOOTER

When you are working with two different types of light, such as window light and a flash, your camera may not render skin tones accurately when you use the automatic white-balance setting. You can read more about this issue on Page 9 of the color insert and find out how to tweak white balance in Chapter 8.

Quick-Snap Portraits

Not all subjects are as cooperative as the beautiful young lady who agreed to pose for the series of window-side portraits featured in the preceding sections. In my family, even getting people to stand still for a quick snapshot is often a challenge. When you don't have time to arrange people, lighting, or the setting as carefully as you'd like, try these tricks:

- For a quick and easy backdrop for kid pics, throw some big pillows on the floor and have the kids plop down on them. In Figure 3.12, for example, I used sofa cushions, placing them next to a sliding glass door to take advantage of strong window lighting.

- For a family grouping, a plain wall or curtain can provide a nice backdrop. If you use a curtained window as the background during daylight hours, however, you may need to adjust your exposure to account for backlighting, as covered in the later section "Outdoor Portraits."

FIGURE 3.12 Sofa cushions placed next to a sliding glass door provided a great backdrop for this snapshot.

- At night, you will need to use a flash even if you switch on room lighting. If your camera offers slow-sync flash or slow-sync red-eye flash, switching to that mode will help brighten the background. (Chapter 6 has details.) That's assuming the background is worth showing—if it's not, leave the flash in regular mode or red-eye mode, and your background will appear dark.

- Speaking of red-eye flash mode, warn your subjects that they will see two bursts of light, and that the second one indicates that the flash has fired. The first light appears to constrict the subject's pupils slightly, which helps reduce red-eye. (See the Technical Aside sidebar "What Causes Red-Eye?" earlier in this chapter.) If you don't give people this warning, they will think that the preflash is the real flash and stop smiling or move before the picture is actually recorded.

- Don't always insist that people face the camera and say "cheese." Instead, look for opportunities to catch a subject enjoying an everyday activity, which almost always offers a truer reflection of a subject's personality and is infinitely more interesting. Also, capturing interaction between people tells more about their relationship than the typical shoulder-to-shoulder arrangement that most people use for their family photos.

- If you're trying to photograph very young children, fire the flash a few times before you really get serious so that they can get used to your presence. After a while, they'll forget that you're there, and you can capture them doing what they do best: being kids.

PRO TIP

Even though I've just spent several pages offering advice about how to improve your own home portraits, don't write off the idea of working with a professional portrait photographer every now and then, especially for important occasions such as an anniversary or engagement. In addition to years of technical expertise, a skilled professional can bring artistic ideas to the table that you may not have considered. And a professional portrait may offer the only opportunity for you to get in the picture instead of standing behind the camera!

?How To

REMOVE RED-EYE

Almost every photo-editing program offers an automated red-eye removal tool. Too bad these tools hardly ever work well. The good news is that doing the job on your own is probably even easier than working with the automated tools. Here's how to do it in Adobe Photoshop Elements 2.0:

1. Duplicate the background image layer so that if you mess up, you can easily return the image to its original state. Just open the Layers palette and drag the background layer to the new layer icon, labeled in Figure 3.13.

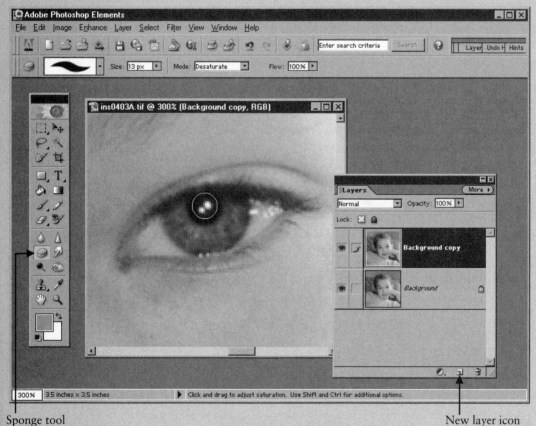

Sponge tool   New layer icon

FIGURE 3.13   Working on a duplicate image layer, first use the Sponge tool to desaturate the red pixels.

2. Select the Sponge tool from the toolbox.

3. On the Options bar, set the Mode control to Desaturate and the Flow setting to 100 percent, as shown in the figure.

?How To

REMOVE RED-EYE *(continued)*

4. Choose a small, hard-edged brush. The brush should be smaller than the red-eye area you want to correct.

5. Click or drag over the red-eye pixels. The program sucks the color out of the pixels you touch, leaving them white, black, or gray.

6. Create a new, empty layer by clicking the new layer icon in the Layers palette. This layer will hold your new eye color. Set the layer blending mode to Color by using the menu at the top of the Layers palette, as shown in Figure 3.14.

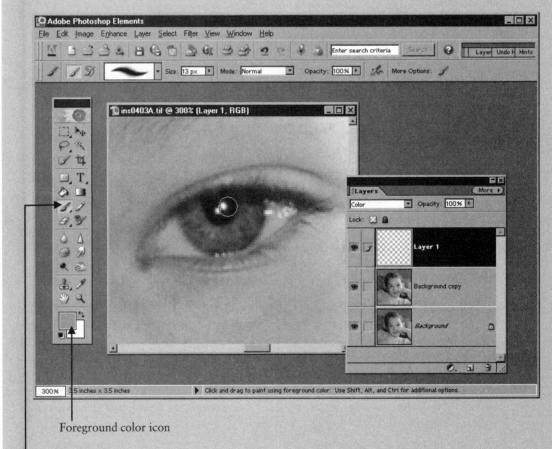

Foreground color icon

Paintbrush

FIGURE 3.14   Paint in the correct eye color on a separate layer set to the Color blending mode.

REMOVE RED-EYE *(continued)*

7. Click the foreground color icon (labeled in Figure 3.14) and choose a color that's close to the subject's natural eye color.

8. Activate the Paintbrush tool, also labeled in Figure 3.14. Again, use a small brush, but this time you may want to work with a soft brush tip so that your paint strokes don't have hard edges.

9. Dab on the new eye color as needed. If you don't see any change, as may be the case when working on animal eyes, switch the blending mode to Normal and reduce the Opacity setting in the Layers palette to about 50 percent.

10. When you're happy with your work, merge the image layers by choosing Layer | Flatten Image.

You can use this same approach with any program that offers a Sponge tool, layers, and the layer blending mode. Don't have any of those tools? If your photo editor offers a hue/saturation filter, try this fix instead: Select the red portion of the eyes and then adjust the color by using the hue control. You also may be able to use a regular color balance filter, which is a basic filter found in every photo editor.

Professional Head Shots

In the business world, people often need a formal head shot, a close-up photo showing just the face and maybe a bit of shoulder. Many social organizations also request this type of photo for their publications.

If you take head shots regularly, I recommend that you invest in at least one professional studio light. Moving a chair next to a window is a good solution for home portraits, but it's a little unpractical in an office, church, or other out-of-home setting. A studio light will also enable you to shoot without a flash, saving you the hassle of having to fix red-eye in every picture.

✂ COST CUTTER

If buying a light blows your budget, you can save some money on your portrait backdrop. Just head to the hardware store and buy a canvas drop cloth to use as your backdrop. You can hang the drop cloth from a curtain rod, clamp it to a storage cabinet door, or just tape it to the wall behind your subject.

With just one light, you can produce a nice head shot, as illustrated by the top image on Page10 in the color insert. Figure 3.15 shows the same image in grayscale along with the relative positions of camera, light, and subject. I used a studio "hot" light, attaching a white reflective umbrella to diffuse the light and prevent harsh shadows.

FIGURE 3.15 A simple, one-light setup produces a nice head shot.

Chapter 1 provides more information about hot lights and other lighting options.

By adding reflectors or a second light—or both—you can make subtle changes to how a face is rendered, as illustrated by the other examples on Pages 10 and 11 of the color insert. Here's a look at the different setups I used and how they affected the portrait:

- **One light with reflector** For the second and third images on Page 10 in the color insert, I placed a large reflector next to the subject, as indicated by the diagram in Figure 3.16. The reflector bounced light from the main light onto the face, reducing the shadows that you see along the subject's right cheek (left side of the photo) in Figure 3.15.

  For the first of the two reflector images (shown in Figure 3.16 as well as on Page 10 of the insert), I used a white reflector. For the second reflector image, I switched to a gold reflector. As you can see from the color plate, the white reflector creates a stronger bounced light than the gold reflector, and the gold reflector adds a subtle warming effect.

- **Two lights** Replacing the reflector with a second light, positioned as indicated in Figure 3.17, creates even lighting across the face. Losing the shadowing on the side

FIGURE 3.16   A reflector positioned next to the subject reduces shadowing on the side of the face that's farthest from the main light.

of the face makes the face appear slightly flatter, however. And although the side shadows are gone, the shadows around the nose and mouth are more pronounced. In addition to being unflattering, those shadows add so much contrast to that area that they pull attention away from the eyes and wonderful smile. Ditto for the heavier shadow that results under the jacket lapel.

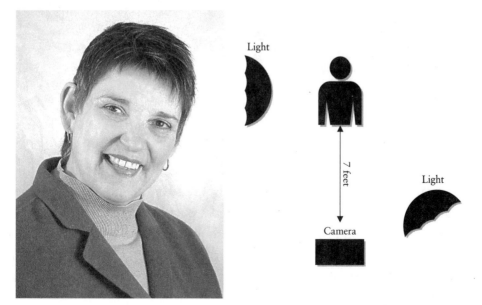

FIGURE 3.17   Replacing the reflector with a second soft light creates even lighting but results in harsh shadows around the nose and mouth and under the jacket lapel.

- **Two lights, low reflector**   To soften the facial shadowing without abandoning the second light, I asked the subject to hold a small white reflector on her lap. We positioned the reflector to bounce light up onto her face, which softened the problematic shadows, as shown in Figure 3.18 and in the middle image on Page 11 of the color insert. But that reflected light source also lightened the neck area, which here has the effect of making the chin and neck appear to blend together. In fact, the whole face starts to take on a two-dimensional appearance.

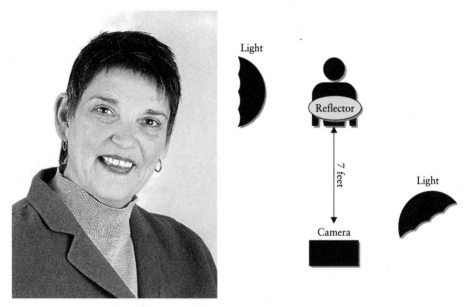

FIGURE 3.18   A reflector placed on the subject's lap throws additional light on her face but also makes the boundary between chin and neck less defined.

For the final image, shown in Figure 3.19 and at the bottom of Page 11 of the insert, we used the same lighting setup but changed the angle of the face and tilted the chin slightly downward. This new orientation solved a couple of problems. First, less of the neck shows, so the illusion of chin blending into neck is gone. Second, with the change in head angle, some soft shadowing appears on the side of the face, bringing some dimension back to the features. Finally, only one earring is now visible, and in a much less distracting way than in the earlier images.

I also took care to pull the neck of the jacket and shirt tight to eliminate the gapping that occurs in the other images. (No sense in fussing with these details until you work out the lighting and all the other issues.)

FIGURE 3.19 Changing the angle of the head produced a more flattering image and made the earrings less of a distraction.

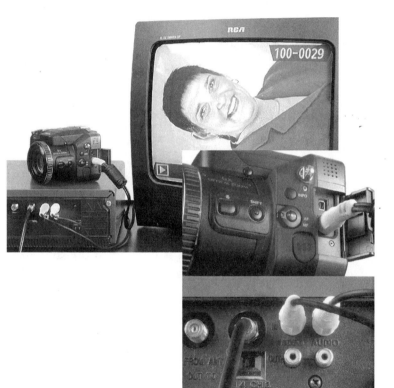

FIGURE 3.20 Connecting your camera to a television offers a better way to evaluate each shot than using the small monitor on the camera.

PRO TIP

If your camera offers a video-out port, you may want to connect the camera to a television or VCR, as shown in Figure 3.20, when shooting formal portraits. You then can preview and play back shots on the TV instead of in the camera's monitor, which is too small to reveal subtle problems with an image. If you position the monitor so that both you and the subject can see it, you can assess each shot together. (If you oriented the camera in a vertical position, however, the image appears lying on its side on the monitor screen, as shown in the figure, unless your camera offers an automatic rotation option.)

To hook the camera to the TV, connect a video cable (usually supplied with the camera) between the camera's video-out port and the TV or VCR video-in jack, as shown in the close-up in Figure 3.20. If your camera records audio, the second plug goes in the audio-in jack.

Outdoor Portraits

Given the option, I always take portraits outdoors during the daytime. Why? Frankly, it's easier than working indoors. The sun provides a convenient (and energy efficient) light source, you don't have to worry about red-eye, and you can usually find a suitable backdrop close by—a stand of evergreens, a garden, or even a brick wall. Your only real challenge is making sure that your subject is properly exposed. The following techniques will help you accomplish that goal:

- The best times of day to work outdoors are in mid-morning and late afternoon. Try to avoid shooting at midday, when the position of the sun can create harsh shadows on the face.

- Position subjects so that they don't directly face the sun. Otherwise, they will have trouble not squinting. Either move your subjects into a shady spot or position them so that the sun is to one side or behind them. Another option is to have someone hold a large piece of cardboard between the sun and your subject—to create your own shade, in other words.

- When your subject is in front of the sun—*backlit*, as we say in the biz—guard against underexposing the image. In normal autoexposure metering mode, your camera takes the entire frame into account when calculating exposure. As a result, strong backlighting results in an exposure that leaves the foreground subject underexposed, as shown in Figure 3.21 and in the top image on Page 12 of the color insert. (This metering mode goes by several different names, by the way: pattern metering, matrix metering, and multi-zone metering are just a few.)

- If your camera offers a choice of autoexposure metering modes, switch to center-weighted or spot metering mode. For a single subject, spot metering usually works best. But for a group of people, center-weighted may be a better option. Spot metering calculates exposure based on a small area in the center of the frame, and center-weighted metering gives preferential treatment to the center of the frame but doesn't completely discount the perimeter.

FIGURE 3.21   In pattern or matrix metering mode, which is the default setting on most cameras, a bright background will cause the subject's face to be underexposed.

- Even with spot metering, you still may need to bring additional light onto your subject's face, as illustrated by the two images in Figure 3.22 (the second and third examples on Page 12 of the color insert). Although spot metering did brighten the exposure, some of the face is still a little dark because of the shadows produced by the brim of the hat.

FIGURE 3.22 Switching to spot metering brightens exposure (left), but a flash is needed to bring the face out of the shadows created by the brim of the hat (right).

Switching on the camera's built-in flash, as I did for the example portrait, usually results in a better exposure both for the face and the background. In my picture, the camera assumed (correctly, in this case) that the subject was close enough to be well-illuminated by the flash, so the autoexposure mechanism dialed down the exposure from what it used for the nonflash picture. So while the face became brighter, thanks to the flash lighting, the background became darker.

- No metering control on your camera? If you have an EV compensation feature, it may be just as useful. Raise the EV value to force the camera to increase exposure beyond what its autoexposure meter says is appropriate.

» TROUBLESHOOTER

Because bright sunlight can wash out a camera's LCD monitor, determining whether you have a decent exposure can be difficult. One accessory that can help is an LCD hood, which casts some shade onto the monitor. (See Chapter 1 for a look at this type of product.) However, even with a hood, don't rely on your LCD monitor as a completely accurate indicator of exposure. Bracket your shots to make sure that you come home with at least one decent image.

- You can also bring along a portable reflector to fill in shadows. A gold reflector brings the added benefit of slightly warming the skin, as described earlier in this chapter.

- To get a more pronounced warming of skin tones, pop a warming filter onto the camera lens. Chapter 8 explores warming filters in detail, but the short story is that they lessen blues and increase reds. You can buy warming filters in a variety of strengths; for the bottom image on Page 12 of the color insert, I used a medium-strength filter that has the oh-so-user-friendly designation of 81B.

- As explored in Chapter 8, you can also apply a virtual warming filter by switching to manual white balance and choosing the setting appropriate for overcast skies. (The name varies among cameras.) If you're working on a cloudy day, however, the camera's automatic white balance feature will likely have already selected that setting. You can always use your photo editor's color-balancing filters to warm tones after the fact, of course. Again, Chapter 8 explores all these options for manipulating colors in greater detail.

4

Exploring Product Photography and Other Still-Life Adventures

Compared to portrait photography, shooting still-life pictures seems like it should be a breeze. When you're taking product shots for your company's annual report, for example, you don't have to worry about a flash reflection causing red-eye, as you do when photographing the CEO. And when you're capturing a city skyline, you don't have to beg the buildings to stop fighting and *sit still for just five minutes* so that you can get a halfway decent picture for the family holiday cards.

Yet, as you know if you've done much still-life photography, some inanimate subjects can prove every bit as challenging as living ones. Objects with shiny surfaces are incredibly difficult to photograph because they reflect not just the bright light of a flash but also everything else in the vicinity—including the photographer. Skyscrapers may be patient posers, but capturing their vertical bones without distortion is often impossible.

This chapter offers the best tricks I know for solving these and other common still-life problems. Of course, the solutions presented in other chapters, such as using the EV compensation control to adjust exposure and changing the white balance setting to remove or apply a color cast, apply to still-life photography as well.

Creating a Still-Life Staging Area

If you regularly take product pictures for your business or you want to pursue fine-art photography seriously, you may want to build a dedicated staging area for shooting your still-life projects. I shoot most of my still-life pictures in my guest bedroom, so I designed a stage that can easily be disassembled when company comes. Shown in Figure 4.1, this setup involves nothing more than adjustable shelving brackets and supports, a pair of white melamine boards, a curtain rod, and some clip-style curtain rings. Total cost: less than $50 and one trip to the hardware store.

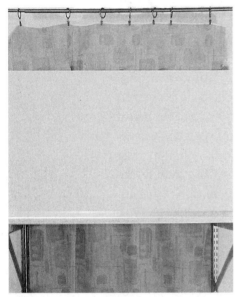

Simple as it is, this arrangement offers all the versatility I need. The shelving supports are 48 inches tall, allowing me to raise or lower the base platform to get the camera angle I want. The white boards serve as a good backdrop for many product shots, but if I need a colored background, I just clamp poster board or matte board from the art-supply store to the melamine boards. (To prevent the vertical board from accidentally falling forward onto whatever I'm shooting, I run a length of cording through screw eyes along the top and tie the cord to the curtain-rod brackets.) For shots that require a fabric background, I take down the vertical board and hang the fabric from the curtain rod.

FIGURE 4.1 You can build a simple yet versatile still-life staging area for under $50.

If you want something more sophisticated, several companies offer commercial solutions for still-life photography. Figure 4.2 shows one such product from Smith-Victor (*www.smithvictor.com*). Dubbed the TST Digital Desktop Studio Kit, this outfit includes the shooting table and frame, clear and white Plexiglas panels, two lights, and dimmer controls. The kit retails for about $450 and is sold through professional photography-supply stores.

FIGURE 4.2 This commercial still-life kit includes a pair of lights and interchangeable base and background panels.

FIGURE 4.3 A busy backdrop doesn't make a plain product more interesting—it only grabs attention from your subject.

Choosing a Backdrop

Just as the right clothing can make or break a portrait, the background you use for a still-life picture can enhance your subject or detract from it. Consider the computer cable shown in Figure 4.3, for example. When you're working with a subject that seems visually uncompelling at first glance, your initial instinct might be to use a patterned backdrop to add some interest to the scene, as I did for this image. But rather than enhancing the image, a busy backdrop just draws the eye from your subject.

For a better result, switch to a plain background and think more creatively about your composition. For the cable image, I decided to play off the idea that computer cables are often described as "snaking" around the office. I fashioned the cable into a shape that resembles a coiled snake, as shown in Figure 4.4, anchoring the "head" and "tail" in position by using transparent plastic thread tied to my curtain rod. The dark black background provides dramatic contrast to the cable without being distracting.

>> TROUBLESHOOTER

If you need both a color and black-and-white version of your product shot, be sure that your background provides not just color contrast, but also tonal contrast. A pale blue subject set on a pale pink backdrop may look great in color, but when you convert the image to black-and-white, subject and background will both appear light gray. If your camera offers a black-and-white special-effect mode, you can use it to check your composition for tonal contrast before you shoot. See Chapter 8 for more tips on converting a color photo to black-and-white.

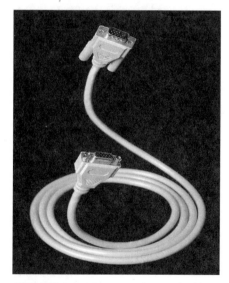

FIGURE 4.4 To create this snake-like form, I secured lengths of invisible plastic thread around the cable ends and then tied them to a rod above.

On occasions when you can't move a subject to improve the background, you may be able to use these tricks to get a better image:

- For small subjects, slip a thin piece of poster board or matte board behind the object.

- You may also be able to hang a temporary fabric background by clamping it to two light stands or other supports.

- When all else fails, use your camera's largest aperture to throw the background out of focus as much as possible. The examples on Page 13 of the color insert show you the impact of this adjustment. You need to switch the camera into either aperture-priority autoexposure or manual exposure mode to control aperture. (Remember, to get a larger aperture, you choose a *lower* f-stop number.) If your camera doesn't offer either mode, try using the portrait scene mode, which also results in a large aperture.

PRO TIP

Small wrinkles in a fabric backdrop will look like major hills and valleys in your picture. (See Page16 of the color insert for an example.) Keep a steamer or iron handy to smooth the fabric before you shoot. Similarly, use a lint brush to get rid of flecks of dust or dirt, which also will be more noticeable in the photo than they may be in real life.

Avoiding Moiré Patterns

Objects and backgrounds that feature strong linear patterns can sometimes result in a distortion known as a *moiré pattern*. The top set of images on Page 32 of the color insert shows two examples; Figure 4.5 shows portions of those images in black-and-white.

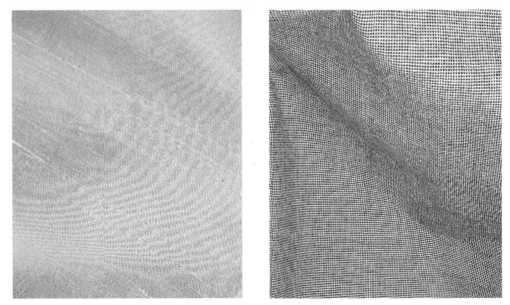

FIGURE 4.5   The wavy lines in these two pieces of fabric are a distortion known as a moiré pattern.

The fabric in the first image is a rough silk in which the threads are running diagonally through the picture; the moiré distortion creates the wavy lines. The second example shows black-and-white checked fabric, a design that is probably the most challenging for a digital camera. Here, the problem shows up not just as a ripple of waves but also stray bits of green and purple throughout the color image.

Many newer digital cameras have built-in moiré-removal filters that automatically attempt to correct the problem. So even if the moiré distortion is visible in the camera's LCD monitor when you preview the shot, it may not prove as significant in your actual image. If you do encounter problems, these remedies may work:

- Adjust the angle of the camera to bring the sensors into better alignment with the pattern of the subject (or background). Turn on the camera's LCD monitor so that you can preview the image, and just keep moving the camera until you see an improvement.

- If your camera offers a choice of sharpening settings, try switching to the setting that applies the least sharpening. The slight blurring that results may make the moiré pattern less noticeable. (Refer to Page 22 of the color insert to see how in-camera sharpening filters affect an image.)

- Of course, the best way to prevent moiré in picture backgrounds is to avoid using backdrops that feature strong linear designs. But if you can't swap out the backdrop, shoot the picture at a short depth of field so that the backdrop will become less focused. Again, you can shorten depth of field by opening up the aperture (choosing a lower f-stop number) and zooming in.

Technical Aside
More About Moiré

Inside your digital camera, the image sensor chips are arranged in a linear pattern. When the pattern of the chips isn't aligned with the pattern in the subject, moiré can occur. The same thing happens with a video camera—this is why you sometimes see the colors in a television guest's clothing appear to be "beating," or twinkling like a tiny movie-theater marquee.

Taming Reflections

One of the toughest challenges in still-life photography is capturing good images of objects that have reflective surfaces, such as the racing helmet featured on Pages 16 and 17 of the color insert. Although in some cases you may want an object to reflect neighboring elements—for example, to show the petals of a water lily reflected in a pond—for most product shots, the goal is a reflection-free shot.

To illustrate the different approaches that you can take when working with metal, glass, water, glazed porcelain, and other highly reflective subjects, the following sections retrace the steps I took when shooting the helmet.

Shooting with Ambient Light   Like anyone with a lazy bent, I first tried shooting the helmet using ambient room light only. I knew it probably wouldn't work, and I was right—there simply wasn't enough light to record the image, even at a slow shutter speed and wide open aperture. But it never hurts to try, eh? Unfortunately, if the ambient room light is bright enough to produce a good exposure, it's also bright enough to cause unwanted reflections.

> **» TROUBLESHOOTER**
>
> Remember that if you're shooting in programmed autoexposure (AE) mode, aperture-priority AE, or shutter-priority AE, you can raise the camera's EV compensation value to force a brighter exposure. Doing so may enable you to get an adequate shot using only ambient light. But if the light is very dim, the camera may already be working at its largest aperture and slowest shutter speed and so can't increase exposure even if you dial up a higher EV.

Flash reflection

FIGURE 4.6   A built-in flash creates a hot spot of reflected light and leaves part of the helmet in shadow.

Using Built-in Flash   For my second helmet shot, I used the camera's built-in flash, which is almost never a good option for shooting reflective objects. The light from a built-in flash is harsh and narrowly focused, which typically results in a bright orb reflected in your subject, as shown in Figure 4.6 and in the top image on Page 16 of the color insert. Even if your camera enables you to lower the flash output, you are likely to get a reflection.

In addition, a built-in flash often results in uneven lighting; notice that left side of the image in Figure 4.6 is much darker than the right half.

On top of that, the flash wasn't enough to bring out the striking purple-blue colors in the face plate, which you can see in the examples on Page 17 of the color insert. With the built-in flash, the face plate appears opaque black.

Working with Auxiliary Flash   As explained in Chapter 1, some advanced digital cameras enable you to attach an auxiliary flash via a hot shoe or cable. If your camera doesn't offer this flexibility, you can use slave flash units, which are triggered when your camera's built-in flash fires.

Although using an auxiliary flash works well for many projects, it probably won't do the trick when you're shooting reflective objects. For the middle image on Page 16 of the color insert, for example, I turned off the camera's built-in flash and attached an external flash head. I aimed the flash head toward the ceiling, which was white. Although bouncing the light off the ceiling reduced the hot spots, the issues with the uneven lighting and the face plate remain.

Switching on Studio Lights   After trying ambient light, built-in flash, and auxiliary flash to light the helmet—and getting poor results all along the way—I decided it was time to drag out the heavy light power. I switched on a studio hot light, using a white umbrella to diffuse the light. (Peek ahead to Figure 4.7 to see the light and umbrella.) The last image on Page 16 of the color insert shows the result. Now the colors in the face plate emerge, and the lighting is more even.

The bad news is that the reflection from the studio light is even more noticeable than the hot spot created by the flash, and with the increased light, the helmet now reflects the patterned area rug and other room elements.

Building a Light Tent for Reflection-Free Pictures   In most cases, no amount of fiddling with various light sources completely eliminates reflections. So save yourself all that experimentation time and do what the professionals do: Shoot the object through a light tent.

A light tent is simply a piece of white fabric that's draped around the subject, with an opening just big enough for the camera lens to peek through. The tent serves not only to prevent reflections but also to further diffuse the light. I stuck with my hot light for the helmet project, but you can use a light tent with any light source except, obviously, a built-in flash.

Figure 4.7 shows my homemade light tent, created out of a pair of white sheets and a white shower-curtain liner. I used a light stand to support the outer edge of the tent. You

FIGURE 4.7 To further diffuse the light and remove any chance of reflections from surrounding objects, I built a light tent around the helmet.

can see the dramatically improved results on Page 17 of the color insert. Note that the white sheets are reflected in the helmet, but the reflection is soft and even and likely won't be noticeable to most viewers.

> ### PRO TIP
>
> *For the helmet images, I wanted a backdrop that meshed with the racing theme, so I went to the fabric store and bought a remnant of gray leather. Well, okay, pleather. (Did I mention that this book is about budget solutions?) I don't know if real leather wrinkles, but pleather sure does, and it stretches out of shape to boot. In the first four helmet images shown in the color insert, the warp in the backdrop creates distracting shadows and highlights. I couldn't remove the wrinkles with an iron, so I pulled the fabric taut and used hardware-store spring clamps to hold it in place before shooting the rest of the images.*

After I got the light tent built, I shot the same image at several different EV compensation values. When you go to this much trouble to set up a shot, bracketing exposures is a no-brainer; you don't want to have to return to the studio to do everything again if you decide that you want a lighter or darker exposure. As you can see from the examples in the color insert, the shifts in exposure affected not just the relative brightness and darkness of the images, but also the colors in the helmet. For all the images, I worked in aperture-priority autoexposure mode, setting the aperture to f/2.8 so that the background would be slightly less focused than the helmet.

CooL TooLs

Building a light tent is easy enough to do with sheets, shower curtains, or drop cloths, but if you need one frequently, save yourself some hassle and buy a commercial light tent or dome. Figure 4.8 shows two such products.

The Cloud Dome (*www.clouddome.com*) has a bracket designed to hold your digital camera in place while you shoot, removing the need for a tripod. An optional extension collar enables you to increase the size of the dome and alter your shooting angle. For larger objects, manufacturers produce light tents in a variety of sizes; the two in the figure are from Westcott (*www.fjwestcott.com*). The Cloud Dome, bracket, and single extension collar sell for $225; Westcott's light tents range from $59 to $160 depending on size.

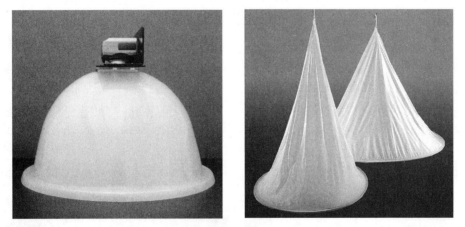

FIGURE 4.8   The Cloud Dome (left) provides a portable light dome for shooting small objects; the Westcott light tents (right) are designed for larger products.

Using a Polarizer to Reduce Reflections

A light tent combined with diffuse lighting works great for eliminating reflections indoors. But what do you use outside, in strong sunshine, with an immovable subject—say, a storefront window like the one featured in Figure 4.9 and on Page 18 of the color insert?

The answer may—and I emphasize, *may*—lie in a polarizing filter. For reasons explained in the sidebar "How Does a Polarizing Filter Work?," the filter may completely eliminate reflections, slightly reduce them, or have no effect at all. The outcome depends on the

FIGURE 4.9 This storefront window reflects the sky, buildings and trees on the opposite side of the street, and a large "Open" flag hanging just outside the window.

angle of the sun, your camera position with respect to the sun and the subject, and the reflective nature of your subject.

In the storefront example, the polarizer reduced reflections almost entirely, as shown in Figure 4.10 as well as in the color insert. (The window frame you see just behind the lettering is a stained-glass window hanging inside the building, not a reflected window.) I was standing at about a 35-degree angle to the front of the window, with the camera

FIGURE 4.10 A polarizing filter virtually eliminated reflections for this shot (but isn't always so effective).

lens at a 90-degree angle to the sun—an arrangement that happens to optimize the effect of a polarizing filter.

If you're new to polarizing filters, here are just a few other basics you need to know:

- Two types of polarizing filters exist: linear and circular. Autofocus cameras require circular polarizers.

- A polarizing filter has a movable outer ring that you twist to find the position of maximum polarization. Depending on your camera, you may not be able to see the effect in the optical viewfinder; you may need to preview the shot in the camera monitor instead.

- A polarizing filter reduces the amount of light your camera sees. If your camera has through-the-lens (TTL) autoexposure metering, as do most newer digital cameras, you shouldn't have to worry about making exposure adjustments; the autoexposure system will make the adjustment automatically. But some inexpensive cameras don't meter the light through the lens itself, which means that you need to tweak exposure manually when you use a polarizer. Check the filter box or package insert to determine the filter factor and how much exposure adjustment the manufacturer recommends. (See Chapter 1 for more details about this topic.) You may or may not be able to preview the filter effects in the monitor on this type of camera. Moral of the story: Always bracket exposures to be safe.

> ›› TROUBLESHO⊕TER
>
> Some autofocus mechanisms are thrown off by polarizing filters. If you have problems, try this trick: Before you twist the polarizer to find the best position, press and hold the shutter button halfway down to set the focus. Then move the polarizer as needed and press the shutter button the rest of the way. If you're in autoexposure mode, however, keep in mind that exposure is also set with your half-press of the shutter button. So you need to raise the EV compensation value a notch or two before you start the process.

SEE ALSO   *Chapter 1 offers tips on buying polarizers and other filters for digital cameras.*

Technical Aside
How Does a Polarizing Filter Work?

When rays of sunlight hit some reflective surfaces, including glass and water, they bounce off the surface and vibrate in a single plane. This reflected light, which is said to be *polarized,* causes glare.

A polarizing filter allows you to screen out polarized light reflections, thereby eliminating glare. This gatekeeper duty is performed by rows of tiny crystals, which work like slats in a window blind to prevent light that's coming from certain angles from entering the camera. The visual effect is just like putting on a pair of sunglasses that have polarizing lenses.

You can't just pop a polarizing filter on your camera and wait for the magic to happen, however. First, you must position the camera lens at a certain angle with respect to both the sun and the reflective surface. For maximum effect, you need to shoot the object from a side angle of about 30 to 35 degrees, with the lens at a 90-degree angle to the sun. You then need to twist the outer ring of the filter until the rows of crystals are aligned with respect to polarized light rays that you want to eliminate. Depending on your camera, you may be able to preview the effect in your camera's monitor or even in the optical viewfinder. If not, just hold the filter up in front of your eye until you find the right position.

In addition to reducing glare, polarizing filters have an added use for outdoor photography: they can make skies appear bluer. Chapter 8 talks more about this benefit.

Photographing Glass

Two of the most common questions I field from people who are new to product imagery relate to glass and art: How do you photograph framed art that's under glass? And how do you photograph glass that *is* the art? So before setting aside the subject of reflective objects, I want to devote a few paragraphs to answering each question.

Shooting Framed Art Under Glass

With framed artwork, the obvious, easy answer is to remove the glass from the frame and then photograph the piece. In many cases, though, that's not an option, and you have to shoot through the glass. If you're not careful, you'll capture your own reflection in the image. As an example, see the painting photos on Page 18 of the color insert. If you look closely, you can see my reflection in the top image.

I took this picture standing about seven feet directly in front of the painting, using one light set a few feet to my left. Although the light itself was diffuse enough to prevent any hot spots like the ones in the helmet image discussed earlier, my reflection caused a ghost-like countenance in the middle of the picture.

You may be wondering why I didn't use a polarizing filter for this shot as I did when photographing the glass window discussed in the preceding section. Unfortunately, a polarizing filter isn't much help in this situation. For a polarizer to have any impact, the reflected light must be polarized, which isn't typical with indoor lighting. Some people use sheets of polarizing material to convert studio lights into polarized light sources and then put a polarizing filter on the camera—a technique called *cross polarization*. But that's a little complicated for my taste and, more important, it can create unwanted color casts.

If you simply light the artwork properly, you should be able to shoot it straight-on without creating much of a reflection, if any. The secret is to use two diffused light sources, one to the left of the art and one to the right. Position the lights at about a 45-degree angle from the art and at about the same height as the art. This lighting setup—known as *cross lighting*—should enable you to stand right in front of the art without creating much of a reflection. But if you still see some hint of yourself or the camera in the glass, put the camera on a tripod and then drape both with a black cloth. Use your camera's self-timer function to take the picture so that you can step out of reflection range before the image is captured.

This is the technique I used to record the second painting photo in the color plate. Notice that the addition of the second light also brought out more of the frame details and eliminated the heavy shadow that falls behind the right side of the frame in the first image.

>> **TROUBLESHOOTER**

Another technique to avoid reflections when photographing framed art is to tilt either the frame or the camera. But this approach distorts the parallel lines in the picture, and you'll need to use your photo editor to correct the problem. See the How-To sidebar "Correct Convergence in Photoshop Elements" later in this chapter for information on how to do this.

Photographing Art Glass

Art glass—that is, decorative glass such as the candle holder on Page 19 of the color insert—offers some special creative photo opportunities, because you can shine light through it as well as on it. By varying the direction at which the light enters the glass, you can produce different effects, as illustrated in the color plate.

The text in the color insert provides details on the lighting setups that I used for each image, so I won't waste space repeating that information in this chapter. But here are a few pointers to help you start planning how you want to photograph your next piece of glass:

- Placing the object on a sheet of frosted glass enables you to light the object from beneath and at the same time diffuses the light to help prevent unwanted reflections. I used this setup, shown in Figure 4.11, to shoot the candle holder.

 **COST CUTTER**

If you don't have any frosted glass lying around, you can buy a can of "frost" in the spray paint section of your hardware store and apply it to a piece of clear glass. Do-it-yourself frosting enables you to control how much light is transmitted through the glass, too.

FIGURE 4.11 Placing your subject on a piece of frosted glass enables you to light it from below.

- For small objects, a portable light box—the kind you use to sort photographic slides—can serve the same purpose as the frosted glass and light.

- Experiment with different lighting positions to see how the resulting shadows and highlights produce varying bands of color throughout the glass. Backlighting usually leads to dark lines along the edges of the glass, for example.

- As when shooting any reflective object, remember that a small, focused light source such as a built-in flash creates harsher shadows and is more likely to produce hot spots than diffuse light.

Shooting Architectural Subjects

Did you notice anything a little off in Figure 4.11? If not, look again, paying special attention to the vertical shelf supports in the picture. They appear to angle inward at the bottom of the picture. In "real life," however, they're perfectly vertical. The distortion in the image is due to a problem known as *convergence*.

When the camera lens isn't on the same horizontal level as the subject, vertical lines can appear to tilt toward each other—to converge, in mathematical language. In Figure 4.11, for example, I stood on a stepladder and angled the camera down to get both the platform and light in the shot. Because the room in which I took the picture is small, I couldn't move far enough away to get the entire setup in the picture without tilting the camera down a little. If I had tilted the camera up instead, the shelf supports would lean in at the top of the frame instead of at the bottom.

Professional photographers use corrective lenses, known as *shift lenses,* to avoid this problem when shooting architectural elements. But these devices are expensive, tricky to use, and not even available for most digital cameras. So how do we ordinary mortals manage to get around convergence? Simple. We cheat.

Almost any photo editing program today offers distortion tools that you can use to get vertical structures back in proper alignment. I used Adobe Photoshop Elements to right the tilting San Francisco towers in Figure 4.12, for example. So when circumstances don't allow you to capture a scene at an angle that prevents convergence, take the picture anyway. Then use the steps outlined in the upcoming How-To section to make it look like you have one of those fancy shift lenses.

FIGURE 4.12   When buildings appear to be leaning on each other (left), you can fix things using a photo editor (right).

❓ How To   CORRECT CONVERGENCE IN PHOTOSHOP ELEMENTS

The following steps show you how to fix convergence problems in Photoshop Elements. You can use the same approach in any photo editor that offers a way to distort an image; check the program's manual for information about a Transform, Perspective, or Distortion tool.

1. For safety's sake, create a backup copy of your original image file before you start. Then close the original and work on the copy.

2. Choose Image | Resize | Canvas Size and enlarge the image canvas by about 25 percent. You may need to stretch the image beyond the current canvas size to fix the converging lines.

3. Choose View | Grid to display a grid of intersecting lines, as shown in Figure 4.13. The gridlines provide some visual guidance as you align the structures in your photo.

FIGURE 4.13 Drag the square handles to stretch the image into shape.

How To **CORRECT CONVERGENCE IN PHOTOSHOP ELEMENTS**
(continued)

4. Choose Select | Select All to select the entire image.

5. Choose Image | Transform | Free Transform. You should see little boxes, called *handles,* around your image, as in Figure 4.13. (If you don't see the boxes, zoom out on the image and then enlarge the image window.)

6. Press and hold the CTRL key (⌘ key on a Mac) as you drag a corner handle. The image stretches in whatever direction you drag. For example, drag the top-right handle outward to pull objects at the top of the image to the right. You can pull both top handles or both bottom handles in tandem by holding down the ALT, SHIFT, and CTRL keys as you drag either of the handles. (Press OPTION-SHIFT-⌘ on a Mac.)

7. Depending on your picture, you also may need to slightly skew or rotate the image. To skew the picture, CTRL-drag (⌘-drag on a Mac) a top- or bottom-center handle sideways or a side-center handle up or down. To rotate the image, drag a corner handle up or down—no CTRL or ⌘ key this time. If necessary, you can stretch the image vertically or horizontally by dragging one of the side or center handles without the CTRL or ⌘ key.

8. When you're satisfied with your results, press ENTER.

9. The transformation likely created some empty canvas area. You can either crop the picture to eliminate the canvas, as I did for my skyscraper picture, or copy some other part of the picture to use as a "patch" over the hole. The Clone tool works well for this job.

5

Capturing Close-ups

TV pundits and editorial columnists are fond of the expression "the devil is in the details." That saying may well apply to congressional bills and budget plans, but in photography, the opposite is often true. When you take a long-distance view of a scene, you may not see anything of obvious visual interest. If you focus your attention more narrowly, however, you may discover incredible beauty in the details.

As an example, take a look at the top image on Page 20 of the color insert. When I first came upon this bed of tulips, I took a wide shot of the flowers, thinking that they offered a pretty color palette. And indeed, the photo is colorful—but other than that, it's nothing special. In search of a more interesting image, I began concentrating on individual flowers. Toward the edge of the bed was a tulip in its last hours of glory, hanging on to two petals. My eye was attracted to the way the sunlight was shining through the petals, playing up their silky texture, sensual form, and subtle blend of colors. So I switched the camera into macro-focusing mode, crouched down to petal level, and snapped away. I love the outcome, shown in the larger image, because it reveals an essential beauty that isn't obvious in a tulip that has all petals intact.

When you want to get up close and personal with a subject, the tools and techniques covered in this chapter can help you capture the image you have in mind. This chapter also contains information about how some common digital camera features, such as the inappropriately named *digital zoom*, affect your close-up photos.

Zooming vs. Moving

If you want to record the details in a subject that's more than a few feet away, you have two options: You can increase the focal length of the lens, either by using your camera's zoom or by attaching an accessory telephoto lens. Or you can simply move the camera closer to the subject.

Which choice you make affects your photo in a few important ways:

- **Angle of view**   As you increase focal length, you narrow the camera's angle of view. That means that your picture will contain less of the surrounding area than if you position the camera closer to the subject and use a shorter focal length. Figure 5.1 and the corresponding color examples on Page 20 of the color insert illustrate this effect.

140mm (equiv.) 35mm (equiv.)

I took both pictures with a camera that has an optical zoom range equivalent to about 35–140mm on a 35mm film camera. I shot the left image from a distance of approximately six feet, with the camera zoomed in to the maximum focal length. For the right image, I zoomed all the way out to the widest-angle setting and moved to within about a foot of the vase.

FIGURE 5.1   A long focal length (left) enables you to capture a subject with less background than a short focal length (right).

The vase and feathers are roughly the same size in both pictures, but the wide-angle version reveals much more of the surrounding area—my living room, if you're interested.

For an explanation of why focal lengths on digital cameras are stated in terms of equivalent numbers on a 35mm film camera, flip to Chapter 1.

- **Spatial relationships**   Moving the camera also changes the spatial relationship of your subject to other objects in the scene. Notice that in the right image in Figure 5.1, the wood cabinet in the background appears to be smaller with respect to the vase than it appears in the left image. (The camera angle is slightly different between the shots, which also has a minor impact here.) If I had taken the right image from the same distance as the left image and merely zoomed out to the 35mm (equivalent) focal length, the size relationship of the cabinet and vase would have remained constant.

- **Depth of field**   Increasing focal length also decreases depth of field (the range of sharp focus). In Figure 5.1, for example, the wood cabinet is much less sharply focused in the zoomed image (left) than in the wide-angle picture. For this subject, the shorter depth of field is helpful because the grain of the wood becomes less distracting.

- **Exposure**   A telephoto lens (long focal length) transmits less light than a wide-angle lens (short focal length). So as you change focal length, the camera needs to adjust aperture or shutter speed accordingly to ensure a correct exposure. In autoexposure mode, the camera handles this adjustment for you; in manual mode, you need to make the necessary changes. Keep in mind that enlarging the aperture (selecting a smaller f-stop number) further shortens depth of field, as explored in Chapter 2. (Also see Page 13 of the color insert.) And a slower shutter speed means there's more possibility of handheld camera shake, so you may want to use a tripod.

- **Distortion**   If you opt for a wide-angle shot, be on the lookout for convergence problems. As explained in Chapter 4, convergence can make vertical lines appear to lean inward. The problem usually gets worse as you shorten the lens focal length. (Chapter 4 shows you how you can fix tilting lines in a photo editor.) In addition, remember that getting too close at a wide-angle setting can distort a subject's proportions, as covered in Chapter 3.

Mind you, there are no right or wrong choices here; the best shooting distance and focal length depend on the artistic goal you have in mind. Also note that when I speak of a zoom lens, I'm talking about a true optical zoom lens—not the so-called digital zoom found on most cameras. To find out why I say "so-called," zoom to the next section.

SEE ALSO

If your camera doesn't offer a zoom lens, see Chapter 1 for information about accessory telephoto lenses.

Snubbing Digital Zoom

When digital cameras first came to market, manufacturers believed that consumers would be less intimidated by the new technology if camera features were described using familiar film terminology. Thus, camera memory cards are often called "digital film," and lens focal lengths are stated in terms of equivalent focal lengths on a 35mm film camera. I can deal with digital film—though it makes no sense at all—and the 35mm-equivalency thing is a logical, if complicated, way to deal with the lack of a standard image-sensor size in digital cameras. (Chapter 1 explains how image-sensor size relates to focal length.) But one term that emerged from the digital-is-just-like-film camp is downright misleading. As you may have guessed from the headline to this section, I'm speaking of *digital zoom.*

A digital zoom works nothing like the zoom lens on a film camera—referred to as an *optical zoom* in the digital-camera world. When you use a digital zoom, the camera simply enlarges and crops the image after you shoot it. The end result is the same as if you were to enlarge an image in your photo editor and then crop away the perimeter. The resulting photo will be of lower quality than it would be if you captured the same subject with an optical zoom, as illustrated by the images on Page 21 of the color insert.

The quality loss occurs because the digital zoom function throws away some of your original image pixels to crop the image. In most cases, the camera then adds new pixels—or, in imaging lingo, it *resamples the photo*—to rebuild the remaining picture area at the original, full-frame size. Adding pixels to an existing photo is always destructive to image details. (Chapter 9 explores the resampling issue in more detail.)

Some cameras do not resample the image but instead simply save the picture file with the reduced pixel count. But as explored in Chapter 2 and illustrated on Page 3 of the color insert, this approach is no better than resampling if you want to print your pictures at a decent size—you simply don't have enough pixels to produce a quality photo.

In addition, angle of view and depth of field aren't affected as they are with optical zoom, because a digital zoom does not change lens focal length. Nor does digital zoom have an impact on exposure, distortion, or spatial relationships. (The preceding section offers more words of wisdom on these issues.)

Again, a digital zoom really should be called *in-camera cropping and enlarging* because that's what this feature does. That's not to say that in-camera cropping and enlarging isn't sometimes useful—if you're printing directly from a memory card, for example, and you don't need top-notch image quality. Just don't buy into the notion that a digital zoom is anything more than a convenience, no matter how the camera ads or sales reps try to convince you otherwise.

>> TROUBLESHO⊕TER

Check your camera manual to find out how your camera's digital zoom function is triggered. In some cases, the camera shifts to digital zoom automatically when you reach the end of the optical zoom range. With other cameras, the digital zoom comes to life only if you press and hold the zoom lever for a few seconds after reaching the optical zoom limit. Some models enable you to turn off digital zoom capability altogether; I recommend you do so if your camera provides this control. You can always turn the function back on for those occasions when you want to take advantage of in-camera cropping and enlarging.

Tweaking Camera Settings for Close-up Work

Along with the aforementioned digital zoom, a few other camera settings call for special consideration when you're doing close-up photography. The next few sections explore the most critical of these options.

Choosing Resolution and Compression

When you're shooting important close-ups, use the highest resolution and lowest compression possible. Defects caused by too few pixels or too much compression are much more noticeable in close-up photos because it's easier for the eye to detect any interruption in the color or design of the subject. In the far-away tulip shot on Page 20 of the color insert, for example, you probably wouldn't be able to spot compression artifacts; they would be lost amid the jumble of shapes and colors. But in the close-up image, compression artifacts would have nowhere to hide.

SEE ALSO

Chapter 2 discusses resolution and compression in greater detail; see Pages 4 and 5 of the color insert for a look at resolution and compression defects.

Focusing at Close Distances

Depending on how close you want to get to your subject, you may need to switch to macro focusing mode. The universal symbol for macro mode is a tiny flower, as shown in Figure 5.2. Check your camera manual for the minimum and maximum camera-to-subject distance to use when working in macro mode; this range varies from camera to camera.

Macro button

FIGURE 5.2 Your camera manual should state the minimum and maximum shooting distance for sharp images in macro mode.

Here are a few additional tidbits to help you achieve sharp focusing at close range:

- If your camera has an optical zoom, you may not be able to use macro mode along the entire range of the zoom. Usually, the camera displays a symbol in the viewfinder or LCD monitor to let you know when you're at a focal length that permits macro focusing.

- Additionally, the zoom position may affect the minimum close-focusing distance. Again, your camera manual should spell out the focusing distances for the various focal lengths available on your camera.

- Throwing more light on your subject can help your camera's autofocus mechanism do a better job. Lighting at close range can be difficult, however, because the camera can get in the way of the light source. For tips, see the section "Lighting at Close Range," later in this chapter. If you have trouble with autofocusing, switch to manual focusing, if your camera offers it, and use a ruler to measure the lens-to-subject distance precisely.

- Many camera lenses produce the sharpest images at a medium aperture setting. However, depth of field is shorter at a medium aperture than at a small aperture, so the range of the scene that is sharply focused will be more limited. Experiment to find out how different f-stops affect your camera's focusing abilities.

- What appears to be faulty focus in an image may actually be a camera movement problem. Any camera shake will register as a slight blur that will be especially noticeable in close-up shots. Use a tripod and snap the picture using the camera's self-timer mechanism to be sure that the camera is absolutely still during the exposure.

Previewing Your Shots

When shooting close-ups, always check your framing in the camera's monitor instead of the viewfinder. The monitor more accurately represents what the camera lens sees.

On most point-and-shoot cameras, the lens and the viewfinder operate independently, and the viewfinder has a slightly different angle on the scene than the lens. This disparity, known as *parallax error,* increases as you move closer to your subject. If you use very tight framing and compose the shot using the viewfinder, your image may not capture the entire subject, as shown in Figure 5.3. Although I could see the entire foreground flower through the camera viewfinder, the outer tips of some petals were actually beyond the vision of the lens.

FIGURE 5.3 Although the entire foreground flower was visible in the camera viewfinder, the lens recorded only the area shown here.

Some cameras force you to frame pictures using the monitor in macro mode. Your viewfinder may also display tiny lines that indicate the actual area that will be captured by the lens at a close distance. However, check your camera manual to be sure that those viewfinder markings indicate the framing area and not the area being evaluated by the camera's autoexposure or autofocus mechanism.

If you own a high-end camera, it may have a *through-the-lens (TTL)* viewfinder. With this arrangement, the viewfinder and lens are supposed to be in perfect synch. Still, framing your shots using the monitor is a good idea because you get a clearer view of the image-to-be.

Sharpening Without Sandpaper

Most digital cameras apply a *sharpening filter* as they record an image. This digital manipulation creates the illusion of sharper focus by boosting contrast along image *edges*. In digital imaging lingo, an *edge* refers to any point where a color change occurs—for example, where the dark blue pixels of an ocean meet the light blue pixels of the sky.

Original   Sharpened

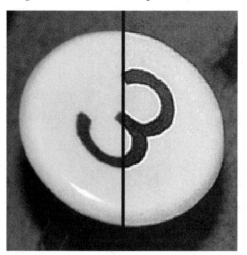

FIGURE 5.4 Sharpening adds light and dark halos along the boundaries where color changes occur.

When a sharpening filter finds an edge, it brightens the pixels on the lighter side of the edge. Pixels on the dark side of the fence line get darker. Figure 5.4, which shows a portion of a close-up photo I took of an antique adding machine, illustrates the effect. The left half of the image is the unsharpened original; the right half has been sharpened.

In the sharpened half of the image, you can see the light and dark sharpening "halos" along the boundary between the number and the button face and also along the border between the button face and the background. When you view the image from a distance, this increase in contrast fools your eye into thinking that the picture is more sharply focused, as illustrated by Figure 5.5.

Although the sharpened image in Figures 5.4 and 5.5 does appear to be better focused, the sharpening in both cases is really overdone. (I purposely applied too much sharpening so that you could clearly see the effect.) With this much sharpening, surfaces that should appear smooth, such as the machine background, take on a sandpaper-like texture. In addition, extreme sharpening halos give the image an "outlined" look—as if someone had traced around the edges with black and white pens. As with compression and resolution defects, oversharpening defects are more noticeable in close-up images than in long shots.

Page 22 of the color insert shows another example of how oversharpening can ruin an otherwise lovely close-up. I took all four pictures with the same camera; like many

Original   Sharpened

FIGURE 5.5 The increased contrast produced by the sharpening filter creates the illusion of sharper focus.

of the latest digital cameras, this one offered a choice of sharpening settings. For the top left photo, I set the sharpening amount to maximum. Every line and crease in the hands is magnified, the skin and the fabric look rough, and you can clearly see distinct light and dark halos along the boundary between hands and background. Hardly the soft, romantic look that I promised when I asked my just-engaged friend to pose for this picture.

Dialing down sharpening to the medium setting improved the picture somewhat, as shown in the top right photo. But even a moderate amount of sharpening has a big impact at this close range. Although the fabric background no longer looks strongly textured, the hands still appear more weathered and dry than they were in real life. (You have to love friends who let you photograph them in an unflattering way!)

For the lower left image, I disabled sharpening altogether. Now the skin has its natural, soft and silky look, and the folds along the fingers are diminished. In addition, the pattern in the fabric is less obvious and so doesn't pull attention away from the hands as it does in the sharpened images.

Many people would find the unsharpened hand image perfectly acceptable. But with no sharpening, some areas of the photo—the ring, in particular—looked a little *too* soft to my eye. So I opened the image in my photo editor and used its sharpening filter to apply a tiny amount of sharpening along the perimeter of the hands. I applied a bit more sharpening to the ring. This selective sharpening made the overall image appear sharper without adding unwanted roughness to the interior of the hands or the background.

If your camera offers a sharpening control, I suggest that you either turn it off or use the lowest sharpening setting when shooting close-ups. Almost every photo editor offers a sharpening filter, so you can easily add sharpening later if needed. And while the camera sharpens the entire image, doing the job yourself enables you to control where and how the effect is applied. For an introduction to a sharpening filter found in many photo editors, see the upcoming sidebar "Sharpen with Unsharp Mask."

PRO TIP

A printed image usually needs more sharpening than an on-screen image. And an image printed on a home inkjet printer typically needs more sharpening than a photo output on a high-quality professional printer.

❓ How To SHARPEN WITH UNSHARP MASK

If you dig through the menus in your photo editor, you may come across a corrective filter called Unsharp Mask. Although its name implies just the opposite, this filter enables you to apply image sharpening with a high degree of control. The name comes from a traditional photographic process that had the same goal but involved a purposely blurred negative. (Don't ask.)

Figure 5.6 shows the Unsharp Mask filter dialog box from Adobe Photoshop Elements. Most programs that offer an Unsharp Mask filter offer the same trio of controls as this one, although the control names may be slightly different.

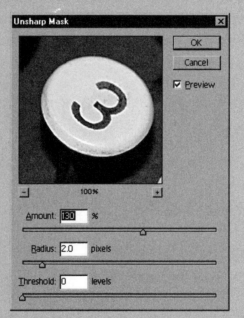

FIGURE 5.6 To get better control over image sharpening, do it yourself using an Unsharp Mask filter.

Each control alters a specific aspect of how the sharpening is applied:

- **Amount** Increase or decrease the Amount value for a more pronounced or more subtle effect.

- **Radius** As discussed earlier, a sharpening filter adds light and dark halos along image edges (areas where a color change occurs). The Radius control enables you to specify how thick you want these halos to be. A smaller halo is less noticeable but also doesn't create as much of a sharpening impact as a thicker halo, obviously. Let your eyes be your guide, but normally, anything above 2.5 is going too far.

?How To

SHARPEN WITH UNSHARP MASK *(continued)*

- **Threshold**   Finally, you can specify how much difference must exist between two adjacent pixels before the program considers their border an edge and creates the sharpening halo. By using a high Threshold value, you limit the effect to areas of strong contrast. For example, the border between a dark gray stripe and a light gray stripe would get the sharpening halos, but the border between a dark gray stripe and a medium gray stripe would not. For portraits, raise the Threshold value if you notice the skin taking on a rough texture.

For a look at how various combinations of these sharpening controls affect an image, check out Page 23 of the color insert. I used the same Amount value for all three of the sharpened images but varied the Radius and Threshold values. Notice that the sharpening halos in the lower two examples, for which I used a Radius value of 4, are significantly larger than the top-right example, for which I used a Radius value of 2. In the final example, raising the Threshold level to 20 sharpened just the high-contrast areas and left the green background largely untouched.

Lighting at Close Range

Getting enough light on your subject can be a special challenge in close-up photography. Here are a few tricks that can help:

- Try to position the camera so that the light source is in front of you. Otherwise, the camera may throw a shadow on the subject or block the light, or both.

- Using a built-in flash probably won't produce good results. At close range, a built-in flash typically blasts one part of the subject with too much light, as shown in Figure 5.7.

  If your camera offers a flash exposure compensation (EV) control, however, you may be able to use your built-in flash successfully. Flash EV enables you to

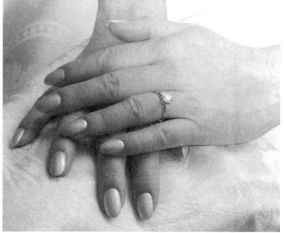

FIGURE 5.7   At full power, the camera's built-in flash lit the upper-right corner of the image much too strongly.

reduce or increase flash output. For the example image, reducing the flash EV to –2.0 solved the problem in the hand portrait, as shown in Figure 5.8. Of course, you may need to increase exposure time (by reducing shutter speed) or open the aperture (by selecting a lower f-stop number) to account for lower flash output.

FIGURE 5.8 By lowering the flash EV to –2.0, I was able to use a built-in flash successfully.

PRO TIP

No flash EV on your camera? You can reduce the impact of the flash by placing a piece of white plastic or thin fabric over the flash head.

- If you do a lot of close-up work, consider investing in a special macro flash unit.

Figure 5.9 shows one example, the Canon Macro Twin-Light, which retails for about $650. This particular unit has two flash heads that you mount to the camera lens via an adapter ring. You can tilt the flash heads in and out and move them around the lens to arrive at the perfect position for even lighting. You can also control the amount of flash output and even have one of the flash heads emit a stronger light than the other. The lower two images on Page 24 of the color insert show you the difference this type of equipment makes in close-up work, especially if your subject contains reflective surfaces.

FIGURE 5.9 A macro flash unit such as this two-head model from Canon enables you to achieve better close-up lighting.

Another type of macro flash, known as a ring flash, has a circular design that puts an even dose of light all around the camera lens. Figure 5.10 shows an example; also from Canon, this flash sells for about $450. A ring flash is especially useful for shooting jewelry and other very small objects.

Note that your camera must have either a hot shoe or flash socket to use most macro flash units. You also may need an adapter to mount

FIGURE 5.10 This ring flash mounts over the camera lens and fires automatically when the camera's own flash fires.

the macro unit onto your camera lens, so check your camera manual to find out whether the manufacturer offers adapters. If not, the flash manufacturer may sell them for your model.

- Don't despair if your camera offers neither a hot shoe nor an external flash socket; several manufacturers offer slave flash units designed for macro photography with digital cameras. As explained in Chapter 1, a slave flash is triggered by your camera's built-in flash, so no hot shoe or socket is needed.

Exploring Macro Photography

As mentioned earlier in this chapter, many digital cameras offer a macro focusing mode. But whether or not you're really getting macro capabilities depends on the camera. Traditionally, the term *macro* was reserved for a lens that could render an image at life size on a 35mm negative. Camera manufacturers are a little sloppy about using the term, though, so your lens may not actually fit that precise definition.

Don't give this issue a lot of thought, however. Because there is no such thing as a standard sized "negative" with digital photography, the whole macro yardstick—er, millimeter stick?—is sort of meaningless. All that really matters is whether the minimum focusing distance of your camera allows you to get as close to your subject as you want to be.

Unless you have a need for extremely detailed close-ups of small objects, the macro mode on your digital camera will likely serve you just fine. Remember that if you're working with a high-resolution digital camera, you can always enlarge the printed image to reveal as much detail as you like.

If you own a low-resolution camera or want to get closer than your lens allows, you have a number of options. Serious professionals use super-macro lenses or attach bellows or extension tubes to their lenses to gain more close-focusing ability. But these solutions are expensive and aren't even possible for most point-and-shoot style cameras.

For those photographers just getting started in close-up photography, a more practical and less costly option is to buy a set of close-up lenses, sometimes called *diopter lenses*. You can see a pair of screw-on close-up lenses from Tiffen in the foreground of Figure 5.11. (More about the other objects in the figure in a moment.) This set sells for about $60. (You may need to purchase an additional adapter to mount the close-up lens onto your camera lens.)

FIGURE 5.11 You can expand your close-up opportunities by using screw-on close-up lenses or just shooting through a magnifying glass or photographer's loupe.

The power of a close-up lens—known as its *diopter power*—is assigned a numerical rating: +1, +2, and so on, just like the reading glasses you can buy in your local pharmacy. The higher the number, the greater the lens power, and the closer you can focus on your subject. You can "stack" several close-up lenses on top of each other to achieve their combined power.

Page 25 of the color insert presents some examples that illustrate the relative strength of a diopter power of +7, +10, and +17. To get the +17 power, I stacked the +7 and +10 lenses.

Camera only

+17 close-up lens

Figure 5.12 shows the difference between an image taken with the camera's macro mode only and with the +17 stack.

However—and this is a crucial however—the impact on your photo depends on two factors: the focal length of the camera lens and the camera-to-subject distance. For the images shown in the color insert, the camera focal length was the equivalent of about 60mm on a 35mm film camera, and the

FIGURE 5.12 Stacking a +10 and +7 close-up lens, for a total diopter power of +17, enabled me to get a super-close view of a bracelet detail.

camera-to-subject distance was about two inches. Of course, both focal length and subject distance by themselves affect how large your subject appears in your image.

As you ponder all this information, keep the following additional tidbits in mind:

- With most close-up lenses, focus is slightly sharper at the center of the lens than around the perimeter. If you need sharp-as-a-tack focus throughout your image, leave a good margin of background around your subject. You can then crop that excess margin away in your photo editor. (Don't forget that using a shorter focal length and smaller aperture extend depth of field, which also keeps more of the picture in sharp focus.)

- You do not necessarily need to set your camera to the macro focusing mode to use a close-up lens. However, doing so usually enables you to move the camera closer to the subject and still achieve sharp focus.

- Look in the guide that comes with your close-up lenses to find out the manufacturer's recommended lens-to-subject distance for sharpest focus. If you are working at your camera's macro setting, you will probably be able to get closer than the guide numbers suggest, however.

- On cameras that don't offer a TTL (through-the-lens) viewfinder, you won't be able to see the effect of the close-up lens through the viewfinder. So use the camera's LCD monitor to compose the image.

- If you stack close-up lenses, put the lens with the highest diopter power closest to the camera lens.

PRO TIP

If you don't do a lot of close-up photography, try shooting through an ordinary household magnifying glass before you invest in a close-up lens. A photographer's loupe—a small magnifying eyepiece used to inspect slides and negatives—can also work as a makeshift diopter, assuming that the camera lens is smaller than the eyepiece on the loupe. Travel back to Figure 5.11 for a look at these alternatives. Hold the magnifying glass or loupe absolutely still to avoid blurring your image.

6

Getting the Tough Shot: Low-Light and Action Photography

In almost every regard, today's digital cameras either match or outdo the capabilities of comparably priced film cameras. But most digital models still fall slightly short of the ideal in two photographic situations: shooting in dim light and capturing moving subjects.

A typical digital camera has a light sensitivity equal to that of ISO 100 film (or, in everyday lingo, 100-speed film). In case you're new to the subject, that ISO number indicates that the camera needs plenty of light to produce a good image. Many digital cameras also offer a limited range of shutter speeds and apertures, which can hamper your ability to adjust exposure to match the light or motion in the scene. Add to these factors the lag time that a digital camera needs to transfer image data to your memory card after each press of the shutter button, and you can see why you may have been frustrated when trying to capture a nighttime skyline or roller-blading teen.

All this is not to say that you should go back to your film camera when you want to work in less-than-ideal lighting or to photograph a moving subject, however. You just need to adapt your technique to your digital camera's personality, which this chapter shows you how to do. With a few changes to your photographic approach, you can produce excellent photos regardless of the lighting conditions or the speed of your subject.

Helping Your Camera Cut Through Darkness

Whether you're shooting with a film or digital camera, taking pictures in dim lighting poses special challenges. After all, a camera works by recording the amount of light in a scene. If the camera's eye doesn't sense much light...well, you see the problem.

Of course, one option is to use a flash or another auxiliary light source. But on many occasions, adding artificial light isn't a viable solution. Most museums don't allow flash photography, for example, and dragging along studio lights to your child's first nighttime piano recital would probably get you booted by auditorium security. Even if you're under no such restrictions, a flash or other artificial light source may be too underpowered to illuminate a subject fully.

When adding light either isn't possible or doesn't solve your exposure problem, you can help your digital camera cut through the darkness in the following ways:

- Raise the ISO setting, which is akin to using a higher ISO film. As explained in the next section, however, this solution sacrifices some image quality.

- Increase the aperture size (by selecting a lower f-stop number) to allow more light into the camera. This choice also changes depth of field, as illustrated by Page 13 of the color insert.

- Select a slower shutter speed, which increases the amount of time that the image sensor can gather light. The upcoming section "Shooting Long Exposures" offers some tips on this tactic.

If you are working in autoexposure mode, you may also be able to tweak exposure by increasing your camera's EV (exposure value) compensation setting, if available. Your camera will then adjust aperture or shutter speed—or both—to produce an exposure that's brighter than what the camera's autoexposure meter suggests is correct. (Some cameras also raise ISO automatically.) Check out Chapter 2 and Pages 9 and 17 of the color insert for more information about EV compensation.

Adjusting Light Sensitivity (ISO)

As I mentioned in the introduction to this chapter, the image sensors on most digital cameras have a light sensitivity equivalent to ISO 100 film, which means that they respond best to brightly lit scenes. In an attempt to give photographers a better chance of recording a good image in dim lighting, newer cameras offer an ISO control that adjusts the camera's light sensitivity.

The ISO control settings typically match the ISO ratings on standard consumer films: ISO 100, 200, 400, and 800. The higher the number, the greater the camera's sensitivity to light.

With a higher ISO film—also called a *faster film* in photography lingo—you can get a good exposure with less light. In bright light, the increased light sensitivity enables you to work with a smaller aperture (higher f-stop number) or faster shutter speed than when using a lower ISO film.

If you're an experienced film photographer, you know that increased light sensitivity comes at a cost, however. As you move up the ISO scale, you increase *grain*—a visual defect that looks like someone sprinkled sand over your photo. The same tradeoff exists with digital cameras, only in the digital world, the resulting defect looks like speckles of random color and is known as *noise*.

You can see examples of how ISO affects both exposure and noise on Page 2 of the color insert. Figure 6.1 shows the detail from the ISO 100 and ISO 800 examples. The amount of additional noise produced when you increase ISO varies from camera to camera; your model may produce significantly more or less noise than what you see in these examples.

ISO 100   ISO 800

FIGURE 6.1   Raising the ISO setting results in a brighter exposure but also introduces noise, giving the image a speckled look.

How much image quality you should sacrifice for increased light sensitivity is purely a personal creative choice. As you debate the issue, keep these points in mind:

- If you're shooting in programmed autoexposure (AE) mode, the camera automatically adapts aperture and shutter speed to your ISO setting.

In aperture-priority AE, the camera changes shutter speed only; in shutter-priority AE, the camera adjusts aperture only.

Remember that the camera can do only so much in this regard, however. If you're shooting in extremely dim lighting, you may not be able to record a good image at a low ISO even if the camera opens the aperture all the way and uses the slowest available shutter speed. (You may be able to brighten the exposure to an acceptable degree after the fact in your photo editor; for a brief lesson, see the upcoming How-To sidebar, "Adjust Exposure with a Levels Filter.")

- Noise is typically most apparent in shadows and areas of flat color, such as the sky in the color insert examples. (This is actually a ceiling painted to look like a sky, but the noise impact is the same.) To be fair, however, at a lower ISO, you may lose all detail in the shadows. Areas that should contain a blend of dark gray to black pixels may all be recorded as black, as you can see in the window archways in the ISO 100 example in Figure 6.1. What can I say—life's a series of tradeoffs, eh?

- Some cameras offer an Auto ISO setting. In this mode, the camera automatically adjusts ISO as the light changes. I recommend that you turn off this option and select a specific ISO setting instead. Most cameras don't inform you when they change the ISO setting, and this control has too big an impact on exposure and picture quality to leave to chance.

- Check your camera manual to find out whether your model offers a noise-reduction feature. This option applies a software filter to erase noise as part of the file processing that occurs as your camera stores the image. Usually, noise removal kicks in only at very slow shutter speeds, however, and also significantly increases the time you need to wait between shots for the camera's brain to do its thing.

- When all else fails, you may be able to diminish or even remove noise in your photo editor by blurring the affected areas. Use your blur tool judiciously, however, or you will blur image details, which is just as problematic as the image noise you're trying to eradicate.

CooL TooLs

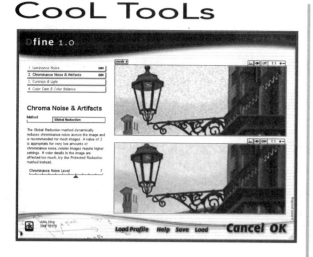

If you find yourself frequently doing noise-removal work in your photo editor, you may want to invest in a specialized utility designed just for that purpose. Products such as Applied Science Fiction's Digital GEM ($79.95, www.asf.com), and nik multimedia's Dfine ($99, www.nikmultimedia.com) provide sophisticated tools that eradicate noise with better results than those found in most photo editors. Both products are *Photoshop-compatible plug-ins,* which means that they work with Photoshop, Photoshop Elements, or any other photo editor that accepts such plug-ins.

How To

?

ADJUST EXPOSURE WITH A LEVELS FILTER

All photo-editing programs offer at least one correction filter that adjusts image exposure. At the basic level, you get a Brightness/Contrast filter, which allows you to make all pixels lighter or darker and to adjust *tonal range*—the overall range of brightness values (shadows to highlights).

FIGURE 6.2 Sunrise and sunset light can be tricky to expose properly; here, the image is too dark and lacks contrast.

A Brightness/Contrast filter is clumsy tool, however, and it usually produces unsatisfactory results. As an example, see Figure 6.2 and the top image on Page 15 of the color insert. I took this shot of an old sugar mill just after dawn, when the light is beautiful but also difficult to capture correctly. In this exposure, the highlights look fine, but the midtones are too

? How To

ADJUST EXPOSURE WITH A LEVELS FILTER *(continued)*

dark and the shadows aren't as deep as they could be. To put it another way, there's a lack of contrast in addition to an underexposure problem.

Figure 6.3 and the middle image on Page 15 of the color insert show the photo after I applied the Brightness/Contrast filter in Photoshop Elements. Raising the Brightness value enough to correct the midtones made the shadows even lighter and blew out the subtle details in the clouds. Again, remember that when you raise the Brightness value, the shadows, midtones, and highlights *all* become lighter.

So what about that Contrast control—it should bring back the lost contrast, and more, right? Nope, sorry. Contrast takes all pixels that are darker than the medium point on the brightness scale and makes those pixels darker. Pixels that are brighter than the midpoint get lighter. So you just wind up blowing even more highlights and losing shadow detail to boot, as shown in Figure 6.3.

FIGURE 6.3   Stay away from simple Brightness/Contrast filters; they reduce tonal range and wipe out shadow and highlight detail.

A better exposure correction filter, known as a Levels filter, allows you to tweak shadows, midtones, and highlights independently of each other. All professional photo-editing programs and many consumer-level programs offer this filter. Figure 6.4 shows the Levels filter dialog box from Photoshop Elements.

A Levels dialog box typically contains a *histogram,* which is a chart that graphs the image brightness values, with shadows on the left and highlights on the right.

123456

SHOOT LIKE A PRO!
35 SECRETS THE PROS KNOW

Keep ISO Low

Your digital camera may offer an ISO adjustment control. As is the case with film, the ISO value indicates sensitivity to light. By raising the ISO value, you can produce a brighter exposure in less light.

Unfortunately, ratcheting up ISO increases *noise*—color defects that give your image a grainy, speckled look. (You get the same kind of degradation when you work with high ISO film.) In most cases, you're better off choosing a low ISO and using your photo editor to brighten exposure if necessary.

PRO TIP

Before you look through your viewfinder, check your camera's ISO, resolution, and file compression settings. For top picture quality, use these settings:

- ISO: 200 or lower

- Resolution: 2 megapixels or more for print photos; fewer for Web pics

- Compression: Minimum or none

ISO 100

ISO 200

ISO 400

ISO 800

3 megapixels

1 megapixel

3

More Megapixels Means Bigger, Better Prints

These images show the difference that a few megapixels can make. Compare the 3 megapixel image on the top with the 1 megapixel version below. Both look fine at the small size on the left. But suppose that you wanted to crop the pictures to the framing indicated by the red borders. The images on the right show a portion of the cropped picture as it would appear when enlarged to a 4x6-inch print. Only the 3 megapixel original has enough pixels left to deliver good results.

Too Much Compression Spoils the Digital Soup

Many digital cameras provide a choice of file formats and compression options, each of which produces a different file size and picture quality.

When you select the JPEG format, the camera applies *lossy* compression, which eliminates picture data to reduce the file size. You typically can choose from several compression levels. The TIFF format either applies no compression or *lossless* compression, which preserves image quality but doesn't reduce file size much.

The images on this page illustrate the difference between an uncompressed TIFF image (top) and a highly compressed JPEG image (bottom). The JPEG image has a compression ratio of 39:1, which means that the file is 39 times smaller than the original. Although that much compression is a bad idea, a little compression doesn't lower quality significantly.

To find out how much compression is safe, take test shots at each compression setting. Because resolution also affects quality and file size, run the test for each resolution setting. As the examples on the opposite page show, various combinations of resolution and compression produce different results. Images in the right column have had a greater degree of compression applied. With the exception of the first row, images in the left column contain fewer megapixels (mp) than their partners to the right.

6 mp, no compression, 18MB

6 mp, heavy compression, 409K

6 mp, no compression, 18MB

6 mp, light compression, 2.4MB

3 mp, light compression, 1.2MB

6 mp, medium compression, 1MB

1 mp, light compression, 670K

3 mp, medium compression, 541K

1 mp, medium compression, 306

6 mp, heavy compression, 409K

5

Add Head Room for Framing Flexibility

Digital cameras produce images with a 4:3 aspect ratio, which differs from that of traditional film prints. If you want to be able to crop portraits so that they fit in a standard-size photo frame, include a margin of background around your subjects when you take the picture, as shown here. The blue line indicates the aspect ratio of an 8x10-inch frame; the red line, a 5x7; and the white line, a 4x6.

Stand Back and Zoom In to Avoid Distortion

Shooting with a wide-angle lens at a close distance to your subject creates facial distortion, as shown in the left image. For the right image, I positioned the subject against a nicer background, zoomed in to a longer focal length, and moved a few feet farther away.

As a result of the increased subject-to-camera distance, the picture included more background than the left image. To make my subject fill the frame, as shown here, I just cropped away some excess background and enlarged the remaining area. (You can see the uncropped original in Chapter 3.)

Increase Shutter Speed for Action Portraits

To record a moving subject in sharp focus, you need to match shutter speed to the speed of the action. For these pictures of a young gymnast friend, a shutter speed of 1/125 second did the trick.

1/20 second

1/60 second

1/125 second

PRO TIP

Light reflecting off a background can affect image colors. In the trampoline pictures, for example, light bouncing off the red wall gives the skin a reddish tint.

7

Try Slow-Sync Flash for Nighttime Portraits

In normal flash mode, backgrounds in nighttime portraits appear dark, as in the left example. If you want the background to be visible, as in the right example, switch to slow-sync flash.

Slow-sync flash enables you to use a lower shutter speed than is possible in regular flash mode. The longer exposure time allows the camera to soak up more ambient light, leading to brighter backgrounds.

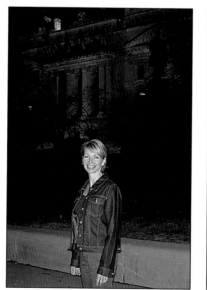

Use Bounced Window Light for Great Home Portraits

Daylight coming through a window can provide the foundation for well-lit portraits at home. For all these portraits, I positioned the subject next to a window on a bright but overcast day.

For the first portrait, I used my camera's built-in flash. The result isn't horrible, although the left side of the face is strongly shadowed. And as is typical with built-in flash, red-eye reflections mar the picture.

Switching to a more powerful, external flash and bouncing the flash off the wall behind the subject eliminated red-eye and brought more of the face into the light. But the brighter flash also created stronger shadows behind the head.

I abandoned flash for this picture, relying on window light in combination with my camera's autoexposure compensation (EV) control. The harsh shadow behind the head is gone, but raising the EV value high enough to get a decent exposure on the left side of the image seriously overexposed the side of the face nearest the window.

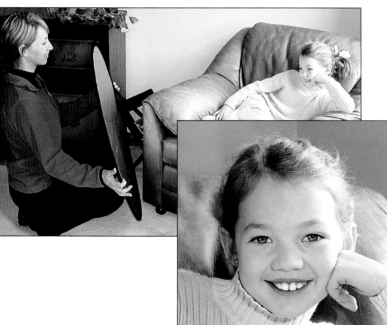

9

Using a gold reflector to bounce some of the window light back onto the shadowed side of the face enabled me to dial down the EV compensation. The result is more even lighting, with just a soft glow on the right portion of the image. Colors are slightly warmer due to the gold reflector.

Watch Out for White Balance Miscues

Each light source lends its own color cast to a scene. Your camera's auto white balance feature is designed to neutralize the light, but multiple light sources can trip it up. For example, in the portraits on the opposite page, the camera assumed that the primary light source was the flash, which casts a slightly bluish light, and adjusted white

balance accordingly. But it didn't compensate for the daylight, which has an even stronger blue color. As a result, skin tones are on the cool side. For the flash-free portraits on this page, skin tones are rendered more accurately because the camera had to deal only with a single light source. Fortunately, most cameras enable you

to switch to manual white balance control if the auto setting doesn't do the job, and you can preview the effects of each option in your camera's monitor.

Shape the Face with Light and Shadow

Your lighting decisions can affect how the shape of a face is rendered. For this series of portraits, I used various combinations of lights and reflectors. You can see the relative positions of each light source in the accompanying figures in Chapter 3.

For this first image, I positioned a single light approximately six feet from the subject, at an angle of about 45 degrees. This setup produces soft shadowing on the side of the face opposite the light (the left side of the photo).

To reduce the shadows, I hung a white reflector to the right of the subject (left of the camera). The reflector bounced light from the main light source onto the face. With light coming from both directions, the face appears somewhat flatter.

Switching to a gold reflector reduced the strength of the bounced light, restoring some of the original shadowing. As a side effect, the gold reflector lent a slightly warmer tone to the image.

For this shot, I removed the reflector and used a second light placed to the left of the camera, about the same distance from the subject as the main light but at a 90-degree angle to the face. The second created even lighting across the entire image. On the downside, the side light created harsh, unattractive shadows around the nose and mouth, while the rest of the face looks even more unsculpted than in the reflector images.

Next I asked the subject to hold a small white reflector on her lap. The reflector bounced light up into the face, reducing those unsightly facial shadows. However, the face now appears almost two-dimensional, and the boundary between neck and chin is less defined.

For this image, I used the same lighting setup as in the preceding image but changed the angle of the head. This shift in position created some soft shadowing on the side of the face and under the chin, bringing dimension back to the features and restoring definition between chin and neck. My subject and I both agreed that this image was our favorite of all the variations.

Conquer Strong Backlighting with Spot Metering and Flash

A bright background may result in an underexposed subject when you set your camera's autoexposure mode to pattern metering (sometimes called *multizone metering* or *matrix metering*), as shown in the top image here. For better results, switch to spot metering. In this mode, the camera bases exposure only on the light at the center of the frame. I used spot metering to catpure the second image. If spot metering doesn't solve the problem completely, as was the case with my picture—or if your camera doesn't offer spot metering—try using a flash. For the third photo here, I used spot metering and flash. The flash eliminated the shadows cast by the hat, bringing the face fully into the light.

Enhance Skin Tones with a Warming Filter

Notice the difference in skin tones between these portraits? The golden glow in the third photo isn't due to the flash or spot metering, but to a warming filter placed over the camera lens. Most people prefer how they look when photographed with a warming filter, which is why many pros never work without one. Depending on your light source, you may also be able to warm skin tones by using your camera's manual white balance control; see Secret #28 for details about this trick.

f/2.8

f/11

Together with shutter speed and ISO, aperture size determines image exposure. Aperture sizes are given in f-numbers; the smaller the f-number, the larger the aperture, and the more light enters the camera lens.

In addition to controlling exposure, adjusting the aperture has a side effect that you can exploit to suit your creative urges. By switching to a higher f-stop, you increase the range of sharp focus, known as *depth of field*. In these two images, for example, the portrait in the background is less sharply focused at f/2.8 than at f/11.

Changing Aperture Affects Both Exposure and Depth of Field

epth-of-field shifts become more ronounced as you move closer to your ubject. For these images, I held the amera about a foot above the flowers nd focused on the center of the yellow lip. The petals around the perimeter f the image are noticeably softer at 2.8 than at f/11.

f/2.8

f/11

Add a Neutral Density Filter to Use a Slow Shutter in Bright Light

To add a nice creative touch to waterfall photos, use a slow shutter, which blurs the water but leaves the rest of the scene in sharp focus. On a bright day, however, a shutter speed that delivers the proper exposure may not be low enough to blur the water, as shown in the first image here, which I shot using a shutter speed of 1/125 second. The secret is to use a neutral density (ND) filter, which reduces the amount of light that enters the camera. You can then slow the shutter enough to get a significant blurring effect. I used this trick to properly expose the waterfall scene at 1/30 second.

1/125 second

1/30 second

1/30 second with ND filter

4 seconds

1 second

1/2 second

Composite

For Nighttime Shots, Slow the Shutter and Raise the Tripod

To photograph a city scene at night, you need a slow shutter speed. I took these Las Vegas shots in early evening, using shutter speeds of 4 seconds, 1 second, and 1/2 second. Notice that the trails of light created by the cars become more blurred as the shutter speed slows.

Whenever you work with a slow shutter, use a tripod to avoid unwanted blurring of still objects. Also, record the scene at several different exposures. If you're not happy with any of the images, you can use your photo editor to combine the

bracketed exposures into one image, as I did for the fourth picture here.

Don't Try to Correct Exposure with a Brightness/Contrast Filter

16

Original

Getting exposure right can be tricky at sunrise and sunset. If you expose for the sky, the foreground may be too dark, as in this picture. But if you increase exposure to make the foreground brighter, light sky areas may go completely white, eliminating interesting color details. The first option is the best solution. You can fix slightly underexposed areas in a photo editor, but bringing back blown highlights is difficult.

When you adjust exposure in your photo editor, don't use the Brightness/Contrast filter. For reasons explored in Chapter 6, this filter can actually destroy contrast and wipe out shadow and highlight details. You can see the disastrous effects of this approach in the second image here.

A more sophisticated exposure tool, called a Levels filter, enables you to tweak shadows, midtones, and highlights independently of each other. I used the Levels filter to produce the third image, deepening shadows slightly, lightening midtones, and leaving highlights untouched.

15

Exposure adjusted with Brightness/Contrast filter

Exposure adjusted with Levels filter

PRO TIP

When fixing exposure problems in your photo editor, keep in mind that pictures appear brighter on your computer monitor than they will when printed. If you plan to print a picture and use it on a web site, create two copies of the image, adjusting one copy for print and one for the screen.

A Light Tent Makes Shooting Shiny Surfaces a Breeze

Photographing reflective objects can be a nightmare. A built-in flash typically is reflected in the object and produces uneven, underpowered lighting. Switching to an auxiliary flash and bouncing the light off a white ceiling can help but may still leave too much of your subject in the dark, as it did in the second example here.

For the third shot, I disabled the flash and switched to a hot light with a white umbrella attached. (Chapter 1 discusses this type of light.) The hot light produced more even lighting and brought out the iridescent colors of the face plate. But the larger light also created a larger reflection, and reflections of surrounding objects became visible in various areas of the helmet. Small wrinkles in the leather background became more noticeable with the stronger light as well.

Built-in flash

Auxiliary flash bounced off white ceiling

Hot light, softened with umbrella

PRO TIP

Your local fabric store is a great source for inexpensive backgrounds for product and portrait photos. Look for the remnant table, where you can find small pieces of fabric at bargain prices—often just a dollar or two a yard. A canvas drop cloth from the hardware store is another great solution when you need a large background.

Light tent, EV 0.0

To get these reflection-free images, I again used the umbrella-softened hot light but put the helmet inside a light tent (see Chapter 4 for a look at the tent). Although the white fabric of the tent is reflected by the face plate, the reflection is so soft and subtle that most people won't notice it unless they are looking for it.

Because this shot took a lot of work to set up, I bracketed exposures to give myself a safety net. I shot the image at five different EV compensation settings, resulting in the exposure variations you see here. Before shooting, I pulled the background taut to remove any wrinkles, using hardware-store spring clamps to keep it in place.

Light tent, EV -0.3

Light tent, EV +0.3

Light tent, EV -0.7

Light tent, EV +0.7

17

Reduce Reflections with a Polarizing Filter

When you're shooting outdoors, using a polarizing filter can reduce reflections in glass, as illustrated by these photos of a storefront window. (The window panes behind the lettering are stained-glass windows hanging inside the store, not reflections.) See Chapter 4 to find out how to get maximum impact from a polarizing filter.

Without polarizing filter

With polarizing filter

Light Framed Artwork from Both Sides

Photographing artwork under glass presents a special problem. If you shoot the frame straight on, you see your own reflection in the image, as in the first example here. You can angle the frame or camera to avoid reflections, but doing so causes parallel lines to appear distorted.

The secret is to light the artwork from both sides, setting the lights at a 45-degree angle to the picture. If you still see your reflection, put the camera on a tripod, drape the equipment with a black cloth, and use the camera's self-timer feature so that you can step away from the camera for the shot. Here, the two-light setup also produced more even lighting and made frame details more visible.

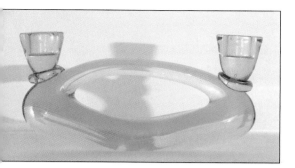

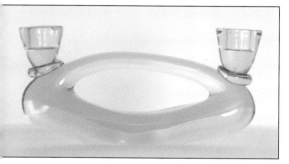

Light position and quality (soft or hard), combined with exposure, have a major impact on your images, as illustrated by this series of photographs. For all these shots, I placed the candle holder on a piece of frosted glass in front of a plain white background.

I used a single light for the top two images, positioning it several feet above and to the right of the candle holder. For the top image, I used a bright, narrowly focused light, which creates a harsh shadow. For the second image, I kept the same light position but added a white umbrella to diffuse the light, which softened the shadow. This image is much improved, but it's pretty lifeless, and the shadow is still a little distracting.

Light Glass from Below to Create a Dramatic Effect

For the third image, I added a second, umbrella-softened light, placing it underneath the glass platform and angling it to shine through the candle holder from the back. (You can see the lighting setup in Chapter 4.) The second light brightens the frosted-glass platform and almost eliminates the shadow from the main light. I also adjusted exposure to make the colors in the glass a little more intense.

To achieve the more dramatic look of the last two images, I switched off the top, side light and reoriented the underneath light. I angled it so that light would hit the candle holder from directly below rather than from behind. Again, I adjusted exposure to create progressively darker images.

Of course, if you're photographing glass that you want to sell, you should strive for a result that most accurately reproduces the object's colors. In this case, the second image on the page does that job best. But my personal favorite from an artistic standpoint is contestant number four.

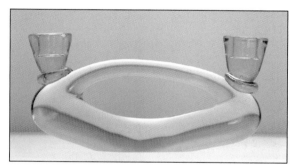

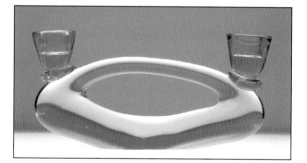

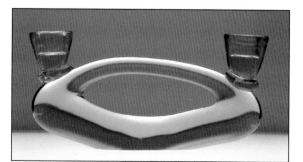

You Can Find Beauty in the Details

Focusing on a single, small element often reveals a better photographic opportunity than trying to capture a broad area. Although the bed of tulips shown here offers a pretty color palette, the picture is otherwise uninspired. Zooming to an extreme close-up view of a tulip with only two petals remaining resulted in a picture that's far more interesting and yet just as dramatic from a color standpoint.

PRO TIP

For great close-ups outdoors, use a large aperture (low f-stop value). The background will appear blurred, as in my tulip photo. A large aperture also enables you to use a fast shutter speed, which helps you capture the main subject sharply even in a slight breeze.

Zoom In to Include Less Background; Move Closer to Capture More

Deciding whether to zoom in or move nearer to your subject affects more than how much energy you expend to get a close-up. Zoom out and move closer to include more background and increase depth of field, as shown in the right example. When you zoom in, you increase the lens focal length, which reduces the amount of background in the frame and also makes that background appear more softly focused. The focal lengths shown here are stated in terms of the equivalent measurement on a 35mm film camera; see Chapter 1 to find out why.

140mm (equiv.)

35mm (equiv.)

Digital Zoom Reduces Picture Quality

All digital cameras offer a digital zoom, a feature that manufacturers like to highlight in their advertisements. Unfortunately, a digital zoom has none of the power of a real—optical—zoom lens. A digital zoom simply enlarges the image and then crops away the perimeter of the picture. The end result is the same as if you cropped and enlarged the picture in your photo editor. In both cases, image quality is reduced.

These four images illustrate why digital zoom really should be called "in-camera crop and enlarge." All four photos come from a digital camera that offers an optical zoom that equates to a 35–280mm lens on a 35mm film camera—an 8x zoom power—plus a 4x digital zoom. At the far end of the optical zoom range (middle image), the photo looks as good as at the wide end (top image). But in the shot captured at the maximum digital zoom setting, quality is seriously degraded. The image looks no better than its twin to the right, which I created by cropping and enlarging the photo taken with the optical zoom only.

35mm (equiv.)

280mm (equiv.)

280mm (equiv.) plus 4x digital zoom

280mm (equiv.) enlarged

21

Beware In-Camera Sharpening Filters

Sharpening, an option found on many digital cameras, tries to create the illusion of sharper focus by boosting contrast along the borders between differently colored areas. You get better results doing your own sharpening in your photo editor because you can more precisely control where and how the effect is applied.

For these images, I used a camera that offers a choice of strong, medium, and no sharpening. At the strong setting, the skin and fabric have a rough look, and lines in the hands are emphasized. In addition, the sharpening created noticeable light and dark halos around the perimeter of the hands. The medium setting produced a better result, but the skin still appears too textured for such a romantic subject.

For the lower left image, I turned in-camera sharpening off, which softened the skin and made the pattern in the material less obvious.

To create the final image, I opened the picture in my photo editor and slightly sharpened just the ring and the boundary between the hands and the dress. That touch of sharpening gave the ring a bit more sparkle and made the hands appear to be in sharper focus without adding unwanted roughness to the skin.

Strong in-camera sharpening

Medium in-camera sharpening

No in-camera sharpening

Selective sharpening in photo editor

Take the Sharpening Reins with Unsharp Mask

The Unsharp Mask filter, offered in many photo editors, gives you complete sharpening control. You can vary the amount of sharpening, change the width of the sharpening halos, and limit the effect to areas of high contrast only. These filter options typically go by the names Amount, Radius, and Threshold.

Examples on this page illustrate how different combinations of these three filter options create different effects. Don't let the scientific-sounding option names scare you off—using Unsharp Mask is very easy. Chapter 5 shows you how.

Original

Amount, 200; Radius, 2; Threshold, 0

Amount, 200; Radius, 4; Threshold, 0

Amount, 200; Radius, 4; Threshold, 20

Built-in flash, flash EV 0.0

Built-in flash, flash EV -2.0

Switch to a Macro Flash for Better Lighting at Close Range

When you're shooting this close to a subject, don't rely on your camera's built-in flash for illumination. The flash is so focused that it typically produces a strong flare at the point of maximum impact, as shown in the top two images. I took both pictures using a camera that offered flash exposure compensation (flash EV), but even reducing the flash output to its lowest setting didn't fix the problem.

Specialized macro flash units enable you to light your subject much more evenly. I took the two images below with a unit that puts two small, adjustable flash heads on either side of the camera lens. At full power, the flash was a little too strong; reducing the flash EV to -1.0 produced a perfect exposure.

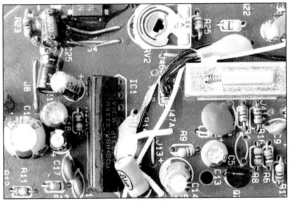

Macro flash unit, flash EV 0.0

Macro flash unit, flash EV -1.0

PRO TIP

Precise focus is critical for close-up photography. If your camera has a video-out port, connect the camera to a television using the AV cables that came in your camera box. You can then preview and review your shots on the TV screen, where focus problems will be more obvious than on the camera monitor.

Boost Macro Power with a Set of Close-Up Lenses

Accessory close-up lenses offer an inexpensive way to get closer to your subject. These lenses work like the reading glasses you find in the drug store, magnifying whatever the camera lens sees.

The power of a close-up lens is indicated by its diopter number; the higher the number, the greater the magnification. Here, you can see the impact of a diopter power of +7, +10, and +17. (The images were cropped to allow me to show them all on the same page.) How much magnification you get at a given diopter power is affected by the focal length of your camera lens, however. For these images, the focal length was equivalent to about 60mm on a 35mm film camera.

Camera only

+7 Close-up lens

PRO TIP

You can mount multiple close-up lenses on your camera to get their combined magnification power. I stacked a +7 and +10 lens to produce the +17 example.

+10 Close-up lens

Stacked +10, +7

25

Manual White Balance Gives You Color Control

Various light sources produce different colors of light. For example, cloudy daylight has a bluish cast, while standard household bulbs generate a warm yellow light. The color cast produced by a light source is known as its *color temperature*.

Color temperatures are measured on the Kelvin scale. As the temperature rises, the light takes on a cooler color cast. This chart shows the approximate color and Kelvin temperature of various light sources.

In Automatic mode, your camera's white-balance control detects the light temperature and makes the necessary color adjustments. But if your camera offers manual white balancing, you can use the control to produce warmer or cooler tones, similar to what you can do with a traditional warming or cooling filter.

I took this picture on a cloudless, sunny afternoon, so the Sunny white balance setting captured the carousel colors correctly.

To produce cooler tones, use a white balance setting appropriate for light that has a lower Kelvin temperature than the actual light. Here, I switched to Fluorescent (left) and Incandescent (right).

Kelvin	Light source
8000	Snow, water, shade
	Overcast skies
	Flash
5000	Bright sunshine
	Fluorescent bulbs
	Tungsten lights
3000	Incandescent bulbs
2000	Candlelight

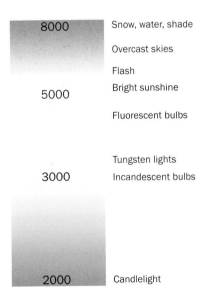

For warmer tones, choose a white balance setting geared to a light source that has a higher color temperature than the actual light source. I used the Flash setting for the left image and Cloudy for the right image.

Warming Filters Aren't Just for Portraits

My favorite time to take pictures outdoors is late afternoon, when the fading sun infuses everything with a warm wash of color. But if my schedule requires shooting earlier in the day, using a warming filter adds similar tones to the scene.

I photographed this architectural ruin around 10 a.m., for example. I recorded the first image without any filters, using automatic white balancing. For the second shot, I used an 81B warming filter, which adds a medium-strength warming effect.

No filter

81B warming filter

No Warming Filter? Create the Same Look in Your Photo Editor!

No filter, color balance altered

No filter, Brilliance/Warmth effect

If you don't have a warming filter, you can get similar results by adjusting color balance in your photo editor. I used this technique to create the left image, aiming this time for more golden tones than I got from the 81B filter.

For the final image, I turned to nik Color Efex Pro!, a Photoshop-compatible plug-in that offers a collection of color effects that mimic traditional photographic filters. Here, I applied the Brilliance/Warmth effect.

A Polarizer Can Turn Gray Skies Blue

No filter

With polarizing filter

On days when Mother Nature doesn't provide perfect weather, you may be able to use a polarizing filter to coax a bit more blue out of the sky. The impact of the effect depends on the camera angle with respect to the sun and sky.

Remember that in addition to altering sky colors, a polarizing filter may also reduce reflections in glass and other shiny surfaces, as it did for the second image here.

If you don't want to use a polarizing filter because you want to retain reflections, you can tint the sky blue in your photo editor. I used the technique outlined in Chapter 8 to produce the third image from my unpolarized image.

No filter, sky tinted in photo editor

Normal saturation

Maximum saturation

Minimum saturation

Some digital cameras offer a saturation control that enables you to make image colors more or less intense. These three images show the same subject recorded at normal, maximum, and minimum saturation. (How much adjustment occurs varies from camera to camera.)

Cool as this option sounds, it doesn't give you as much control as your photo editor. You're limited in how much change you can make, and you can't adjust some colors and leave others alone, as you can in a photo editor.

29

Tweak Saturation in the Digital Darkroom, Not in the Camera

32

Here's an example of the advanced control you enjoy when you adjust saturation in your photo editor. Starting with the normal saturation image at the top of the page, I applied the Photoshop Elements Hue/Saturation filter.

First, I increased saturation of yellows, which gave the lemon and green onions a bit more pop. Then I lowered the saturation of blues and cyans to make the plate a little less important in the composition.

Selective adjustment in photo editor

Shoot in Color, Even If You Want a Black-and-White Photo

Most digital cameras offer an option that produces a black-and-white photo. But you get more control over the tones in your photo when you do the color conversion in your photo editor.

To understand why this is true, remember that a digital image is made up of three color channels: red, green, and blue. Each color channel is just a grayscale image that reflects the amount of red, green, or blue light in the image. The three grayscale pictures on this page show you the red, green, and blue channel images for the full-color photo.

When you do an in-camera conversion, your camera mushes all three channels into one, taking a certain amount of brightness information from each channel. This approach, which doesn't account for the varying importance of different channels from image to image, has an averaging effect that can reduce the overall tonal range and eliminate subtle details.

RGB composite

Red channel

Green channel

Blue channel

The first image on this page shows the result of the simple color-to-grayscale conversion applied by most cameras. Notice that some details that are visible in the individual channel images get lost in the conversion. The striations in the green onions, for example, are vivid in the blue channel, but become much more muted in the conversion. By doing the conversion yourself, you can pick and choose the channel details that you want to emphasize.

You can produce custom color conversions using a number of different techniques. For the second image, I used the Photoshop Elements Hue/Saturation filter, using the technique described in Chapter 8. (Don't use the standard Grayscale Mode command; it produces results similar to the in-camera converter.)

Advanced photo editing programs offer even more options. One popular technique is to convert the image to the Lab color mode and then retain just the lightness channel, as I did for the lower-right image.

As another alternative, you can create the grayscale composite using just one of the RGB color channels. Or you can custom-blend the channels, specifying how much of each channel you want to use. I took this approach for the lower-left image, using the Adobe Photoshop Channel Mixer filter.

These examples, by the way, aren't intended to imply that any one result or technique is the right answer. I purposely varied the outcome of each image to emphasize the degree to which you can control your photos when you take the grayscale reins. Which method or result you prefer is your artistic choice!

Standard conversion to grayscale mode

Hue/Saturation selective conversion

Adobe Photoshop Channel Mixer

Lightness channel from Lab image

31

When Patterns Collide, Moiré Ensues

Digital cameras, like video cameras, sometimes have trouble capturing fabrics that have strong patterns. The problem occurs because the chips in an image sensor are arranged in a linear design. When the chips and the fabric's pattern aren't aligned, the camera may produce a third, distorted pattern known as *moiré*. This flaw shows up as wavy lines and weird color striations, as shown here. If you notice moiré occurring, try changing the camera angle slightly and softening focus.

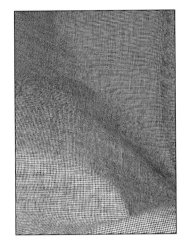

GIF, 256 colors,
62K, 23 seconds

GIF Makes Good Colors Go Bad (So Does Heavy Compression)

Pictures that you want to use on the Web must be saved in a browser-friendly file format. JPEG is the best option for photos because it retains all image colors. The other popular format, GIF, can preserve a maximum of 256 colors, which usually results in the color-blocking effect that you see in this GIF example.

When you save a picture as a JPEG file, the Quality setting determines how much the file is compressed. As illustrated by these examples, compression affects picture quality, file size, and download times. (The download times shown here assume a modem speed of 28.8Kbps.)

JPEG, Minimum Quality
8K, 4 seconds

JPEG, Medium Quality
30K, 11 seconds

JPEG, Maximum Quali
113K, 41 seconds

How To

ADJUST EXPOSURE WITH A LEVELS FILTER *(continued)*

The vertical axis of the chart shows the concentration of pixels at each brightness value. For example, Figure 6.4 shows the histogram for the sugar mill image in Figure 6.2. The histogram clearly shows a lack of pixels at the darkest end of the brightness spectrum—there are no true black pixels.

The specific method you use to adjust your image using the Levels filter varies from program to program. In Photoshop Elements, you can just drag the triangle sliders underneath the histogram, as follows:

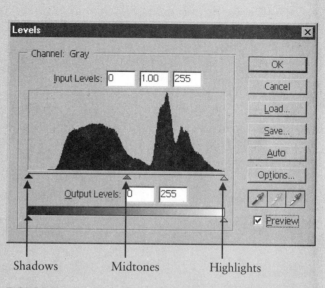

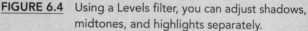

Shadows   Midtones   Highlights

FIGURE 6.4   Using a Levels filter, you can adjust shadows, midtones, and highlights separately.

- Use the left slider to adjust shadows. Drag right to make the darkest pixels even darker. In some programs, this control is called the Black Point control.

- Use the right slider to manipulate highlights. Drag left to make the lightest pixels brighter. This control is sometimes known as the White Point control.

- Use the middle slider, sometimes known as the Gamma or Midpoint control, to adjust midtones. Drag right to make midtones darker; drag left to make them lighter. (In some programs, including Photoshop Elements, dragging either the shadow or highlight control also shifts the midtones. You can always move the midtone slider later, if necessary.)

Figure 6.5 and the bottom image on Page 15 of the insert show the original sugar mill picture after I adjusted shadows and midtones, moving the sliders to the positions shown in the Levels dialog box that accompanies the image. This change lightened the midtones, deepened the shadows, and left highlights untouched. The

How To ADJUST EXPOSURE WITH A LEVELS FILTER *(continued)*

result is an image that appears brighter and has a broader tonal range, yet still shows detail in the highlights.

FIGURE 6.5 Moving the shadows and midtones sliders to the positions shown in the Levels dialog box produced a better exposure and tonal range.

The Levels filter has one unwanted side effect: it can make your picture look a little washed out. You can use a Saturation filter to strengthen colors if necessary; Chapter 8 discusses this filter in detail. Levels may also shift image colors slightly, a problem that you can easily remedy using your photo editor's Color Balance filter.

I've provided just the briefest introduction to Levels, so check your software manual to find out what other features your version of the filter may offer. In Photoshop Elements, for example, you can apply the filter as an adjustment layer, which enables you to adjust exposure without permanently altering image pixels.

Shooting Long Exposures

Somewhere in your camera manual—look in the back few pages, in the list of camera specifications—you should find information about the range of shutter speeds available to you. The longer your camera allows you to keep the shutter open, the darker the scene that you can photograph successfully.

≫ TROUBLESHOOTER

Don't have any way to control shutter speed on your camera? Check to see whether the camera offers a nighttime scene mode. In that mode, the camera automatically uses a slow shutter speed. On some cameras, this scene mode shifts you to slow-sync Flash mode, explained later in this chapter. But on other cameras, you can disable the flash for an even slower shutter.

Page 14 of the color insert shows four images that feature a nighttime subject that's been a favorite of generations of photographers: the Las Vegas "strip." For the first three images, I used shutter speeds of 4 seconds, 1 second, and 1/2 second, respectively. At the longest exposure, the sky appears a dark blue—a little lighter than it looked to my eye at the time. In the shorter exposures, the sky goes black, shadowed areas in the foreground virtually disappear, and the city lights don't burn as brightly.

PRO TIP

If you bracket exposures in your nighttime shots, you can blend the images together in a photo editor. This technique allows you to combine the shadow details from the brightest exposure and the highlight details from the darkest exposure into one image that has a broader tonal range than you could get from any one shot. The fourth Las Vegas image on Page 14 of the insert offers an example. First, I copied the sky from the 4-second exposure into the 1-second exposure. Then I replaced some of the lighted signs that were too bright with darker ones from the 1/2–second exposure. For this technique to work, you must make sure that you don't move the camera between exposures; otherwise, the elements in the scene won't match up when you merge the images.

As with ISO adjustments, you need to consider the following caveats when using a slow shutter speed:

- Most people can't hold a camera still enough to capture an image without blurring at exposures longer than about 1/60 second. On a good day—one that doesn't involve lots of caffeine, for example—you may be able to get away with 1/30 second if you lean against a wall or other support while taking the picture. But to ensure the sharpest images, use a tripod or put the camera on a solid surface before you press the shutter button.

- Speaking of pressing the shutter button, take advantage of your camera's self-timer function, if available. The slight press of a finger on the camera can create enough camera shake to blur the image, and using the self-timer enables you to take a hands-free shot. Some cameras can be triggered with a remote-control unit or shutter-release cable as well.

- Even if the camera remains perfectly still, any objects moving through the scene will appear blurry in long-exposure images. The longer the exposure, the greater the blur. For example, notice the car lights in the Las Vegas images, shown in Figure 6.6 in grayscale. (In the 1/2-second example, the cars in the center of the image are waiting at a stoplight; you can see light trails from the crossing traffic near the right side of the frame.)

4 seconds   1 second   1/2 second

FIGURE 6.6 Shutter speed determines not only exposure, but also how much blurring occurs from moving objects, such as the cars in these images.

PRO TIP

If you want more blur but don't want the brighter exposure that a longer shutter speed would produce, stop down the aperture (select a higher f-stop number). Another trick is to use a neutral density filter to reduce the amount of light that enters the camera, as discussed later in this chapter in the section "Using Blur to Emphasize Motion."

- Some cameras offer a *bulb* setting, which keeps the shutter open as long as you keep the shutter button pressed down. However, the camera may put a limit on the amount of time you can keep the shutter open—1 minute or 5 minutes, for example. Dig through your camera's menus to see whether you can adjust the bulb duration limit.

- Image noise, explained in the preceding section, typically increases as exposure time lengthens. You can keep noise down as much as possible by setting the camera's ISO control to its lowest setting and by switching on the noise reduction feature, if available. Of course, you need to select a slower shutter speed or larger aperture (lower f-stop number) to get the same exposure at a lower ISO than at a higher ISO.

Using Slow-Sync Flash

Chapters 3, 4, and 5 discuss techniques for using a flash when shooting portraits, product shots, and close-ups. For nighttime and other low-light photography projects, you should get acquainted with a flash option that I haven't yet introduced: *slow-sync flash*.

To get a proper exposure, the flash and shutter speed must be synchronized so that the light from the flash hits the subject at the precise moment when the shutter is fully open. On most cameras, you're limited to using a relatively fast shutter speed—say, 1/60 to 1/125 second—when flash is enabled. This setup ensures that the subject is lit primarily by the flash and not ambient room light. Slow-sync mode enables you to use your flash at slower than normal shutter speeds, letting ambient light play a bigger role in the exposure.

Switching to slow-sync flash has two effects on your photograph: First, a background that would otherwise appear dark becomes visible. Second, you can get a good exposure with less flash power, which usually translates to softer, less contrasty foreground lighting. Figure 6.7 and the bottom pair of images on Page 7 of the color insert offer two examples of the impact of slow-sync flash.

FIGURE 6.7 With regular flash, the background appears dark, and foreground lighting may be harsh (top). Switching to slow-sync flash results in softer, more even lighting throughout the scene (bottom).

Whether or not you opt for slow-sync flash depends on your creative goal. Take the scene in Figure 6.7, for example. In this image, the house in the background is distracting, so standard flash is the better choice. But slow-sync flash works better in travel photos and in other scenarios where you want to emphasize the location of the subject. In the color insert image, for example, the Indiana state capitol in the background helps place the subject in Indianapolis (well, to Hoosiers familiar with that government building, anyway).

How you implement slow-sync flash and the extent to which you can control the feature varies from camera to camera. Here are a few options and limitations you may encounter:

- In programmed autoexposure mode, the camera automatically reduces shutter speed when you switch to slow-sync flash and increases shutter speed when you go back to regular flash mode.

- If your camera offers manual exposure control, check your owner's manual to find out what shutter speeds you can use with slow-sync flash and standard flash.

- In normal flash mode, the flash fires at the beginning of the exposure, which is why this mode is sometimes called *front-curtain sync*. (The curtain part comes from the name given to the part of the shutter that opens and shuts when you press the shutter button.) Some cameras also offer *rear-curtain sync*. In this mode, known sometimes as *trailing sync*, the flash fires at the end of the exposure.

The difference between the two modes becomes apparent only in long exposures of moving objects, such as the Las Vegas images shown in Figure 6.6. With rear-curtain sync, the ghostlike trails that emerge from moving objects appear to follow the objects, the arrangement that has come to serve as the traditional way to indicate motion in a still picture. If you use front-curtain sync, the motion streaks precede the object, which looks a little bizarre—sort of like buildings falling down before the windstorm hits. For this reason, most cameras automatically take the rear-curtain approach when you use slow-sync flash mode. But on high-end cameras, you may be able to choose between the two options.

>> TROUBLESHO⊕TER

Because of the slower shutter speed, always put the camera on a tripod or other steady surface to avoid blurring when using slow-sync flash mode. All the other cautions mentioned in the earlier section on long-exposure photography apply to slow-sync mode as well.

Capturing Motion

When you want to catch a moving target through your camera lens, you can go in two creative directions: you can use a slow shutter and purposely blur the image to create a heightened sense of motion, or you can set the shutter speed high enough to "freeze" the subject at a particular instant in time. (Experienced photographers also know to claim that they were trying for the former if the latter doesn't work as intended.)

The rest of this chapter provides some tricks to use for both approaches.

Using Blur to Emphasize Motion

If your camera offers manual exposure control or shutter-priority AE (autoexposure), achieving the amount of blur you want is easy: just experiment with slower and slower shutter speeds until you're satisfied with the results. (Read the earlier section about long-exposure photography for tips on getting the best image quality.)

Of course, as you reduce shutter speed, your camera senses light for a longer period of time. So you should also reduce aperture size (by shifting to a higher f-stop setting) to avoid overexposing the image.

If your digital camera offers only programmed AE—or programmed AE and aperture-priority AE—you may be able to use these workarounds to get the slow shutter needed to produce the blur:

- In programmed AE, try switching to nighttime scene mode, if available. As discussed earlier, this mode typically forces a slower shutter. You may wind up with too much light in your image, though; try using a negative EV value to compensate.

- In aperture-priority AE, set the f-stop to its highest number, which results in the smallest possible aperture opening. The camera will shift to a lower shutter speed to account for the smaller aperture.

The one tricky aspect of using a blur-inducing shutter speed is getting a good exposure in very bright light. Even if you stop the aperture all the way down, a shutter speed that's slow enough to produce the effect you want may overexpose the image. As an example, see the waterfall photos on Page 14 of the color insert, repeated in Figure 6.8 in grayscale.

1/125 second   1/30 second   1/30 second with ND filter

FIGURE 6.8 To give a waterfall a misty look, use a slow shutter. In bright light, you may need to add a neutral density filter to avoid overexposing the image.

For the first image, I set the shutter speed to 1/125 second, with an aperture of about f/5.6. The exposure was fine, but I wanted the water to be more blurred, which gives it a misty look. To achieve that effect, I needed to slow the shutter to 1/30 second. But I was shooting on a very sunny day, and 1/30 second resulted in a too-bright image even when I used the smallest possible aperture. This level of overexposure is beyond what you can successfully correct in a photo editor.

A special lens filter, called a *neutral density* (ND) *filter*, comes in handy for this situation. The filter reduces the amount of light without altering image colors. You can see the difference the filter made in the third waterfall image. (See the sidebar "Understanding Neutral Density Filters" for details about this type of filter.) A polarizing filter can serve the same purpose; if you don't want the polarizing effect along with the darkening impact, just turn the outer ring of the filter until the polarizing effect disappears.

 SEE ALSO

Chapter 4 explains how to use a polarizing filter to reduce glare; Chapter 8 shows you how to use the filter to make skies appear bluer.

>> TROUBLESHOOTER

Some advanced digital cameras have a built-in neutral density filter that serves the same purpose as a real lens filter. Usually, the filter works only when you select a slow shutter speed.

Technical Aside

Understanding Neutral Density Filters

Neutral density filters reduce light transmission to enable you to use a slower shutter speed or larger aperture in bright light without overexposing your image. These filters come in varying strengths, which are indicated by a *density number*.

Density numbers typically range from .10 to 4.00, with a higher number indicating more light reduction. As with close-up lenses, you can stack neutral density filters to enjoy their combined light-reducing strength. I used a single filter with a density number of .6 for my waterfall image in Figure 6.8.

You may also see ND filters rated in terms of *filter factor*. As explained in Chapter 1, this value indicates how much increase in exposure is required to produce the same image that you would get without the filter. Again, just remember that the higher the number, whether it's density number or filter factor, the more you reduce the light entering your camera. The .6 ND filter that I added for the waterfall photo has a filter factor of 4X, meaning that you need four times the light to get the same exposure with the filter as without.

Freezing Action with a Fast Shutter

If your photo collection is like most, it contains scads of images that were unintentionally blurred because the subject moved too fast for the camera to capture clearly. You may as well go ahead and toss those pictures, as I do, because no amount of fiddling in a photo editor can fix them.

For future pictures, follow these guidelines to freeze a subject in motion:

* Switch to shutter-priority AE or manual exposure, if available on your camera, so that you can match the shutter speed to the pace of your subject. Until you get a feel for the shutter-to-action relationship, you'll need to experiment to find the right setting. For the subject featured in Figure 6.9, for example, a shutter speed of 1/20 second was much too slow; 1/60 second nearly stopped the action, but some blurring was still visible around the hands, feet, and bottom of the shirt. At 1/125 second, my young friend appears cleanly suspended in mid-jump. You can see the color version of these images on Page 7 of the color insert.

1/20 second   1/60 second   1/125 second

<u>**FIGURE 6.9**</u> Match shutter speed to the pace of your subject. Here, a shutter speed of 1/125 second froze the jumper cleanly in mid-air in the far-right photo.

>> TROUBLESHOOTER

Don't forget that you must add more light as your raise shutter speed, either by shifting to a larger aperture (lower f-stop number) or by increasing the power of whatever artificial light source you may be using. Otherwise, your image will get progressively darker.

- If your camera doesn't offer manual shutter control or shutter-priority AE, but it *does* provide aperture-priority AE, you can increase shutter speed by shifting to a lower f-stop. Doing so opens the aperture and lets in more light, which causes the camera to increase shutter speed in response.

- No way to control either aperture or shutter speed? Check to see whether your camera offers a sports or action scene mode. This mode automatically shifts your camera to a higher shutter speed.

Speeding Up Your Camera's Response Time

Although many digital cameras offer shutter speeds high enough to capture just about any moving subject, some other camera functions can slow you down. Try these tricks to kick your camera into a higher gear:

- On most models, you must wait for the camera to write the current image to the memory card before you can take a second picture. Even when this lag time is brief, it can cause you to miss a great shot when you're shooting action. To keep the lag time as short as possible, use the lowest resolution setting that will produce the quality and picture size that you need. The more pixels the camera captures, the longer it takes to write the picture to the camera's memory card.

- Turn off specialty image-processing functions, such as noise reduction (explained earlier in this chapter) and color effects (covered in Chapter 8).

- If you can get by without it, turn off your camera's flash. You can't take a picture during the time it takes the flash to recycle between shots.

- Turn off instant picture review, which displays an image briefly on the camera monitor after each shot. Most cameras prevent you from taking the next shot during the picture review period.

- Make sure that your batteries are fresh. Low-powered batteries can make a camera behave sluggishly.

- When using autofocus and autoexposure, frame the image and set the exposure and focus (by pressing the shutter button halfway down) in advance of the action. That way, you don't have to wait for the autoexposure/focus mechanism to do its thing when the moment you want to capture happens. Just keep the shutter button pressed halfway down and then press it the rest of the way when the action occurs. If your subject isn't already in the frame at the time, set the focus and exposure by pointing the camera at something that's at the same distance and in similar lighting as your subject will be.

- If you just can't get the timing of the shutter right, you may want to consider switching to movie mode, if your camera offers one. This mode records a brief digital video segment, just like a digital camcorder. You can then pull a single frame from the video clip to use as a still photo. Unfortunately, most cameras limit you to low-resolution images and don't permit the use of flash in this mode. Movie mode also creates large image files, so make sure you have a high-capacity storage card in your camera.

7
Creating Panoramic Images

You're standing on the rim of the Grand Canyon, looking out on a spectacular vista. The light is perfect, your camera batteries are juiced up, and you've found the perfect vantage point for photographing the scene. But when you look through your camera's viewfinder, you realize that your lens can see only a small slice of the landscape, resulting in a picture that's nowhere near as powerful as you had envisioned.

When you can't fit a subject into a single frame, consider capturing it in a series of pictures and then using your computer to join the images into a panoramic photo. Whether you want to record a jaw-dropping natural wonder, a towering cityscape, or just your own street, this chapter shows you how.

Setting Up for Panoramic Photography

Your film camera may offer a panorama setting that produces a photo that's much wider, but also shorter, than a regular picture. This type of panorama is easy to do but limits you to a specific image size.

With a digital camera and image-stitching software, you can create as large a panorama as your creative heart desires. I stitched together five images to produce the urban panorama shown in Figure 7.1, for example. (You can see the five separate images in Figure 7.9, later in this chapter.)

FIGURE 7.1   I built this panoramic image from five individual photos.

In addition to flat panoramas like the one in Figure 7.1, you can create virtual-reality (VR) panoramas, sometimes also referred to as *immersive* images, which provide a 360-degree view of a scene. When you open the panorama in a VR viewer, you can spin the display to see the subject from all angles, creating the illusion that you have stepped into the middle of the image. Figure 7.2 shows a panorama displayed in Apple's QuickTime Player, a free utility that you can use to view immersive images as well as digital movies and other media.

The panorama creation process is the same whether you're making flat or VR panoramas. You photograph the first segment of the scene, rotate the camera right or left to shoot the next segment, and keep going until you've captured each area that you want to include in the panorama. Then you open the images in a stitching program on your computer and glue them together. Most stitching programs create the pieced-together image without much interaction from you; after you specify a few options, such as the type of panorama, you can sit back while the program quilts together the images.

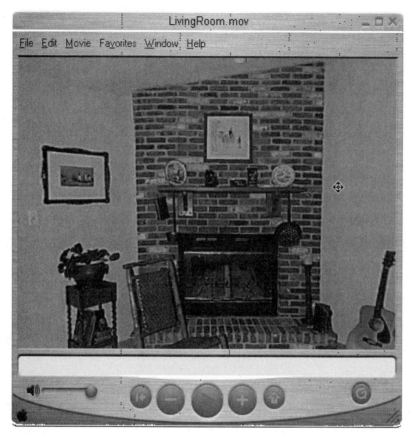

FIGURE 7.2 Apple QuickTime Player is a popular tool for viewing VR panoramas.

For the stitching software to sew a seamless panorama, however, you have to feed it good raw material. You must be careful about how you take each picture, or the panorama will look like a crazy quilt of distorted lines, blurry objects, and odd shifts in perspective, focus, and exposure. The next several sections give you the information you need to do your part of the job.

Rotating Around the Nodal Point

When you rotate the camera between shots, the axis of rotation is critical. You must rotate the camera with respect to the optical center of the lens, called the *nodal point*. Otherwise, you get large shifts in perspective from one shot to the next, which results in alignment errors that are difficult or impossible to remove in the stitching process.

Nodal point

Rotation axis

FIGURE 7.3 When you mount your camera on a tripod, the lens nodal point is several inches away from the axis of rotation.

If you put the camera on a standard tripod head, as shown in Figure 7.3, the axis of rotation will be several inches away from the nodal point. The same problem occurs when you handhold the camera and merely rotate your body to take each shot.

To solve this problem, manufacturers such as Manfrotto (*www.manfrotto .com*) or *www .bogenphoto.com*), Kaidan (*www .kaidan.com*, and Peace River Studios (*www.peaceriverstudios .com*) sell panoramic tripod heads. These heads have sliding plates that allow you to position the camera so that it rotates around the nodal point, as shown in Figures 7.4 and 7.5. The figures feature Manfrotto's QTVR kit, which sells for about $325 and includes a base unit that helps keep the camera level— another important component of a successful panorama. Most panoramic heads, like this one, also enable you to lock in a particular degree of rotation to guide you in framing each shot. (See the section "Shooting the Pieces of Your Panorama" for more about leveling and framing issues.)

Nodal point and rotation axis aligned

FIGURE 7.4 Special panoramic tripod heads enable you to position the camera so that it rotates around the lens nodal point.

FIGURE 7.5 This panoramic head also offers guides to help you level the camera and properly frame each shot.

Although a panoramic head isn't cheap, it's an investment you should make if you shoot panoramas regularly. The heads tend to be heavy, so you should also get a sturdy tripod; cheap, lightweight models marketed to casual photographers can easily tip over with the combined weight of the head and camera. Also be sure that the head is designed for use with the type of camera body that you plan to use. Some heads are engineered to work with larger, single-lens reflex (SLR) cameras or video cameras. Finally, don't confuse a panoramic head with a panning head—the latter is designed to enable smooth, easy movement of the camera but doesn't offer nodal-point positioning rails and other panoramic features.

COST CUTTER

If a panoramic head isn't in your budget, try this technique to make sure that you rotate the camera around the lens nodal point. Find a flat, stable surface on which you can place the camera while shooting your panoramic series—a tabletop, fence railing, or ladder step, for example. Place a coin on the surface to mark the axis of rotation you want to use. For each shot, reposition the camera so that the lens nodal point is always on top of the coin.

When you want to use a tripod, put the coin or other marker on the ground. Before each shot, move the tripod as necessary to keep the lens nodal point directly over the marker. Some photographers use a string that has a weight at the end to help in this positioning. You tie the unweighted end of the string around the lens barrel and let the weighted end dangle down to the nodal-point marker.

How To

CHECK NODAL POINT POSITIONING

Whether you work with a panoramic tripod head or use one of the cost-cutter solutions described, the following steps will help you determine whether the camera is properly positioned to rotate around the nodal point.

1. Find a scene that includes two vertical objects that are several feet apart—a lamppost and the side of a house, for example, if you're outside. Inside, an open closet door located across the room from a window frame will do.

2. Position yourself so that you're close to one of those objects, with the other in view. (If you're doing the door/window frame setup, you should be close to the door.)

CHECK NODAL POINT POSITIONING *(continued)*

3. Look through your camera's viewfinder and frame a shot so that the two objects appear side by side, as shown in Figure 7.6.

FIGURE 7.6   For the first step in your nodal point test, line up two vertical structures side by side in your camera's viewfinder.

4. Pan the camera to the right until the objects are at the left edge of the frame. Then pan left until the objects are at the right edge of the frame. If the two objects remain joined at the hip, as shown in Figure 7.7, you're good to go—the camera is rotating around the nodal point.

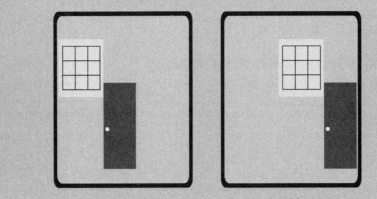

FIGURE 7.7   The relative position of the vertical structures should remain constant as you pan the camera from side to side.

If the relative positioning of the objects shifts when you pan the camera, as shown in Figure 7.8, the nodal point is either in front of or behind the rotation axis. Reposition the camera and try again. Otherwise, the stitching program won't

How To

CHECK NODAL POINT POSITIONING (continued)

be able to join the images correctly because of the variation in perspective between the shots.

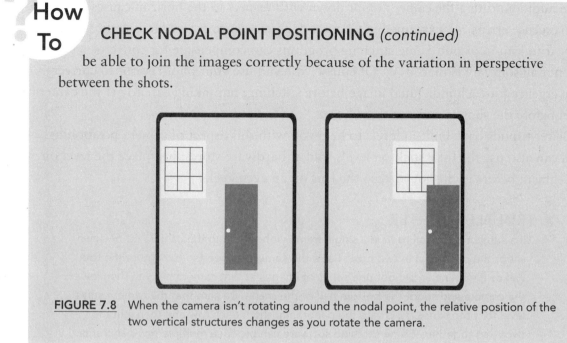

FIGURE 7.8   When the camera isn't rotating around the nodal point, the relative position of the two vertical structures changes as you rotate the camera.

Shooting the Pieces of Your Panorama

In addition to rotating your camera with respect to the lens nodal point, shooting good panoramic images involves several other important considerations. The following sections tell you what you need to know.

Shoot in Vertical Orientation

When you stitch together your images, the stitching software probably will shift some of the images up or down to achieve a good seam, just as you do when hanging patterned wallpaper. This results in ragged edges at the top and the bottom of the panorama, which you then have to crop away. (See Figure 7.14, toward the end of the chapter, to see what I mean.)

Because you'll ultimately be cropping away some of the scene, shoot your panoramic images with the camera in a vertical orientation, rather than in normal horizontal orientation. After the stitching software does its cropping, your panorama will have more height than if you started with horizontally oriented images.

Keep the Camera Level to the Horizon

For best results, keep the camera level to the horizon line. If the camera strays significantly off level, you'll have trouble getting good seams because the horizon line will shift between images.

In addition, tilting the camera up or down with respect to the horizon causes convergence errors. As explained in Chapter 4, convergence errors cause vertical lines appear to lean in or out. Some stitching programs can compensate for convergence, but not all software is that savvy. Of course, you can use your photo editor to correct convergence for each individual image before stitching, but taking care to get the camera level before the shot spares you that chore.

Better tripods have built-in levels to help you with this aspect of camera positioning. You can also use the little stick-on levels sold at hardware stores; just place the level on the camera before each shot to keep the lens on an even keel.

> **» TROUBLESHOOTER**
>
> If a subject is too tall to fit in a single frame without tilting the camera up or down, shoot the panorama in two rows. Raise the camera as needed to capture the top half of the scene and shoot one series of images at that camera height. Then lower the camera and shoot the bottom half of the scene. Be sure that the camera stays level for both series. To create the panorama, stitch each row and then join the two rows together. (Some stitching software can produce multiple-row panoramas, but if yours can't, you can combine the two rows using your photo editor's copy-and-paste functions.)

Overlap Each Shot

Each shot should overlap the previous one in the series, as illustrated by Figure 7.9, which shows you the raw images that I used to create the panorama in Figure 7.1. The overlap gives the stitching software the data it needs to glue the images together. You don't need to be precise or use the same amount of overlap for each picture. However, you should check your stitching software to find out the recommended amount of overlap. A 30 to 50 percent overlap is the norm.

If you're working with a panoramic tripod head, it likely offers a mechanism that helps ensure that each frame includes the right amount of overlap. You adjust a locking pin or other control to specify a percentage of overlap, and when you rotate the tripod head, it stops when it reaches the correct position.

> **PRO TIP**
>
> *Check your camera manual to find out whether the camera can display a grid to help you align shots. Some models also display a portion of the previous shot to help you see where the next one should begin.*

FIGURE 7.9　Each shot should overlap the previous one.

Maintain Constant Distance and Focal Length

Position the camera so that the lens-to-subject distance remains constant throughout the series of images. In an interior setting, for example, put the camera in the middle of the room.

For best results, don't use an extremely wide-angle lens or long telephoto lens. Both can produce heavy distortion in the stitched panorama. A medium focal length works best. If you're working with a zoom lens, try to hit the middle of the zoom range.

> ≫ TROUBLESHOOTER
>
> Don't change the focal length between shots. When you do, you move the lens nodal point, throwing the camera off the proper rotation axis.

Lock in Focus

Use consistent focusing throughout the series. For example, don't focus on an object 10 feet away in one shot and on something that's 30 feet away in the next. If your camera offers manual focusing, switch to that mode. If you must use autofocus, be sure to set the focus at the same distance for each shot.

>> TROUBLESHO⊕TER

Remember that aperture size affects the range of sharp focus (depth of field). The smaller the aperture, the greater the depth of field. On cameras that don't offer a way to control aperture, try switching to the landscape creative scene mode, which should reduce the aperture size.

Take Control of Exposure

Working in autoexposure mode can cause problems unless the lighting is even throughout the scene. As an example, see Figure 7.10, which shows two frames from a 360-degree VR panorama of a living room. Because of differences in ambient light between the two shots, the overlapping area is darker in one shot than the other. In the stitched panorama, this creates an abrupt change that makes the seam noticeable, as shown in Figure 7.11.

FIGURE 7.10 When light isn't consistent throughout a scene, shooting in autoexposure mode can result in significant shifts in brightness levels from frame to frame.

Shooting panoramas in automatic exposure mode may create shifts in focus between frames as well as lighting breaks. Again, when aperture size changes, depth of field changes as well. For more on this issue, see Chapter 2.

The best solution is to work in manual exposure mode, basing the exposure on the average lighting conditions throughout the panoramic view. If your camera doesn't offer manual exposure, see whether it provides autoexposure lock, which tells the camera to keep using the same exposure setting until you specify otherwise.

FIGURE 7.11 In the stitched panorama, the exposure difference makes the seam noticeable.

For cameras that don't offer either feature, aim the camera at an area of medium brightness as you set the autoexposure for each shot. After you press the shutter button halfway down to set the exposure, reframe the shot as necessary. Remember, however, that some cameras set focus as well as exposure when you depress the shutter button half way.

As with any photographic project that involves tricky exposure issues, always bracket your shots, taking each image at three different exposures. You can use the camera's EV (exposure value) control or autobracketing feature, if available, to adjust image brightness between shots.

PRO TIP

Shooting outdoor panoramas on overcast days helps solve the exposure variation problem because the clouds eliminate strong highlights and shadows. If you want a clear sky in your panorama, shoot at midday, when the sun is directly overhead and doesn't cast strong shadows on the landscape.

Keep an Eye on White Balance

When not all areas of the scene are lit by the same type of lighting, pay careful attention to how colors are rendered from one shot to the next. Automatic white balancing can result in color inconsistencies in this situation. If one frame includes an area that's lit by daylight coming through a window, for example, and the next frame is lit by both daylight and incandescent bulbs, colors in the overlapping area may be slightly mismatched.

You can take control of white balance by switching from the automatic to manual setting. Preview each shot to see what white balance option maintains the same color balance as the preceding frame.

SEE ALSO

Check out Chapter 8 for tips on using your camera's manual white balance options to manipulate colors.

Watch Out for Moving Objects

Scenes that contain moving objects pose difficulties for the panorama photographer. After the image is stitched, a moving object may show up as a ghostly apparition, as shown in Figure 7.12. This ghosting usually results when the movement occurs in the area of overlap and is captured in only one of the frames—for example, someone walks into the camera's view as you're taking your first shot but is out of the frame for the second.

FIGURE 7.12   People moving through a scene can show up as a ghostly blur in a stitched panorama.

On the other hand, if you catch a moving object in several nonoverlapping frames, it will appear multiple times throughout your stitched panorama. The moral of the story is to be patient and wait for bypassers to get out of the frame before you press the shutter button.

Stitching Your Panorama

As I alluded to earlier, the difficult part of creating a panorama is taking the pictures correctly. Compared with finding the lens nodal point, keeping the camera level, and all the other preparations you need to take, running the images through a panorama-software sewing machine is a breeze. The remainder of this chapter outlines the few important things that you need to know to get the job done.

Stitching Software

If you are creating a simple, two- or three-image flat panorama, you may wonder whether you need any special software at all. You could simply copy and paste the pictures together, just as if you were building any photo collage—right? In theory, the answer is yes. However, stitching software goes beyond simple image-stapling. It also warps the individual images as necessary to correct any slight distortions that may occur due to the slightly different lens perspective of each shot. You can do these corrections in your photo editor, too, but you'll get better, faster results using a stitching program.

Because panoramic imaging has become popular among digital photography enthusiasts, many photo editors now offer a basic panorama-building tool. Figure 7.13 shows the Photoshop Elements panorama utility, which goes by the name of Photomerge. This tool, like most stitching utilities, provides on-screen guidance to help you get the best results. (Choose File | Create Photomerge to try it out.)

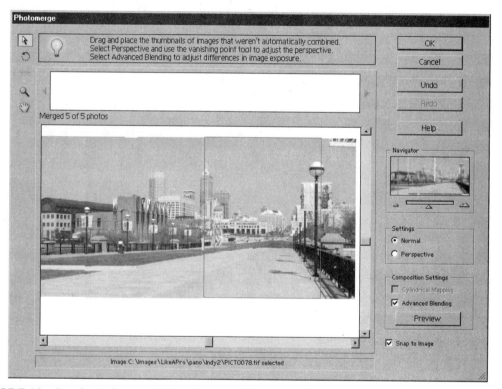

FIGURE 7.13   Simple stitching tools like this one in Photoshop Elements can produce flat panoramas only.

For flat panoramas, a simple stitching solution like Photomerge works just fine. But not all basic programs can create 360-degree VR panoramas; for that, you need more sophisticated software. Fortunately, sophisticated doesn't necessarily translate to expensive. Figure 7.14 shows a popular VR stitcher, The Panorama Factory, a shareware program that costs just $35; you can download a trial copy at *www.panoramafactory.com*. Also check out ISeeMedia's Photovista, which sells for $30 (*www.iseemedia.com*).

FIGURE 7.14 More advanced tools such as The Panorama Factory enable you to produce 360-degree VR images.

You will have to move up the software price ladder to produce immersive imaging that incorporates the kind of elements you find in video games and other high-end digital media—audio tracks, interactive elements, and the like. Many professional VR artists use Apple QuickTime VR Authoring Studio, which sells for about $400. This type of imaging is beyond the scope of this book, but if you're interested, visit the Apple web site (*www.apple.com*) for more information.

Preparing Your Images (and Computer)

Before you bring your images into the stitching program, make sure that they all have the same pixel dimensions (pixels wide by pixels tall). The images must also be in the correct orientation; if you shot the pictures with your camera oriented vertically, as recommended, that means that you have to rotate the pictures 90 degrees. (Some stitching programs offer a rotate command that you can use to take care of this step.)

You should also check your images for exposure consistency. Some stitching programs include exposure correction tools that automatically adjust brightness to a consistent level, but if your software doesn't include this feature, make the exposure adjustments in your photo editor before you begin the stitching process.

SEE ALSO

To avoid degrading your picture, save your edited photo in the TIFF format if your stitching software can work with files in that format. TIFF does not degrade image quality like the other popular image format, JPEG. See Chapter 10 for more information about JPEG and its effect on image quality. Chapter 6 explains how to correct exposure.

Before you launch your panorama software, shut down any other major programs that are running on your computer. Image-stitching places a big demand on your computer system, and closing other programs makes the maximum system resources available to the stitching software.

Stitching the Seams

After preparing your images and system, just follow your stitching software's instructions to open and stitch the images. I'm sorry to be vague here, but every program uses different commands to set panorama options (size, type, file format, and so on) and launch the stitching software. Fortunately, most programs offer a wizard that guides you through these steps; see the next section for more information about file formats.

When the program finishes stitching the panorama, you may need to give your input about how you want to crop the image to trim off any ragged edges that are created by the image-alignment process. You also may be given the option of manually fixing alignment problems, depending on the level of software you're using. The last step is to save the panorama; file format options are explained in the next section.

PRO TIP

Some stitching programs offer a blending control that allows you to specify how much image manipulation you want the software to perform when creating a seam. Adjusting this control can correct ghosting or obvious shifts in color or exposure.

Also, most stitching tools ask you to specify the type of camera and lens focal length you used to shoot your images. Fiddling with these options can also improve your panorama. You may in fact get better results by choosing a different focal length than you actually used.

Choosing a Panorama Format

When you create a flat panorama, most programs enable you to save the stitched image as either a JPEG or TIFF file. For web use, choose JPEG, following the file-saving tips outlined in Chapter 10. If you instead plan to print the panorama, TIFF is a better choice, for the image-quality reasons just mentioned. You may want to make a copy of the panorama in both formats just in case you want both a print and web version. (Save to TIFF first, and then make a JPEG copy.)

VR panoramas can be saved in a couple of formats, the two most common being the QuickTime VR format, better known as QTVR, and IVR, a format that was developed a few years ago by MGI Software (now a part of Roxio software). Some stitching programs also have their own proprietary format.

Among other things, the format you choose dictates how the program builds the image, which is why you usually have to choose the format *before* you stitch the panorama. QTVR maps the images around a cylindrical projection, for example, while IVR uses a spherical projection. Each format also supports a different list of VR features, such as the option of adding audio tracks and identifying "hot spots" that a viewer can click to jump to another part of the image. (As mentioned earlier, these advanced VR elements require professional-level software.)

Most important for panoramas that you want to share with others, the format dictates what software you need to use to view the image product. Thankfully, the viewers can be downloaded at no charge from the Internet; check your stitching software's help system for information on where to get the appropriate viewer.

8

Manipulating Color

In the film world, knowledgeable photographers manipulate colors to suit their artistic vision through their choice of film. Some types of film emphasize blues and greens, for example, while others subdue those same hues and enhance warmer tones. A huge array of color lens filters provide additional control over how a scene is rendered.

Digital photographers obviously can't swap out image sensors the way that film photographers change film. But filter manufacturers such as Tiffen and Kenko now offer a variety of traditional filters in sizes to fit digital camera lenses. In addition, you can use your camera's white-balance control to give pictures a warmer or cooler tone. Some cameras even provide controls for fine tuning color saturation.

This chapter explores just a few of the ways that you can manipulate color with traditional filters, digital features, or both. You'll also find some easy techniques for producing similar results in your photo editor.

Tweaking Colors with White Balance

Every light source emits a particular hue, influencing the colors of the objects it illuminates. Candlelight infuses a scene with warm, reddish tones, for example, while cloudy daylight adds a bluish tint.

The color of a light source, often referred to as its *color temperature*, is measured on the Kelvin scale. You can see an approximation of the colors of common light sources on Page 26 of the color insert. Read the sidebar "Measuring Degrees of Color" if you want to know more about the Kelvin scale.

Our human eyes are pretty good at compensating for the various colors of light. We perceive a white shirt as being white whether we're looking at it across a candlelit table or outdoors on an overcast day. But cameras need a little help in this area.

In the film world, specific films are produced for use with different light sources. On a digital camera, the light-compensating function is performed by the white-balance control. If you leave this control set to automatic, the camera adjusts to the color temperature of the light source for you.

As a rule, white-balance mechanisms do a pretty good job in automatic mode. But if you're working with multiple light sources that have different color temperatures—say, a flash plus window light—the camera can get confused. For this reason, most cameras offer a manual white-balance control that enables you to select from five or six specific light sources. Typically, you get a setting appropriate for cloudy/overcast skies, flash, bright sunshine, fluorescent lights, and incandescent light (household bulbs). Some advanced cameras also offer a setting for studio lights that use tungsten bulbs.

In addition, some cameras provide an auto white-balance compensation feature. This feature works similarly to exposure compensation, enabling you to make the exposure a little warmer or cooler than one of the standard settings provided. For example, if you're working on a partly cloudy day, you can choose "Cloudy +3" or "Cloudy –3" if you want the image to be slightly warmer or cooler than the Cloudy setting produces.

Although the main purpose of white balance is to enable you to record colors accurately in any lighting, you also can use the feature as a sort of virtual warming or cooling filter, as follows:

- For warmer colors, choose a white-balance setting appropriate for a light source that's higher on the Kelvin scale than your actual light source. In bright sunlight, for example, choose the setting for flash or clouds. (Fortunately, your LCD monitor will show you how your image colors shift as you cycle through the various white-balance settings, so you don't need to memorize the Kelvin chart.)

- For cooler colors, choose a white-balance setting appropriate for a light source that has a lower color temperature than your actual light source. Again, on a sunny day, the incandescent or fluorescent setting would produce cooler tones.

I used this approach to create the variations on my carousel image on Page 26 of the color insert. Note, however, that how much color shift you get varies from camera to camera.

Of course, if you're working on a cloudy day and you're already using your camera's cloudy setting, you can't get any warmer. Nor can you go cooler if you're shooting in incandescent light and using the incandescent setting. The next two sections discuss some other options for times when you're maxed out in the white-balance department.

PRO TIP

You can use a traditional warming or cooling filter in conjunction with manual white balance to produce a more pronounced color shift than either delivers alone.

Technical Aside
Measuring Degrees of Color

Named for a Victorian-era scientist (Baron Kelvin of Largs, born William Thomson), the Kelvin scale is a thermodynamic temperature scale. On the Kelvin scale, the zero point is what scientists refer to as *absolute zero,* which translates to −273.15 degrees on the Celsius temperature scale.

The importance of all this to photographers is that the colors emitted by various light sources have been plotted on the Kelvin scale, enabling us to describe light in specific terms. The science behind the concept is complex, but the gist involves a black object—called a *black body*—that radiates different colors as it is heated. When photographers speak about the color temperature of a light source, they're referring to the Kelvin temperature at which the black body emits the same color as that light.

Light sources that you encounter on a daily basis range from about 2000 to 8000 kelvin. (The scientific community decided in the late 1960s that we shouldn't use the word *degree* or the degree symbol when discussing this temperature scale—just *kelvin* or K.) Toward the low end of the color temperature range, light emits a reddish cast. As temperature increases, the light color changes, moving from yellow to white to blue.

Discussions of color temperature can be confusing because photographers use the terms *warm* and *cool* to describe actual photo colors. Warm indicates a reddish color,

Technical Aside
Measuring Degrees of Color (continued)

and cool refers to a bluish tone. It seems backwards that a light source with a high temperature adds a cool color cast to a scene, and vice versa, but that's what happens.

In practical terms, you don't need to worry about the Kelvin temperature of a light source—you just need to know what color cast to expect. Use the chart on Page 26 of the color insert as your guide.

Warming Image Colors

In photography lingo, the term *warm colors* refers to hues in the red-to-yellow range. *Cool tones* refers to hues in the blue-to-green range.

As discussed earlier in this chapter, you can add warmth to image colors by switching to a white-balance setting that's appropriate for a light source with a higher color temperature than the actual light source—for example, using the cloudy or overcast setting to capture a subject lit by household incandescent bulbs. (Your camera's LCD monitor will reflect the color changes as you shift the white-balance setting, so you don't need to be a student of light temperatures to use this trick.)

If fiddling with white balance doesn't produce the warming effect you're after, try these alternative techniques:

- Go the traditional route and place a warming filter over your camera lens. These filters cut down on the amount of blue in the light and give your image a rosy cast, as illustrated by the top right image on Page 27 of the color insert. Although warming filters are most often used to warm skin tones in portraits, as I did for the last image on Page 12 of the insert, I also sometimes use them in scenic shots to approximate the light that you get around sunrise and sunset—the so-called golden hours for photography. The top right image on Page 27 shows an example. Warming filters, like other color filters, are available in different strengths; for both example pictures, I used an 81B filter, which indicates a medium-impact filter.

➤➤ TROUBLESHO⬦TER

After you take a shot with a warming filter (or any filter, for that matter), review the image on your LCD monitor to double-check the exposure. If your camera uses through-the-lens (TTL) exposure metering and you're working in autoexposure mode, the camera should automatically adjust exposure to account for the filter. If not, you need to handle that task manually. The filter package should tell you how much exposure adjustment is needed. (Look for the filter factor number; see Chapter 1 for an explanation of what this number means to exposure.) Remember that in autoexposure mode, you can raise the EV value to produce a brighter exposure.

- If you're comfortable with computers, you can adjust image colors after the fact using your photo editor's color-balancing tools. The lower left example on Page 27 of the color insert offers an illustration. For this image, I used the Photoshop Elements Color Variations filter, shown in Figure 8.1. To produce a warming effect, decrease blue and cyan, and increase red and yellow. I added a bit more yellow than red in my example image to produce a more golden tone than created by the 81B warming filter.

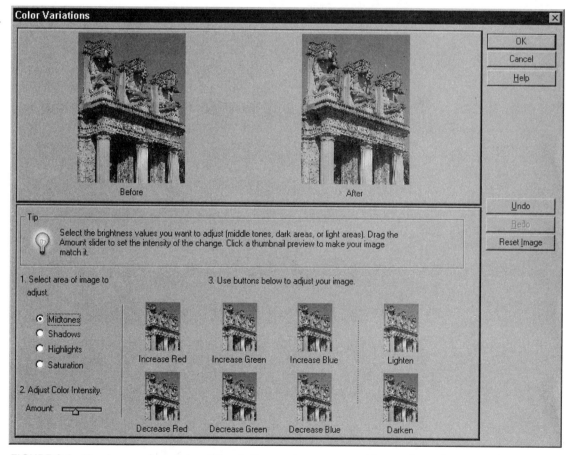

FIGURE 8.1 You can produce color shifts similar to what you get with a traditional warming filter by using your photo editor's Color Variations or Color Balance filter.

Some color-balancing tools, including the Photoshop Elements Variations filter, enable you to adjust shadows, midtones, and highlights independently. If you want to mimic the look of a real warming filter, keep all tones in the same ballpark.

Note also that the Photoshop Elements Variations filter, as well as similar filters in some other programs, appears at first glance to provide controls for adjusting the amount of red, green, and blue only. But when you decrease red, green, or blue, you simultaneously *add* the color that's in the opposite position on the color wheel. In case you're not familiar with the color wheel: Red is opposite cyan; green is opposite magenta; and blue is opposite yellow. So if you want to add yellow, for example, you decrease blue.

CooL TooLs

If you're really into digital color manipulation, check out color-effects packages such as those in the Color Efex Pro! line from nik multimedia. I used the Brilliance/Warmth filter, shown here, from the Complete Collection to produce the final image on Page 27 of the color insert, adding a golden glow to the ruins without also toning down the sky. Like most effects filters, the ones in the Color Efex Pro! family are Photoshop-compatible plug-ins; they work with any photo editor that accepts such plug-ins, not just Photoshop. Prices range from $70 to $300, depending on the version of the product you choose. For more information and free demos, visit *www.nikmultimedia.com.*

Making Gray Skies Blue: Using a Polarizing Filter

On days when skies are less than photogenic, you may be able to coax a little more blue out of the clouds by using a polarizing filter. In clear weather, the filter can make blue skies even more so.

SEE ALSO

Chapter 4 provides a detailed description of how polarizing filters work.

As an example, see Page 28 of the color insert. The top image shows the sky as it really was on the day I took this picture—mostly cloudy, with just the vaguest hint of blue. With the help of the polarizing filter, the lower left image shows a respectable amount of blue. It's not ideal, but it's certainly more pleasing than the first image, assuming that you're not going for that life-is-dismal, all-is-lost mood.

A polarizing filter is not always effective, however. If skies are completely overcast, don't bother—the filter will reduce the amount of light coming into your camera, but that's all. Even on a clear day, the impact of the filter will be negligible unless the sun, camera lens, and subject are in a particular alignment.

For best results, your lens must be at a 90-degree angle to the sun. Unless the sun is directly overhead, that means that it is at either your left or right shoulder. But that's not the only complication. Even when you're positioned properly, the polarizer has maximum impact on a narrow arc of sky at a 90-degree angle to the sun. At noon, for example, the sky at the horizon line receives the filter's full-strength color boost; the effect fades out above that line. Figure 8.2 may help you make sense of this whole issue if you're not a math major.

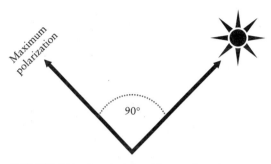

FIGURE 8.2 A polarizing filter makes the maximum impact on the arc of sky that's at a 90-degree angle to the sun.

PRO TIP

To determine what band of sky will be most affected by a polarizing filter, make an "L" with your thumb and forefinger, pointing your thumb at the sun. Now rotate your wrist in and out. The arc that your finger travels will receive the maximum polarizing impact.

Bear in mind that a polarizing filter not only affects sky color, but also may eliminate reflections in glass and other shiny surfaces. As discussed in Chapter 4, this glare-reducing function also depends on the angle of camera, sun, and shiny surface.

In my example image, shown in grayscale in Figure 8.3, notice the glass panes in the building (that's the Indiana State Museum, in downtown Indianapolis). When I first considered this view, the glass was reflecting surrounding buildings. I thought that would be a cool juxtaposition of structures, so I snapped the picture without the polarizer. Unfortunately, because of the camera angle, the reflections weren't quite strong enough to be clearly visible in the image. So I opted to use the polarizer for the next shot, which not only pulled more blue out of the sky but also eliminated most of the subtle reflections, giving the glass its more dramatic, almost black appearance. Notice, however, that reflections in the canal that runs in front of the building are only slightly diminished; the angles of the water, lens, and sun weren't right for the filter to make much impact there.

Without polarizer   With polarizer

FIGURE 8.3 When deciding whether to use a polarizing filter to intensify sky colors, remember that the filter may also eliminate reflections in glass and other shiny surfaces.

One final tip related to using polarizing filters: If you're trying to capture sunlight sparkling on water, leave the filter off; it will reduce those sparkles. On the other hand, if you're trying to photograph something that's *in* the water—a koi swimming in a water garden, for example—the filter can help you get a clearer image. Also keep in mind that while eliminating reflections in a photo editor is tricky, shifting the sky color is usually fairly easy. See the How-To sidebar "Paint the Sky" for some easy techniques you can use.

?How To   **PAINT THE SKY**

Adjusting the color of a sky in a photo editor isn't terribly difficult—some programs even have special-effects filters that automatically create a mix of sky and clouds. (Look for a Clouds filter.) The biggest challenge is to select just the sky pixels so that only they receive the color change. In most cases, the best selection tool for this task is the Magic Wand, which selects pixels based on color. Depending on your software, the tool may go by the name Color Wand, Color Selector, or something similar.

The following steps show you how to select the sky and then add a natural blue tint in Photoshop Elements:

1. With your image open, click the Magic Wand in the toolbox (see Figure 8.4).

How To

PAINT THE SKY *(continued)*

Magic Wand

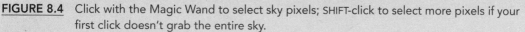

FIGURE 8.4 Click with the Magic Wand to select sky pixels; SHIFT-click to select more pixels if your first click doesn't grab the entire sky.

2. On the Options bar, select the Contiguous check box and set the Tolerance value to 20, as shown in the figure.

3. Click on a sky pixel. The program automatically selects any pixels that are similar in color to the one you clicked *and* contiguous to that pixel—that is, no pixel of another color comes between them and the clicked pixel. A dotted outline appears to show you what areas you selected.

4. If the tool didn't select all the sky areas you want to adjust, press SHIFT as you click on those unselected regions. The program adds the clicked pixel and any contiguous, similarly colored pixels to the selection. Keep SHIFT-clicking until you grab all the sky pixels.

?How To

PAINT THE SKY *(continued)*

5. If necessary, adjust the Tolerance value between clicks. At a lower value, the tool selects only pixels that are very close in color to the clicked pixel; at a higher value, the tool is less discriminating.

6. Open the Layers palette, shown in Figure 8.5, and click the New Layer icon. This new layer will hold your sky color. Set the layer blending mode to Color, as shown in the figure, using the menu at the top of the palette.

Eraser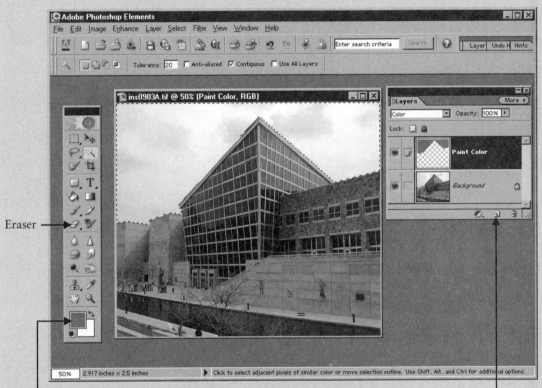

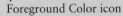
Foreground Color icon

New Layer icon

FIGURE 8.5 Put your new sky color on a separate layer, setting the layer blend mode to Color.

7. Click the Foreground Color icon in the toolbox, labeled in Figure 8.5, to open the Color Picker, and choose your desired sky color.

8. Press ALT-BACKSPACE (Windows) or OPTION-DELETE (Mac) to fill the selected area with the foreground color. (You also can choose Edit | Fill and select the Foreground Color option from the Use drop-down list in the resulting dialog

? How To **PAINT THE SKY** *(continued)*

box.) Because you set the layer mode of your new sky layer to Color, the program retains the highlights and shadows of the original sky, producing a natural-looking effect.

9. To tweak the sky color further, you can repeat the process and choose a different color in the Color Picker. Or choose Enhance | Adjust Color | Hue/Saturation and drag the Hue slider to shift the basic sky tint; drag the Saturation control to adjust color intensity.

10. If those techniques don't deliver the effect you want, change the layer blending mode to Normal and reduce the layer opacity by using the Opacity control in the Layers palette.

11. If you accidentally colored nonsky pixels, use the Eraser tool (labeled in Figure 8.5) to dab away the blue on the new layer.

12. When you're happy with your paint job, choose Layer | Flatten Image to fuse the new sky layer with the original.

Strengthening Saturation

Your digital camera may offer a control that enables you to adjust color intensity, or *saturation*. I recommend that you capture the image at the normal saturation setting and do any adjustments on a copy of the image in your photo editor, however.

Why wait? Because your photo editor gives you more control. On most cameras, you can increase or decrease overall color saturation by a few degrees, or you can completely desaturate the image, which produces a grayscale picture (black-and-white, in everyday lingo). Page 29 of the insert offers an example. I used the camera's normal setting for the first image, maximum saturation for the second image, and minimum saturation for the third image.

Your photo editor's Hue/Saturation filter, on the other hand, enables you to ramp saturation up or down as much as you see fit, putting no arbitrary limits on your artistic options. In addition, many programs enable you to adjust saturation of one range of colors—blues or magentas, for example—but leave other colors untouched.

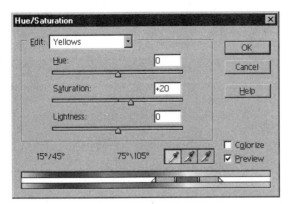

FIGURE 8.6 The Photoshop Elements Hue/ Saturation filter enables you to tweak saturation of one range of colors while leaving others untouched.

In the fourth image on Page 29, I used the Photoshop Elements Hue/Saturation filter, shown in Figure 8.6, to adjust the image. I boosted the intensity of yellows, which affected the lemon and the onions the most. Then I lowered the saturation for blues and cyans to make the plate a little less vivid. This fine-tuning of saturation isn't possible with in-camera adjustments.

PRO TIP

If your photo editor offers layering, give yourself even more flexibility by duplicating the background layer and applying the Hue/Saturation filter to the duplicate. You can then adjust the opacity of the filtered layer or change the layer blend mode to produce different effects. In Photoshop Elements, you also can apply the filter as an adjustment layer, which enables you to keep your original pixel colors intact and to copy the adjustment to other images.

Technical Aside
Exploring RGB Color

Digital cameras, scanners, computer monitors, and digital projectors create images by combining red, green, and blue light, which is why digital photos are said to be *RGB* images. In this light-based color factory, full intensity red, green, and blue create white; zero red, green, and blue makes black. Equal amounts of each color in any other intensity produces a shade of gray.

When you take a digital photo, your camera reads the amount of red, green, and blue light in the scene. The light values are stored in separate *channels* in the image file—one channel each for the red, green, and blue data. If you view each channel by itself, as you can in high-end photo editors such as Adobe Photoshop, you see a simple grayscale image, as illustrated on Page 30 of the color insert.

Bright areas in a channel image indicate a heavy concentration of that color of light. For example, the lemon rind in the example image contains lots of red and green, but very little blue. So it appears bright in the red and green channel images but dark in the blue channel image.

Converting from Color to Black-and-White

If you dig through your camera's color options, you should find a control that tells the camera to create a black-and-white image instead of a full-color photo. As with saturation adjustments, I'm not a fan of this option except in situations when you need to ship someone a black-and-white image immediately and don't have access to your photo editor.

Perhaps the biggest reason to capture your pictures in color instead of black-and-white is flexibility. You can always make a black-and-white copy of your color original, but you can't create a convincing color photo from a grayscale original. Sure, you could use your photo editor's painting tools to infuse your grayscale pictures with color, but creating a true, photo-realistic image requires a huge amount of time and skill. Converting a color image to a grayscale image, on the other hand, is painless.

But let's assume for the sake of argument that you know you'll never need a particular shot in full color. If you want the best possible black-and-white photo, you still should capture it in color and then do the conversion in your photo editor.

As detailed in the sidebar "Exploring RGB Color," a digital camera produces an image that contains three color channels—red, green, and blue (hence the RGB moniker). When the camera creates a grayscale photo, it combines the color values from the original red, green, and blue color channels into one channel, using a standard formula that gives the brightness values from each channel a particular weight. This one-size-fits-all conversion approach doesn't take into consideration that the most important details in a picture

Technical Aside

Grayscale versus Black-and-White

What most people refer to as a *black-and-white* photo is called a *grayscale* image by people with a digital graphics background. In the computer graphics world, a black-and-white image can contain only black and white, while a grayscale image contains black, white, and shades of gray. I use the terms interchangeably in this book but thought I'd give you a heads-up so that you'll know what's what if you get in a discussion with someone who's from the graphics side of the tracks.

Also note that your photo editor may offer a command that converts your image to the Grayscale color model, which produces an image with 256 colors—again, black, white, and shades of gray. When I speak of the Grayscale color model, with a capital G, I'm referring to this particular type of file.

aren't always found in the same channel. It also has an averaging effect that tends to reduce the tonal range of the image.

As an example, study just the garlic clove in the images in Figure 8.7. The top left image shows the result of the standard grayscale conversion; the other three images show the original contents of the red, green, and blue channels. Some of the best shadow detail from the blue channel didn't survive the journey to the composite.

Composite gray

Red channel

Green channel

Blue channel

FIGURE 8.7   You can split a digital camera image into its individual color channels, which reflect the amount of red, green, and blue light in the picture.

By making the grayscale conversion yourself, *you* control how much brightness data comes from each channel. This enables you to pull out particular details that you want to emphasize—to custom blend your own grayscale recipe.

To do a custom blend, you have to look beyond the standard color-to-grayscale conversion found in every photo editor. (In Photoshop Elements, this command is Image | Mode | Grayscale and it converts the picture to the 256-color Grayscale mode discussed in the earlier sidebar "Grayscale versus Black-and-White.")

The following list offers just a few of the other, better ways of going gray. You can compare the results on Page 31 of the color insert. Note that which techniques you can use depends on your photo software. For all but the first one, you need a program that gives you access to individual color channels. (Photoshop Elements and most comparably priced programs don't provide this feature.) Also, I didn't attempt to give each of the conversions the same tonal qualities because I wanted you to see just how much variation you can achieve.

- In Photoshop Elements, use the Gradient Map command in combination with the Hue/Saturation filter, as explained in the How-To sidebar "Create Custom Grayscale Conversions in Photoshop Elements."

- Convert the image to the Lab color mode. This color mode, used primarily by imaging professionals, also comprises three color channels: a Lightness channel that stores just the pixel brightness data, plus two other channels for storing color information. The Lightness channel by itself often produces an excellent grayscale image. However, because photo printers are geared to outputting RGB images, you should copy the contents of the Lightness channel to a new RGB image instead of saving the file in the Lab mode. The red, green, and blue channels in your new image will all contain the same brightness values. (Again, see the sidebar "Exploring RBG Color" if all this channel stuff is foreign to you.)

- You also may find that the original red, green, or blue channel contains just the grayscale tones that you're after. If so, just copy that channel to a new RGB image.

- In Adobe Photoshop, the Channel Mixer command enables you to specify exactly what percentage of each RGB channel you want your grayscale image to contain. Other advanced imaging programs also offer this feature, although it may go by a different name.

? How To

CREATE CUSTOM GRAYSCALE CONVERSIONS IN PHOTOSHOP ELEMENTS

To control your color-to-black-and-white conversions in Photoshop Elements, follow these steps. Work on a copy of your original image file, as always.

1. Set the foreground and background colors to black and white, respectively. You can do this quickly by just pressing the D key (*D* for default colors).

2. Open the Layers palette and click the Layer Adjustment icon, labeled in Figure 8.8. Choose Gradient Map from the menu that appears.

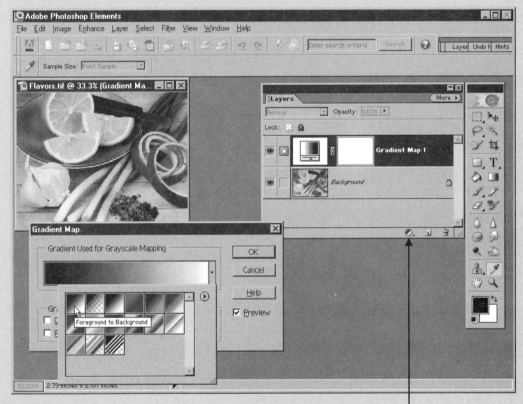

Layer Adjustment icon

FIGURE 8.8   The first step in the custom conversion process is to apply a black-to-white gradient map.

3. When the Gradient Map dialog box appears, choose the Foreground to Background gradient icon in the top drop-down list, as shown in Figure 8.8, and click OK. The program then *maps* your original image colors to a black-to-white spectrum. In other words, the darkest pixels become black,

CREATE CUSTOM GRAYSCALE CONVERSIONS IN PHOTOSHOP ELEMENTS (*continued*)

the lightest pixels become white, and the other pixels are spread across the range in between.

4. If you don't want your final grayscale image to have that complete contrast range, choose Edit | Undo to get rid of the gradient map and set the foreground and background colors to match the darkest and lightest shades you want the image to have. Then repeat Steps 2 and 3.

5. The next step is to add a Hue/Saturation adjustment layer *underneath* your new Gradient Map adjustment layer. To do so, click the Background layer in the Layers palette and then click the Layer Adjustment icon. Choose Hue/Saturation from the menu to create the adjustment layer and display the Hue/Saturation dialog box, as shown in Figure 8.9.

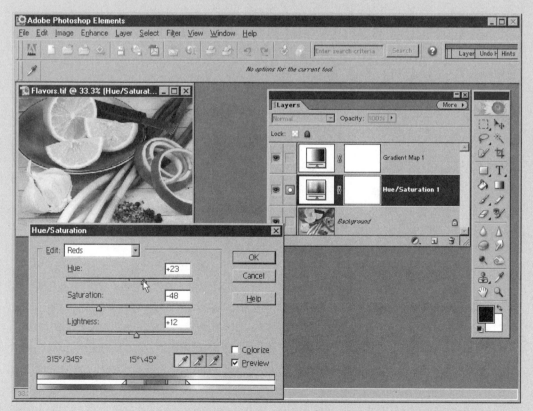

FIGURE 8.9   After adding a Hue/Saturation adjustment layer between the Gradient Map layer and the Background layer, use the Saturation, Lightness, and Hue controls to adjust image tones.

?How To CREATE CUSTOM GRAYSCALE CONVERSIONS IN PHOTOSHOP ELEMENTS *(continued)*

6. In the Hue/Saturation dialog box, choose Red from the Edit drop-down box, and select the Preview check box, as shown in the figure. Now watch the image window as you drag the Saturation, Lightness, or Hue slider. You should see a tonal shift in any areas of the photo that were originally red.

7. One by one, make your way through the other color ranges available via the Edit drop-down list to shift the tones of those pixels as well. You also can click in the image to select that color for editing.

   Be careful not to ramp up Saturation too much, or you may wipe out subtle details. Let your eyes be your guide.

8. When you finish adjusting your picture, flatten the image by choosing Layer | Flatten Image. If you think you may want to do more work on the tones in the grayscale image later, however, first save a copy of the image in the Photoshop Elements native format (PSD) to retain the two adjustment layers separate from the original, full-color background layer.

As noted earlier, you should leave your newly gray photo in the RGB color mode if you will be printing it on an RGB printer. Keeping the image in RGB also enables you to add a color tint to the picture—for example, to add a sepia tone or create a hand-painted effect.

Creating Color Effects

Your photo editor likely offers a collection of special effects that play with the colors in an image. You can buy additional, third-party collections from companies such as the previously mentioned nik multimedia.

As a rule, I'm not fond of special effects, because they detract too much from the subject of the picture. But effects can be helpful for rescuing a problem image. If you have a slightly blurry or noisy photo, for example, applying a filter that produces the look of a watercolor painting or pencil sketch can hide the defect.

Because the focus of this book is photography, not photo manipulation, I don't want to spend much space discussing software effects. The filters typically are easy to use, anyway—you just choose a filter from an effects menu or palette and then let the program do its thing. In some cases, you may be offered a few controls for adjusting the effect.

I want to share with you a few color-effect tricks that may not be immediately obvious, however:

- To add a sepia tint to your photo, create a new image layer and set the layer blending mode to Color. Fill the new layer with the sepia color you want to apply. In Photoshop Elements, you can also simply select the Colorize check box in the Hue/Saturation dialog box (featured in Figure 8.6, earlier in this chapter) and drag the Hue slider to adjust the tint color.

- Another fun color play is to use the Gradient Map command, discussed in the How-To section "Create Custom Grayscale Conversions in Photoshop Elements," but set the foreground and background colors to something other than black and white. In Photoshop Elements, if you apply the change as an adjustment layer, you can play with different layer blending modes to alter the effect.

- To give your picture a hand-tinted look, first do your color-to-gray conversion as explained earlier, leaving the gray image in the RGB color mode. Create a new, empty image layer, again setting the blend mode to Color, and use a paint tool to dab color on the scene. Adjust the layer or paint opacity to control color intensity.

- If your photo editor's Saturation filter allows you to adjust individual color ranges, experiment with desaturating all color ranges except one or two. For example, keep the blues and cyans but turn everything else to gray.

- Finally, here's a color effect that involves no computer at all: Just use a slow shutter speed and move your camera slightly during the exposure. The result is a Monet-like image like the one that decorates the cover page of the color insert. To create this image, which features the flowers shown on Page 13 of the insert, I positioned the camera lens a few inches above the flowers and set the shutter speed to 2 seconds.

PART III

Printing and Sharing
Your Photos

9

Becoming a Master Printer

Now that digital cameras are commonplace, nearly every retail outfit that offers film processing can make prints from your camera's memory card. Online services such as Ofoto and Shutterfly provide another convenient way to turn a batch of image files into frame-ready photos.

Although I often turn to these commercial printing services for everyday pictures, I take the printing reins myself for special images. It's not that the quality offered by commercial services isn't good; it's just that asking someone else to translate my raw image file to paper is a little like mixing up the ingredients for a soufflé and then trusting the baking to a stranger. Just as a stand-in chef may not share my philosophy about the perfect time to remove that soufflé from the oven, a lab technician may have a different idea than I do about what constitutes the best print of a particular scene.

For times when you want start-to-finish control over your pictures, this chapter shows you how to master the art of digital photo printing, from choosing a printer to matching colors between screen and printer. I'll also share some advice for getting better results when you do hand over printing responsibilities to a lab.

Buying Your Next Photo Printer

As someone who's tested photo printers since the first models were presented for public consumption, I've seen my share of clunkers. Among the first and second generations of machines, even the cream of the crop didn't live up to their claims of "photo-quality" printing. In the past couple of years, however, manufacturers have refined their products to the point that I rarely see a photo printer that *doesn't* impress.

The point is, if you've been waiting for do-it-yourself printing technology to mature before you invested in a new printer, you can now buy with confidence. However, you do need to shop carefully, because photo printers come in different flavors, and not all of them may suit your needs.

Although I don't have room in this book for a full-fledged buying guide, I want to provide some basic information to get you started on your printer search. Appendix B points you toward some web and print resources that offer additional shopping advice, including detailed printer reviews.

Picking a Printer Type: Inkjet, Dye-Sub, or Laser?

Color printers for the home and office fall into three main categories: inkjet, dye-sub, and laser. Your first step in finding the right printer is to decide which of these technologies fits the kind of printing you want to do. The next three sections give you my take on each type of printer, but here's the short story:

- Inkjet printers offer the best solution for most home and small-business users who need a machine that can handle light-to-moderate document printing as well as photos.

- Dye-sub printers produce excellent photo quality but can't be used for document printing.

- Laser printers provide acceptable photo quality and are better than inkjets for heavy-duty document printing.

Inkjet Printers: All-Around Champs

Inkjet printers spray tiny droplets of ink onto the paper to produce a print. They can print on plain paper, on glossy photo stock, and on specialty media such as watercolor paper, silkscreen-type fabric, and the like. On high-quality paper, inkjets deliver output that equals that from a professional lab. In fact, many professional photographers now use inkjets to print photos that they sell in galleries.

Good photo inkjets range in price from about $150 to $700, with choices ranging from tiny, snapshot printers to wide-format models that can output supersized prints. For a look at just two options, see Figure 9.1, which shows a Hewlett-Packard PhotoSmart 230 snapshot printer and the larger Canon i950. The first sells for about $200; the second, $240.

FIGURE 9.1   Inkjet printers come in all shapes and sizes; shown here are the Hewlett-Packard PhotoSmart 230 snapshot printer and the Canon i950.

✂ COST CUTTER

Higher priced inkjets offer added features such as networking capabilities, memory card slots (for printing directly from a memory card), and even small monitors on which you can preview the images on a memory card. But spending more doesn't necessarily buy better print quality because manufacturers often use the same print mechanisms in entry-level models as they put in their priciest offerings.

In a small office, an inkjet printer can do dual-duty as a document printer. Some manufacturers even offer all-in-one printer/scanner/copier/fax machines, which can be a great solution in a cramped office. For heavy document production, though, a laser printer is a better choice. Inkjets are slower than lasers, and inkjet text doesn't appear as crisp laser-printed text. Also note that not every all-in-one machine offers good photo quality, so read reviews and ask to see a sample print before you buy.

CooL TooLs

Because inkjet printers are far and away the best selling machines for photo printing, a wide variety of specialty art papers are available for them. In addition to those offered by the major printer manufacturers, several fine-art paper companies also offer some terrific papers. Shown here is an array of papers from Pictorico (*www.pictorico.com*). Others to try come from Ilford (*www.ilford.com*), Lumijet (*www.lumijet.com*), and Legion Paper (*www.legionpaper.com*). Check camera and art stores for these products, as most aren't sold in electronics or office-supply stores.

Dye-Sub Printers: Glossy Photos Only

Dye-sub printers use a heat-based process to transfer solid dye from ribbons or a sheet of plastic film onto specially coated paper. Before inkjet printing technology was refined, dye-sub was *the* technology to use for the best possible photo quality. Some experts think dye-sub prints still outclass inkjet prints, while other people lean the opposite direction.

For the record, I don't lean either way—both dye-sub and inkjet look darned good to me. However, if you're considering buying a dye-sub printer, be aware that you can't use these machines to print text documents, nor can you print on plain paper or specialty art media. Only the specially coated dye-sub media works.

Dye-sub printers tend to be slow beasts, too. The paper has to pass through the printer multiple times because each dye color—usually, cyan, magenta, yellow, and black—is applied separately. Some printers send the paper through the works an additional time to apply a clear, protective overcoat.

Most dye-sub models offered to consumers are snapshot-size printers and cost in the neighborhood of $200. You can find a handful of larger-format dye-subs, such as the $500 Olympus P-400, which can output prints at sizes of approximately 7½×10 inches.

Laser Printers: Office Players

Laser printers turn data into print via a technology that involves a laser beam—hence, the name. Instead of ink or dye, laser printers affix toner to the paper. You can print on plain paper as well as on glossy photo stock. Figure 9.2 gives you a look at one offering from the latest crop of lasers, the Minolta-QMS magicolor 2300W, which retails for $700.

Engineered primarily as heavy-duty document machines, laser models have long been the leading technology for office printing, but in the past they have not rivaled inkjet or dye-sub machines for photo quality. Because imaging is becoming increasingly important in office settings, laser manufacturers are now paying more attention to photo-printing capabilities.

Although photo quality still lags slightly behind inkjet and dye-sub output, it's getting closer to the mark every year. In fact, I daresay that if you weren't comparing prints from the various technologies side by side, you'd probably be pretty satisfied with your laser photos.

Color lasers don't come cheap, however; $700 is about the minimum you can expect to pay. Remember that you're buying a highly capable document machine for that price, not just a photo printer. In addition, most laser printers offer document collating, two-sided printing, networking capabilities, and other features that are important in an office environment.

(Photo courtesy Minolta-QMS, Inc.)

FIGURE 9.2 New laser printers such as this model from Minolta-QMS offer greatly improved photo-printing capabilities than earlier generations of lasers.

Sorting Through Printer Specs

Choosing a printer technology is the easy part of printer shopping. Finding the right printer in a particular category is a little more difficult. To help you narrow the field, the following list offers advice about the various specifications and features that you'll encounter when you browse the printer aisles.

Inkjet Ink Configuration

For inkjet printers, don't accept anything less than four ink colors: cyan, magenta, yellow, and black. Printers that skip the black do a poor job reproducing shadows. Six- and seven-color inkjets deliver even better photos than four-color printers.

>✂— **COST CUTTER**
>
> Ink costs are usually lower with a printer that uses separate ink cartridges for each color. With multi-color cartridges, you often run out of one color before the others are gone, leading to ink waste.

Print Speed

Check the printer specs to find out how long you'll have to wait for your pictures to appear each time you click the Print button. Understand, though, that manufacturer data gives you a best-case scenario, and printing at the highest quality setting may be significantly slower.

Borderless Printing

Some printers can produce borderless prints, while others insist on adding a small margin of paper around the image. With some models, you must use special paper that has perforated tabs around the edges to get a borderless print. The tabs provide the printer with something to grab onto as the paper passes along the print path. After printing, you tear away the tabs.

Card Input

Many photo printers offer slots that enable you to print directly from your memory card. Most printers offer slots for CompactFlash and SmartMedia cards only, so if you use some other type of card, double-check to be sure that the printer offers a matching slot.

✂ COST CUTTER

Printers that have memory-card slots can serve as a card reader. When computer and printer are connected, you can copy files from the card to your computer's hard drive as you would from a floppy disk or CD-ROM.

Technical Aside
Direct Printing with DPOF

Most new photo printers and digital cameras offer a feature known as Digital Print Order Format, or DPOF (*dee-poff*) for short. DPOF enables you to include printer instructions in an image file. When you print directly from a memory card, the printer reads the DPOF data and automatically prints the images according to your specifications.

Preview Monitor

Printers that have memory card slots sometimes also offer a tiny monitor that you can use to review your images and select photos for printing. If you plan on printing directly from your memory card on a regular basis, the monitor is a great feature. In some cases, you can even do basic editing, such as cropping the picture, using the monitor as a guide.

Printer Resolution

Printer *resolution* refers to how many dots of ink, dye, or toner the printer can squeeze into a linear inch of paper. Printer resolution is measured in dots per inch, or *dpi*.

Printer manufacturers make a big deal about resolution, but that doesn't mean that you should pay much attention to this number. First off, resolution requirements vary depending on the printer technology. Prints from a 300-dpi dye-sub printer look just as good as prints from an inkjet offering 1440 dpi resolution, for example. And while it's true that with inkjet and laser printers, a higher printer resolution theoretically means sharper prints, many other factors affect print quality. So simply choosing a printer based on dpi is not a smart move.

Cost Per Print

One reason why printers are relatively inexpensive is because manufacturers profit each time you buy ink and paper—*consumables,* in industry lingo. Over the life of your printer, you'll likely spend far more on consumables than you did on the printer itself.

Unfortunately, calculating an exact cost-per-print is simply impossible because the amount of ink, dye, or toner used depends on the image and the print settings you use. You can get a general idea about cost-per-print from printer brochures, but these figures are loose estimates, and no standard industry formula exists to calculate costs.

> ≫ TROUBLESHOOTER
>
> Before you buy a printer—or any digital photography equipment, for that matter—ask whether you can return the product without paying a restocking fee. Many merchants, especially online stores and computer superstores, charge as much as 15 percent of the product price if you want to return the equipment. Defective goods can be exchanged without a restocking fee, but if you decide that the product just doesn't meet your expectations, you'll have to pay. Most camera stores do not charge restocking fees, but double-check to be sure.

Inkjet Printing for the Long Haul: Archival Solutions

When the first high-quality photo inkjet printers became available, digital imaging artists were overjoyed. Finally, we had a way to produce sale-quality prints in the studio, enabling us to exert total control over our images, not to mention save money and drive time to and from the lab.

The rejoicing, though, was short lived. Although prints looked terrific when fresh out of the printer, they quickly began to fade or shift colors. Mind you, traditional film prints degrade over time, too, but they last between 10 to 60 years, depending on the paper and printing process and the environment in which they're stored. Our inkjet prints started to look sad in a matter of weeks, sometimes days.

Fortunately, the printer industry responded to the loud wails from the photographic community and worked to develop more stable inks and papers. Thanks to their efforts, you now can produce inkjet prints that should last as least as long as traditional photographs, if not longer.

However, to give your photos a long life span, you have to select both inks and paper carefully. The two work together to determine print stability. Newer photo papers often state print-life estimates on the package; read the fine print to discover what printers and inks you need to use to achieve that durability.

(Photo courtesy Epson America, Inc.)

FIGURE 9.3 A favorite with fine-art photographers, the Epson Stylus Photo 2200 uses special archival inks for long-lasting prints.

For maximum print life, you may want to invest in a printer that uses pigment-based inks, which offer more stability than the dye-based inks used by most inkjets. Note, though, that pigment-based inks have a down side: They can't reproduce as broad a color range, or *gamut*, as dye-based inks. Always a catch, eh? It may help to know that traditional film prints can't match the color gamut offered by dye-based inks, either.

One popular printer in the pigment-ink category is the Epson Stylus Photo 2200P, shown in Figure 9.3. Priced at about $700, the 2200P can make prints up to 13×44 inches and even has an attachment that allows you to print on uncut rolls of photo paper. This printer is the younger sibling of the Stylus Photo 2000P, which offered an amazing 100-year print life. Some photographers thought the color gamut just wasn't acceptable with the 2000P, so Epson reconfigured the ink set for the 2200P, sacrificing some life expectancy for better color reproduction. Print life on the 2200P is estimated at 44 years on Epson's glossy media.

Let me offer a few additional points that may help you sort out the archival issue:

- If you're not sure what to expect from your printer or paper, point your web browser to the site of the leading authority on print life, Wilhelm Research (*www.wilhelm-research.com*). Test results for popular printers, papers, and inks are posted on the site.

- Most people think that light exposure is the main cause of print degradation, but pollution, heat, and humidity are equally destructive, if not more so. You can extend print life by framing your pictures under glass and not displaying them for long periods of time in direct sunlight. Or store them in archival albums, in a dry, clean, cool environment. (These precautions apply to your traditional film photos as well.)

- Although plenty of testing is being done by Wilhelm Research and others, no one can really say for sure how long any digital print will last. We just haven't been printing digital images long enough to know whether the aging factors introduced in laboratory tests will hold true in real life. The rapid pace at which manufacturers develop new technologies makes testing even more difficult—by the time researchers devise a set of testing protocols for a particular printing technology, that technology has been replaced by something newer and better.

- Finally, remember that as long as you retain your digital original, you can always make a new print if the old one starts to look worse for wear. This safety net doesn't help for prints you plan to sell, but for cherished family memories, you can rest easy as long as you take care of your image files.

SEE ALSO
Chapter 1 offers tips for archiving your original image files.

Preparing Your Picture for Printing

When you print a document from a word processor, you don't need to do any preparatory work—you just click the Print button and wait for the printer to do its thing. Printing a digital photo, however, requires a bit more input on your part.

Before printing your picture, you need to use your photo software to specify two key values:

- The print size.

- How many pixels you want to pack into each linear inch of that print. This value is the *output resolution* and is measured in *pixels per inch* (ppi).

In the upcoming How-To box, you can find instructions for setting print size and output resolution. Although the steps are specific to Photoshop Elements, the basics apply no matter what software you use.

Don't jump to the How-To information, however, until you digest the next two sections. They explain some background concepts that are critical to getting the best prints from your image file.

Balancing Output Resolution, Print Size, and Photo Quality

As explored back in Chapter 2, output resolution plays a large role in print quality. How many pixels you need for good prints varies from printer to printer; most personal photo printers do their best work with 300 ppi files, but commercial printing labs often ask for 200 ppi files.

Assuming that you keep the number of image pixels constant, output resolution is inseparably linked with print size as well as print quality. As output resolution goes up, print size goes down, and vice versa.

Figure 9.4 illustrates this concept. I produced both photos from the same 800×600-pixel image file, simply changing the output resolution between prints. For the large image, I set output resolution to 200 ppi. For the small image, I increased the resolution to 300 ppi, which in turn reduced print size.

Again, the codependent relationship between output resolution and print size assumes that the number of original image pixels remains constant. Most photo editors also enable you to add or delete pixels to achieve a particular output resolution at a given print size. Changing the pixel count—or *resampling* the image—is not always a wise move, for reasons explained in the next section.

800×600 pixels, output at 300 ppi

800×600 pixels, output at 200 ppi

FIGURE 9.4   When print size goes up, output resolution (ppi) goes down.

Adjusting Output Resolution by Resampling

Suppose that your image is 1280 pixels wide by 960 pixels tall. You like the image so much that you decide you want to make a large print—for the sake of easy math, let's say 10×7½ inches. At that print size, the output resolution is just 128 ppi. (1280 divided by 10 is 128; 960 divided by 7.5 is 128.) Your printer, however, needs 300 ppi to produce good print quality.

You have two options: You can live with the print quality that you get at the low output resolution, or you can tell your photo editor to resample the image, adding enough new pixels to get you to 300 ppi.

Adding pixels sounds like a good solution, but in practice it's not likely to improve print quality. Image sharpness and detail typically get lost as the photo software goes through the process of rebuilding the image at the new resolution. In fact, you may find that your low-resolution original looks better than the resampled, higher resolution image. Compare the images in Figure 9.5, for example. The first picture has an output resolution of 128 ppi; for the second picture, I resampled the image to 300 ppi. The lower-resolution print appears slightly sharper than its resampled cousin.

128 ppi   Resampled to 300 ppi

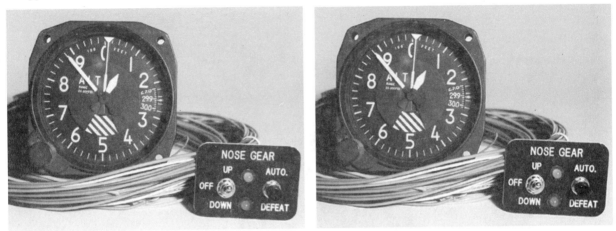

FIGURE 9.5 Resampling an image to achieve a higher output resolution usually doesn't improve print quality, and may even degrade quality.

That said, I do sometimes *slightly* upsample a picture if I'm sending the file to a client or lab that requires a specific output resolution. But I'm talking about adding just a handful of pixels—going from 275 ppi to 300 ppi, for example.

Having more pixels than you need is less problematic. You can safely eliminate pixels without worrying about doing noticeable damage to image quality. If the output resolution isn't too excessive, though, you can just print the image file as is, assuming that you're not sending the file to a lab that has specific resolution requirements. However, the larger the image file, the more muscle your computer and printer need to process the data, so ideally, you don't want a massive oversupply of pixels. Be sure to make a copy of your image file *before* you dump pixels in case you ever want to print the image at a larger size in the future.

SEE ALSO

Because resampling is a standard part of preparing an image for screen display, instructions for this process appear in Chapter 10.

How To SET OUTPUT RESOLUTION AND PRINT SIZE

These steps show you how to set output resolution and print size in Photoshop Elements. The basic approach is the same for other programs, although the specific command used to access the controls may be different.

?How To **SET OUTPUT RESOLUTION AND PRINT SIZE** *(continued)*

Note that these steps assume that you do not want to resample the image (add or delete pixels). If you do want to adjust the pixel count, Chapter 10 provides instructions.

1. Choose Image | Resize | Image Size to open the dialog box shown in Figure 9.6.

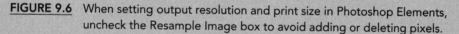

Image Size

Pixel Dimensions: 3.09M
Width: 900 pixels
Height: 1200 pixels

OK
Cancel
Help

Document Size:
Width: 3 inches
Height: 4 inches
Resolution: 300 pixels/inch

☑ Constrain Proportions
☐ Resample Image: Bicubic

FIGURE 9.6 When setting output resolution and print size in Photoshop Elements, uncheck the Resample Image box to avoid adding or deleting pixels.

2. Make sure that the Resample Image box is not selected. If it is, click the box to disable the option.

3. Enter the desired print width or height in the Width or Height box. When you change one value, the other automatically changes by a proportionate amount. The value in the Resolution box also changes to reflect the number of pixels per inch at the new print size.

4. Click OK to close the dialog box. If your picture doesn't change size on-screen, don't be alarmed—you've just changed the output size of the photo, not the screen display size. Display the rulers along the top and side of the image window (View | Rulers), and you can verify that the output size has been correctly set.

Choosing Printer Properties and Other Printing Tips

I'm assuming that if you're comfortable enough with technology to have picked up this book, you're already schooled in the basics of using your software's Print command. So I won't bore you with Printing 101 here.

I do want to urge you, though, to read your software and printer manuals thoroughly so that you really understand the controls that may be available to you. Those controls vary so much from system to system that I can't provide any specific instructions. I can, however, offer a few troubleshooting tips that may make the printing process go more smoothly.

- For the best prints, use top-quality photo paper. You'll be amazed at the difference that a change in paper can make. In my experience, name-brand papers produce better results than generic, store-brand papers.

- When you're working your way through the printer options that appear after you choose the Print command, be sure to select the right media type for the paper you're using. Most paper manufacturers include in the paper package a sheet outlining the best settings to use with various printers.

- Any resolution options found via the Print dialog box relate to the printer resolution, *not* the image output resolution. Some printer manufacturers mistakenly use the term *ppi* when describing the printer resolution, an error that adds to the confusion over this issue. (See the earlier sections about output resolution for more information.) For most printers, the highest printer resolution translates to the top print quality but also a slower print speed.

- Many printers provide you with a way to tweak saturation, brightness, contrast, and sharpening. These changes affect only the current print job; for lasting changes to your image, you need to use your photo software's editing tools.

- If you're having trouble getting printed colors to match what you see on-screen—and who doesn't?—check out the next section for help.

Solving Color-Matching Problems

Getting the colors that come out of your printer to match what you see on your computer monitor is one of the toughest challenges in digital-photo printing. The next few sections offer some techniques you can try to get things more in sync.

Understanding the Limits of Color Matching

My first word of advice about color matching is to get your expectations in line. Don't drive yourself nuts trying to make printed colors look absolutely identical to your on-screen image—it's a battle you can't win.

As explained in Chapter 8, computer monitors and other electronic displays are *RGB devices,* which means that they create colors by mixing red, green, and blue. Printers use a different color model, either CMY or CMYK. With CMY, the primary colors are cyan, magenta, and yellow. CMYK includes those same three colors plus black. (Black is called the *key* color, thus the *K* in CMYK.)

But more important than the differences in the primary colors used by displays and printers is the role that light plays in the equation. Monitor colors are pure, projected light, while the colors you see on a printed page are the result of light reflecting *off* the ink (or dye or toner) and paper. Because of this inherent difference, you simply can't reproduce in print the most vibrant colors in the RGB model.

Although getting your print and display colors in the same ballpark is entirely doable—and a good idea—your ultimate concern should be how a photo looks in the medium in which you intend for it to be viewed. If the colors on the printed page look great, don't worry if they look different on-screen, and vice versa.

Calibrating and Profiling Your Monitor

One easy step you can take for better color matching is to use a monitor-calibration and profiling tool, such as Adobe Gamma, which is installed automatically with the Windows-based versions of Adobe Photoshop Elements and Photoshop. On the Mac side, Apple ColorSync, provided as part of the Mac OS, performs the same function. These calibration utilities tune your monitor to a set of specifications that are designed to create a neutral canvas for your images.

After calibrating the monitor, the software creates a *color profile.* The profile is a data file that tells your system more about your monitor so that images can be displayed as accurately as possible. Depending on your printer and photo software, the profile may also be used to help the printer understand how the image colors appear on-screen, enabling it to reproduce those colors more accurately.

The upcoming How-To box walks you through the steps of using Adobe Gamma to calibrate and profile your monitor. If you're working on a Mac, start the ColorSync calibration and profiling process by choosing Control Panels | Monitors from the Apple menu. In the dialog box that appears, click the Color icon and then click the Calibrate button to launch the Monitor Calibration Assistant, a wizard that guides you through the rest of the process.

Whichever system you use, follow these tips to get the best results:

- Let your monitor warm up for at least 30 minutes before calibrating.

- Perform the calibration in the light you usually use to view your images.

- Because monitor colors shift over time, you should recalibrate every month or so.

CooL TooLs

(Photo courtesy Monaco Systems)

The one flaw in calibration utilities such as Adobe Gamma and Apple ColorSync is that they rely on the user's visual judgments about the monitor's display characteristics. Because of ambient room light and other factors that affect color perception, what looks right to your eye may not be the completely neutral canvas that calibration is designed to achieve.

If you want a less subjective analysis of your display, you need a *colorimeter*. When attached to your monitor screen, this device records precise color, brightness, and contrast measurements. Shown here is one such device, the MonacoOPTIX, from Monaco Systems (*www.monacosystems.com*). This product, which sells for about $225, can calibrate and profile both CRT monitors and LCD monitors.

How To — CREATE A COLOR PROFILE WITH ADOBE GAMMA

Adobe Gamma is installed automatically when you install Adobe Photoshop Elements, Photoshop, and certain other Adobe products on Windows-based computers. But the utility isn't immediately obvious because the icon that launches it is tucked away in the Windows Control Panel. To open the Control Panel and run the software, follow these steps:

1. Click the Windows Start button and then click Settings | Control Panel. The Control Panel window opens.

2. Double-click the Adobe Gamma icon.

?How To

CREATE A COLOR PROFILE WITH ADOBE GAMMA (*continued*)

3. In the dialog box that appears, choose Step by Step to launch a wizard that walks you through the calibration process. This option is best if you're new to monitor calibration. But after your first few times through the process, you may want to instead click Control Panel. You then see the dialog box shown in Figure 9.7, which puts all the calibration controls in a single panel. If you need help with any of the controls, click the Wizard button.

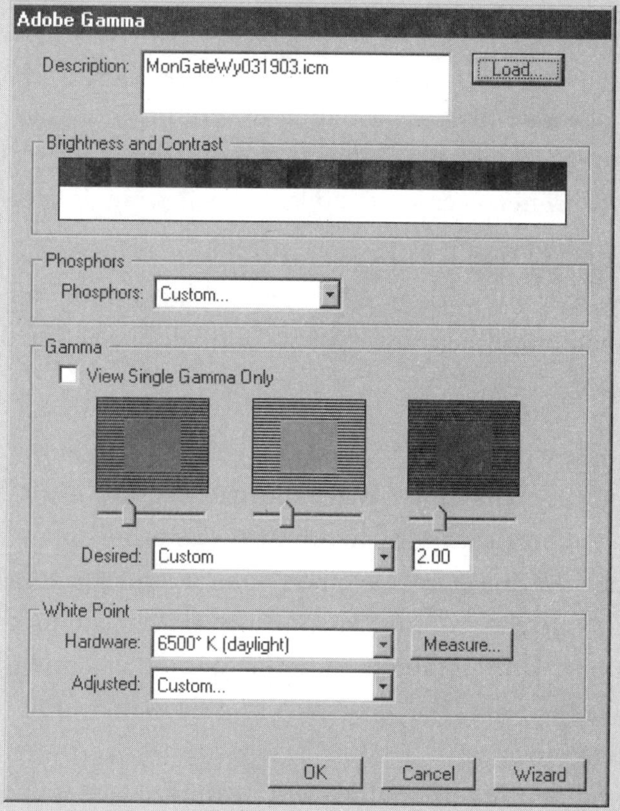

FIGURE 9.7   Use these controls to adjust your monitor so that it provides a neutral canvas for your images.

At the end of the process, be sure to save the profile. So that you can easily distinguish the profile from other profiles that may be on your system, use a name that tells you something about the profile's purpose—for example, something like MyMonitor17 for a 17-inch monitor.

Fine-Tuning Printer and Monitor Colors

Calibrating your monitor gets you started on the road to improved color matching, but if you want to bring screen and printed colors even closer, follow these tips:

- When you choose the Print command, the resulting dialog box should offer a Properties button that enables you to access the printer's own software. Many printers provide controls for adjusting color balance, brightness, and saturation. Play with these options to fine-tune your printed output, and then record the settings when you find a combination that works well. With some printers, you can save the settings so that you can easily apply them the next time you print.

- Colors vary depending on the paper stock. Color-matching tends to be better with glossy photo stock than with plain paper because the paper itself is brighter and whiter, closer to the canvas that your monitor provides. In addition, you often get better color matching when you use paper made by the same company that made the printer, because the inks and software drivers are specifically tailored to those papers.

- If you're working with an inkjet printer, make sure that the print has fully dried before you judge the color match. Colors look slightly different when the print is still wet.

Here's one last secret that will probably get me in trouble with purists in the color-management community: When all else fails, just use Adobe Gamma or some other monitor-adjustment utility to adjust the screen display to what your printer produces. Open the image in your photo editor, launch the calibration utility, and hold the print up next to the monitor. Then just tweak the amount of red, green, and blue in the display, along with brightness, contrast, and other settings, until the on-screen image looks more like the print. You may even be able to accomplish this using controls for your computer's video card.

Keep in mind that if you go this route, your image colors will look different if you display the photo on another monitor, print on some other printer, or use a paper that's significantly different from what you used as your color-match guide. You're also introducing a monitor bias, so the screen may no longer show the colors as your camera captured them. As a result, you could wind up making unnecessary or incorrect corrections to your image colors and exposure. But if all you want is an accurate preview of how your print is going to look, this approach seems as logical as any.

Diving into Color Management

Color management is an innocent-sounding term for a highly complex subject. Entire books have been written on the subject, so consider this just a brief taste to help you determine whether color management is something that you need.

Color management is a software-driven system that attempts to ensure color consistency as an image travels from digital camera or scanner to monitor to printer. Each device can produce a different color gamut, or range of colors. A color-management system—CMS, for short—helps ensure the best possible translation of colors from one device to the next.

A CMS involves two components:

- **Color profiles for each device**   A color profile contains data that describes a device's color gamut. You can create custom profiles using products such as Monaco EZColor ($300, *www.monacosystems.com*). Many hardware manufacturers also provide profiles for their products; often, these profiles are installed automatically when you install the hardware driver software. In some cases, you have to download the profile from the manufacturer's web site.

> **PRO TIP**
>
> Color profiles are also known as ICC profiles because they follow standards set out by an organization called the International Color Consortium. Software that supports profiles is said to be ICC compliant.

- **Color management module (CMM)**   After building device profiles, you use the CMM to apply an input profile and output profile to your image. Also known as a *color engine*, the CMM compares those profiles with your monitor profile and adjusts the screen display to approximate how your picture will look when printed. (This print preview feature is known as *soft proofing*.) When you print the picture, the CMM again references the profile data to translate the input colors to the printer's color gamut.

In systems that don't have a CMM, the computer's operating system handles screen-to-print color translation, using profiles that are added to the system when you install hardware. You do sometimes get lucky and get good color matching from the system's internal color brain. But more often than not, colors are off because the translation is based on generic, one-size-fits-all profiles.

If you want more capable color management, you need photo software that's *fully ICC compliant*. Professional imaging programs such as Adobe Photoshop meet this standard, but entry-level programs do not.

Some intermediate programs, including Photoshop Elements, can read and preserve custom profiles, but they don't offer profile application or soft proofing. However, color-profiling programs usually include a basic utility that provides these missing CMM functions. Figure 9.8 offers a look at Monaco ColorWorks, the utility that ships with Monaco EZColor.

FIGURE 9.8 If your photo software doesn't provide soft proofing or allow you to tag images with custom profiles, you can use a utility such as Monaco ColorWorks.

The theory behind the color management system seems simple enough, and it can be for a so-called *closed system*—a single user who works with one scanner, camera, monitor, and printer. But color management is most critical for situations in which many people need to review, edit, and print the same image, each using a different monitor and printer. Each user has to be schooled in color management and, just as important, use the exact same profile settings when working with the image.

Getting that kind of system-wide compliance among users can be difficult, especially because organizations that have a CMS tend to work with Photoshop and other high-end imaging programs. Such programs offer a huge assortment of options that enable the user to tweak color rendering, both on-screen and for print. Figure 9.9 shows the main CMS dialog box from Adobe Photoshop—and this is just one of several related dialog boxes! Some users just can't ignore the temptation to play with all those controls, and when they do, color consistency can suffer.

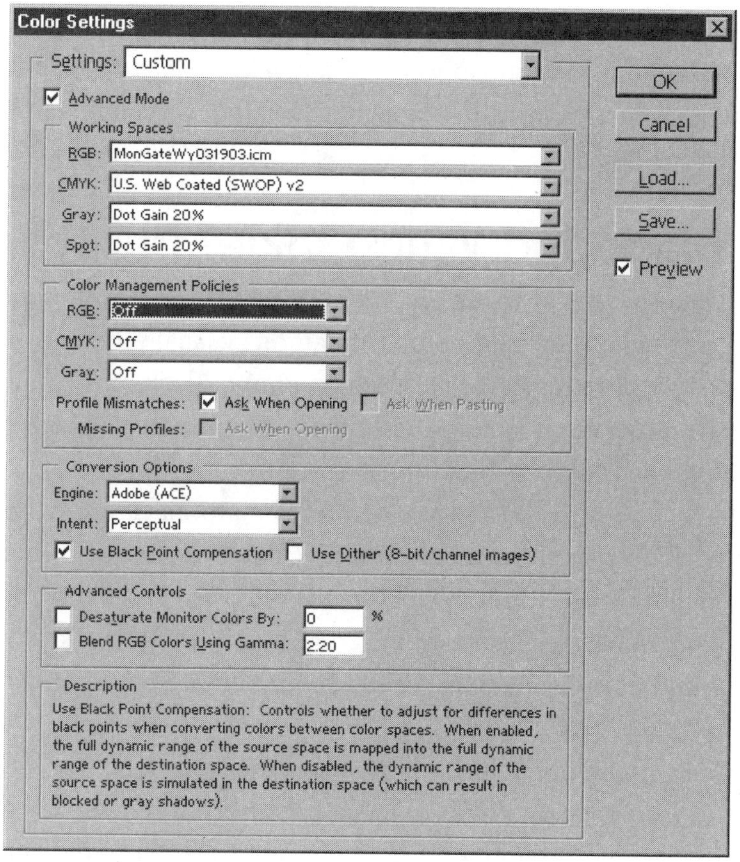

FIGURE 9.9 Adobe Photoshop offers a host of options for specifying how profiles should be used when you edit, view, and print images.

To sum up a very long story, if you're a single user who's interested in getting closer color matching between camera, scanner, monitor, and printer, an entry-level color management product such as EZColor is worth a look. ColorVision (*www.colorvision.com*) also offers packages geared to beginning and intermediate users. Understand, though, that if you want to be able to soft proof images in your photo editor, as opposed to editing them in the photo editor and then proofing them in the color-management utility, you'll need to move up to Photoshop or another program that offers full CMS support.

If you're in the position of having to implement a CMS in a multiuser workflow, try to get advice from other folks who have done so. Ask what products they think work best and, just as important, what tactics they've used to get good results from those products. When you introduce the CMS to your team, make sure that everyone is well trained in the basics, and emphasize that if they follow your guidelines, they can trust the system to work.

Photoshop users can find extensive information about its CMS tools in advanced books about the program. The Adobe web site (*www.Adobe.com*) is another good resource for a better understanding of color management in general and how to implement it in Photoshop.

Printing Black-and-White Inkjet Photos

Black-and-white imagery has always been a favorite with fine-art photographers, but recently it's also enjoyed a resurging popularity among casual picture-takers—in part because you no longer have to decide between color and black-and-white before you take the picture. You can shoot in color and then easily produce a black-and-white version of the picture in your photo editor.

As you may have discovered with your own forays into black-and-white photography, however, getting a good print from a color inkjet printer can be problematic. If you use the printer's normal, all-inks output setting, prints often have a slight color tint. The reason is that color printers produce neutral grays by blending the exact same amount of each ink color, and most printers just aren't precise enough to maintain that balance throughout the print.

Setting the printer to use only black ink removes the color tint. But this approach has its own drawback: the image quality is reduced because you're only using ink drops from a single cartridge, when the printer is engineered to produce the photo using ink drops from all cartridges together.

You may decide that your best bet is to take your important black-and-white images to a lab for output. But first, try these techniques to improve your own printer's black-and-white performance:

- Don't convert your image to the grayscale color mode. Instead, leave it as an RGB image, using the techniques discussed in Chapter 8 to remove the color components from the picture. Inkjet printers are designed to output RGB files, so they work best when fed that type of file.

- Check the status of your color inks. If one ink color is depleted, the printer can't create neutral grays. Most people think that the black cartridge is empty when they see a color tint, but it's more likely that one of the color inks needs replacing.

- Remember that the light in which you view your print can affect the colors you see.

- If you are a serious black-and-white enthusiast, you can explore the option of replacing the ink cartridges in your printer with a third-party black-and-white ink set, such as the Quad Black ink sets sold by Lyson, Inc. (*www.lysonusa.com*). Other companies to shop include Luminos (*www.luminos.com*) and MediaStreet (*www.mediastreet.com*). However, when you make this switch, you have to thoroughly clean the print heads to remove all traces of the old ink, which can be expensive and time-consuming. So you should really set aside one printer just for this purpose.

- Adding a sepia-tone or other subtle tint to your images can be a nice way to get around the problem entirely. Such tints have long been used to good artistic effect in traditional printmaking, and they're easy to apply in a photo editor. See Chapter 8 for details.

>> TROUBLESHOOTER

Printer manufacturers advise against using third-party inks, and not just because they'd like to keep you as an ink customer. The print heads and other vital components in a printer are engineered around the manufacturer's own ink formulas, and when you put another brand of ink into the system, you can wind up with clogged print heads and other malfunctions. In addition, the results you get from various print settings and media may change significantly. For these reasons, most printer warranties become void if damage occurs due to third-party inks.

With that warning in mind, I should in the interest of fairness tell you that many photographers say they use third-party inks with no problem. However, most of the folks I know who are doing so are working with specialty inks from companies that are pursuing the high-end photography market. These products are designed for specific artistic goals, such as black-and-white printing, rather than for cost-cutting, like the cheap inkjet refill products advertised on late-night TV. I would caution you to stay away from those cheap refill kits if you care about either your printer or your print quality.

Working with a Lab

Love the picture-taking side of digital photography but not the printing side? You'll be happy to know that you can get great prints from your digital images at a reasonable cost at just about any place where you used to drop off your film for processing.

You can choose from four basic types of digital-printing services:

- Most one-hour labs can make prints from digital memory cards or a CD, typically for about 40 cents a print.

- If you can't wait an hour for your pictures, many labs and convenience stores have do-it-yourself kiosks for instant printing. These kiosks have tools that you can use for basic image correction, such as cropping and color adjustments, too. You pay about $7 for one 8×10-inch sheet of photos; how many pictures fit on that sheet depends on the print size you select for each image.

- Online photo services, for example, Ofoto (*www.ofoto.com*) and Shutterfly (*www.shutterfly.com*), offer another printing solution. You upload your image files to the web site, and your prints come in the mail a few days later. If you create a personal album page at these sites, your friends and relatives can also order prints of your files, which saves you the hassle of making and mailing the prints to everyone who wants a copy. Print prices average about 45 cents for a 4×6-inch print to $4 for an 8×10, not including shipping.

- If you live in an urban area, you can take your image files to a commercial imaging lab for output. Most labs can color-match the prints to proofs that you make on your home printer. For that reason, when I elect to have to lab prints made, I typically choose this option. Expect to pay slightly more for the benefits of color-matching; labs in my area charge about $7 for an 8×10-inch print but offer good discounts if you print more than one copy of the same image. Many pro labs also offer the same kind of one-hour printing offered at retail photo labs, at competitive prices.

All these services use printers that output your images on traditional photo paper, so you can expect the same print life as you get from film prints. Assuming that the lab uses archival photo paper, which is the norm, that's about 60 years if you safeguard the print from heavy light exposure, moisture, heat, and environmental pollutants.

>> TROUBLESHO⊕TER

Before taking your images to the printer, be sure to find out what output resolution and file format you should use when preparing the image files. For one-hour photo printing and do-it-yourself kiosks, you usually can take in your raw, unedited image files; the printer automatically sets the output resolution to whatever ppi is needed to output the image at the size you request. (Remember that a good print requires an output resolution of 200 to 300 ppi.) But with an online printing service or professional imaging lab, you need to follow specific file-prep guidelines.

SEE ALSO

Don't forget that traditional photo sizes—4×6, 5×7, 8×10, and so on—have a different aspect ratio than the image files produced by most digital cameras. That means that the printer may need to crop your photo or add a blank border to produce the print. See Chapter 3 for more on this subject.

10

Putting Pictures on the Screen

When Hollywood producers decide to take a popular novel to the big screen, they hire a screenwriter to pare the book content to movie length. You likewise need to whittle down digital photos destined for the screen. Otherwise, your pictures will contain too many pixels, resulting in images that are too big to fit on the screen. If you're sharing the pictures via the web or e-mail, pixel-heavy images also cause long download times.

This chapter shows you how to perform this vital image-reduction surgery. In addition, you'll find information about saving your screen pictures in the two main web file formats, JPEG and GIF, and you'll get a look at some great ways to share your pictures online.

Setting the Image Display Size

When you prepare a digital photo for screen display, you can't set picture size the same way you do for printed photos. The next few sections explain why a different approach is necessary and walk you through the steps involved in establishing the size of your screen pictures.

Screen Pictures and ppi

Chapter 9 explains how output resolution, measured in ppi (pixels per inch), affects both print size and print quality. For screen images, output resolution is completely irrelevant.

This concept is critical, so let me repeat: *Output resolution plays no role in either the size or quality of screen images.*

I know that you've heard many people say that you must set the output resolution of web or e-mail pictures to 96 ppi or 72 ppi. But this recommendation is an example of bad information spreading so widely that people perceive it as truth. (The sidebar "Tracing the Origins of the 96/72 ppi Myth" explains how the notion originated.)

Here's the real story: A display device, whether it's a computer monitor, television screen, or multimedia projector, builds everything that you see on-screen out of pixels, just like a digital camera. When presenting a digital picture, the device pays no attention to the output resolution value that you may have established in your photo editor. Instead, it simply uses one screen pixel to reproduce each image pixel.

Figure 10.1 proves the point. Both images on the web page have 300 horizontal pixels and 150 vertical pixels. Before adding the pictures to the web page, I used my photo editor to set the output resolution of the left image to 96 ppi and the right image to 300 ppi. As you can see, the two pictures display at the same size. Notice, too, that a higher output resolution does not improve image quality. Nor would adding more pixels affect quality—it would simply increase the size of the picture on-screen.

The only instance in which the one-to-one relationship between screen and image pixels changes is when you open the picture in a photo editor and use a zoom tool to magnify the image. You must set the zoom magnification to 100 percent to view the image at the size that it will appear when placed on a web page, sent via e-mail, or used for some other on-screen purpose. In many photo editors, this 100-percent view is called *Actual Pixels.*

If you view the picture on another monitor, however, it may display at a different size than the unmagnified size you see on your screen. This happens because the size of the screen pixels used to display the image depends on the *screen resolution*, as explained in the next section.

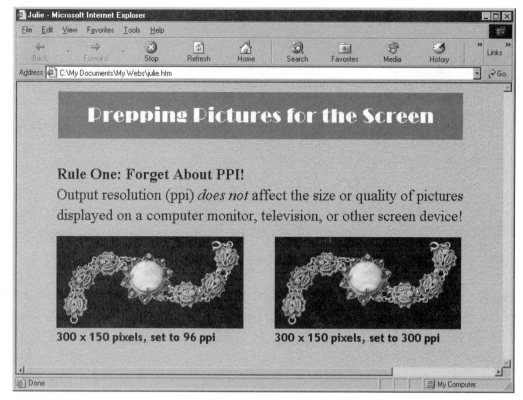

FIGURE 10.1 Output resolution has no effect on display size; all that matters is the number of horizontal and vertical pixels.

How Screen Resolution Affects Display Size

To emphasize an earlier point: Output resolution (ppi) *does not* affect the size of a screen image. The display size depends only on the following two factors:

- The image pixel dimensions (pixels wide by pixels tall)

- The resolution of the screen itself

As I mentioned in the preceding section, the phrase *screen pixels* refers to the display device pixels. *Screen resolution* refers to the total number of screen pixels. Screen resolution, like digital camera resolution, is stated in terms of pixel dimensions.

On a computer monitor, the user can adjust screen resolution. Most systems offer a range of resolution settings; standard options for a 17-inch monitor, for example, are 640×480, 800×600, 1024×768, 1280×1024, and 1600×1200. In Windows, you set resolution via the Display Properties dialog box (right-click an empty area of the desktop and choose Properties). On a Mac, you access resolution controls by choosing Control Panels | Monitors from the Apple menu.

At a high screen resolution, images display at a smaller size than they do at a low screen resolution. As an example, compare Figures 10.2 and 10.3. For both figures, I set the Windows wallpaper (desktop background) to display a 640×480-pixel photograph. The first figure shows how the desktop looks when the screen resolution is 640×480. Because of the one-to-one relationship between screen and image pixels, the picture fills the entire screen. (The bottom

FIGURE 10.2 A 640×480-pixel image fills the monitor when the screen resolution is also 640×480.

of the picture is hidden by the Windows taskbar, which I left visible so that you could tell you were looking at a computer screen.)

Figure 10.3 shows that same 640×480-pixel image on a monitor running at a screen resolution of 800×600. At that resolution, the number of screen pixels increases, which means smaller pixels. Your 640×480-pixel image appears smaller because the screen pixels used to display it are smaller. And, of course, your photo consumes only 640 of the 800 available horizontal screen pixels, and 480 of the 600 vertical pixels, so the image no longer fills the entire screen.

FIGURE 10.3 Displayed on a monitor set to a screen resolution of 800×600, the 640×480-pixel photo no longer consumes the entire screen.

Technical Aside
Screen Resolution Terminology

In discussions about digital cameras, monitors, and digital projectors, you may hear the terms *VGA, SVGA, XGA, SXGA,* and *UXGA* used to describe resolution capabilities. The following table lists the pixel dimensions indicated by each term, as well as the name behind the acronym, which is important only for purposes of sounding like a techie.

RESOLUTION LABEL	FULL NAME	RESOLUTION
VGA	Video Graphics Array	640×480 pixels
SVGA	Super Video Graphics Array	800×600 pixels
XGA	Extended Graphics Array	1024×768 pixels
SXGA	Super Extended Graphics Array	1280×1024 pixels
UXGA	Ultra Extended Graphics Array	1600×1200 pixels

Establishing the Image Display Size

Most of us are used to stating the dimensions of a photo in inches, picas, centimeters, or some other traditional unit of measurement. When you specify the size at which you want a picture to appear on-screen, however, you do so in terms of pixels.

Remember that a one-to-one relationship exists between the pixels in your image and the screen pixels of the display device (computer screen, television, or digital projector). So to set the display size of an image, just figure out how much of the screen you want your picture to cover and adjust the image pixel dimensions to match. For example, if you want to fill the screen of a monitor that's set to a resolution of 800×600, you need an 800×600-pixel photo.

The catch, of course, is knowing the screen resolution of the device that will be used to display the photo, which is impossible if you're preparing an image for the web or e-mail. Most web designers create pages with a 640×480 screen resolution in mind because that's the lowest resolution at which most people run their monitors today. For e-mail, I usually make pictures no bigger than 300×300 pixels. This size ensures that the recipient can see the entire image without scrolling. (Remember that the browser or e-mail window consumes some of the available screen space.)

In most cases, you'll need to dump pixels—*downsample,* in imaging jargon—to get the picture to the appropriate screen size. The upcoming How-To sidebar walks you through the downsampling process, but before you head there, here are a few final bits of advice:

- For web images, smaller is better. Every pixel in your image adds to the file size, increasing download time.

- Always make a backup copy of your image file before you downsample. You'll want all your original pixels if you later need to print the photo.

PRO TIP

I include the word Web *in the file name of a screen copy of a photo. That way, I can easily distinguish the screen version of the picture file in the future.*

- Some digital cameras can create a screen-sized photo and a high-resolution image each time you press the shutter button. Depending on your camera and how large you want your screen image to be, though, the smaller image file may still contain more pixels than you need.

- Finally, one last reminder for good measure: More pixels does not translate to improved on-screen picture quality, as it does for printed photos. More pixels simply makes a bigger screen picture. If the recipient of your picture needs to make a quality *print* from the file, however, you must send a high-resolution image, preparing the print size and output resolution as described in Chapter 9.

PRO TIP

If you want to apply a sharpening filter to your photo, wait until after you set the display size. The amount of sharpening needed often changes after an image is resampled.

≫ TROUBLESHOOTER

Many photo editors, including Photoshop Elements, offer a web optimization tool that you can use to resample the image and save the file in the JPEG format at the same time. However, if you want the option of applying a sharpening filter (or any other edits) after you resample the image, don't set the size via your web optimization tool. Otherwise, your picture will undergo two rounds of JPEG compression—once when you set the image size and save the file and again after you apply your final edits and resave the image. See the section "Using JPEG Wisely" for information on why multiple rounds of compression are bad for your photos.

? How To

ADJUST THE PIXEL COUNT (RESAMPLE A PHOTO)

In most photo editors, you can change the pixel dimensions of an image in the same dialog box where you set print size and output resolution. The difference between the two procedures is that for screen prep, you need to turn on the resampling function, which enables you to add or delete pixels.

These steps detail the process in Photoshop Elements. The approach is the same in any program, but the specific menu commands and control names may vary.

1. Save a copy of your image and use the copy for your screen photo. That way, you can always access all the original image pixels later if needed.

2. Choose Image | Resize | Image Size to open the Image Size dialog box.

3. Select the Resample Image option, as shown in Figure 10.4. When this option is active, the Width and Height boxes in the Pixel Dimensions section at the top of the dialog box become available.

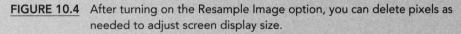

FIGURE 10.4 After turning on the Resample Image option, you can delete pixels as needed to adjust screen display size.

4. Select Bicubic from the drop-down list next to the Resample Image check box. This option determines the algorithm the program uses to rebuild the photo at the new pixel dimensions. Bicubic produces the best results.

5. Select the Constrain Proportions check box to preserve the picture's original width-to-height ratio.

? **How To**

ADJUST THE PIXEL COUNT (RESAMPLE A PHOTO) *(continued)*

6. Enter the new pixel dimensions into the top set of Width and Height boxes. In the figure, I set the pixel dimensions to 300×200. (Note that in Photoshop Elements, the file size value shown at the top of the dialog box is *not* the actual file size, but the amount of memory the program needs to work with the photo while it's open. Other programs may treat this issue differently.)

7. Click OK to resample the image and close the dialog box.

To see your photo at the size at which it will display on-screen, choose View | Actual Pixels. Remember that the display size will differ on a monitor that's not running at the same screen resolution as yours.

Technical Aside
Tracing the Origins of the 96/72 ppi Myth

Like any good myth, the one that suggests that you prepare a picture for the screen by setting the output resolution to 96 or 72 ppi has some basis in fact. In the early years of computers, monitors came in few sizes and offered only one or two screen resolution settings. Most new PCs shipped from the factory set to a screen resolution that resulted in 96 screen pixels per viewable inch of the screen. Macintosh systems used a default setting that translated to 72 screen pixels per viewable inch.

Because these standards existed, you could set your image size in the same way you did for print output. If you wanted the picture to have a display size of 2 inches square, you set the print width and height values to 2 inches. Then you turned on your photo editor's resampling option and specified an output resolution of 96 or 72 ppi, depending on whether you were going for a PC audience or a Macintosh audience. The program eliminated or added pixels as necessary to give you that 96 or 72 ppi resolution.

Although the result was indeed a screen image that was 2 inches square, the display size didn't have anything to do with the output resolution or print width and height values that you set. As explained earlier in the chapter, display devices simply light up one screen pixel for each pixel in the image. Resampling the image to 96 or 72 just gave you the right number of pixels to fill a 2-inch square area on a monitor that itself was producing 96 or 72 screen pixels per viewable inch of the screen.

Technical Aside
Tracing the Origins of the 96/72 ppi Myth (continued)

Even if display devices could interpret the width/height/output resolution values used for printing, this method of setting display size is based on an outdated formula. We're way past the days when all monitors adhered to the standard of 96 or 72 screen pixels per inch. In addition to a much wider range of monitor sizes, we now have video cards that offer many more screen resolution options, so the number of screen pixels per inch varies widely. On my laptop computer, for example, I have a 12-inch screen that has a viewable area of 10×7½ inches. At a screen resolution of 800×600, that means about 80 screen pixels per inch. On my 19-inch monitor, which has a viewable area of 14×10½ inches, that same 800×600 setting results in about 57 screen pixels per inch.

Saving Your Image in a Screen File Format

After you edit a digital photo, whether it's to adjust the display size or to perform retouching or creative work, you need to save the file in a format that is compatible with programs used to display screen pictures—web browsers, e-mail programs, presentation programs such as Microsoft PowerPoint, and the like.

A handful of file formats are screen friendly:

- **JPEG**   Introduced back in Chapter 2, JPEG is the default format used by digital cameras. JPEG is the leading format for web and e-mail photos because it offers file compression, which shrinks download times. Upcoming sections explain more about this format.

- **GIF**   This format is a web-only creature. Among other things, GIF is used to create GIF animations, those blinking graphics that web designers love and most web users hate. GIF also enables you to make part of your picture transparent, allowing the web page background to show through.

  Like JPEG, GIF produces small files, which is what you want in a web format. Unfortunately, GIF images can contain only 256 colors. That's fine for text-based graphics and simple line art, but as illustrated by the GIF example on Page 32 of the color section, a 256-color limit doesn't give you enough shades to reproduce subtle color transitions found in a photograph. The resulting color-block effect is known as *posterization*.

GIF may be an option for photos that you convert to the grayscale color mode. Read the upcoming section "256-Color Grayscales: JPEG or GIF?" for details.

- **BMP (Windows) and PICT (Macintosh)**   These two formats are primarily used for incorporating images into program help systems, screen savers, and other graphics that are displayed by the Windows or Macintosh operating systems. For some of these uses, JPEG works as well, but check your help system to be sure. If BMP or PICT is required for a task, follow the help system's guidelines for choosing specific format options when you save the file.

PRO TIP

Most presentation programs also can work with BMP or PICT images. I prefer JPEG, because I can use the same image file for the web or e-mail as well as in the presentation.

- **PNG and JPEG 2000**   Imaging experts are currently developing these two formats, both designed to produce better image quality at smaller file sizes than JPEG and GIF. However, neither of these new players is recognized by older web browsers and e-mail programs, so stay away for now.

Using JPEG Wisely

When you save your photo in the JPEG format, you'll encounter some complex-sounding options. Before I explain them, I need to share some strong words of warning about this format:

- As explained in Chapter 2, JPEG is a destructive format. JPEG applies compression to the image, which eliminates picture data to reduce file size. The greater the compression, the more your picture quality suffers. But even the lowest amount of compression does some damage.

- Because of the data loss that occurs with JPEG, *don't* use this format to save a picture between editing sessions. Each time you edit and resave your photo, you lose a little more picture information. (Merely opening and closing the photo file is perfectly safe.)

- Save your photos in a nondestructive format, such as TIFF, until you're completely finished editing the picture. Your photo editor's own format—such as PSD in Photoshop Elements—is probably an even better choice, because it's designed for full support of all program features. (In some programs, TIFF can't preserve image layers and other advanced imaging features. Never overwrite your final, edited photo file with the JPEG version. Always keep a backup copy of the photo in the original, nondestructive format.

With those warnings out of the way, the next sections show two different methods for creating your JPEG copy and explain the various JPEG options in detail.

Creating a JPEG Copy of Your Photo

Many photo editors, including Photoshop Elements, offer a *web optimization* utility. This tool offers the best way to create a JPEG copy of your image, because you can preview how your picture will look at a different levels of compression.

Figure 10.5 shows the Photoshop Elements version of this feature. To access it, choose File | Save For Web. (A couple of the important controls aren't labeled in the dialog box, so use the figure as a map.)

> **PRO TIP**
>
> *Some web optimization tools, including the Photoshop Elements Save For Web feature, automatically save your JPEG file as a copy of the original picture. After you save the JPEG file, your original remains open in the program window. If you want to view the JPEG image, you need to close the original and open the JPEG file.*

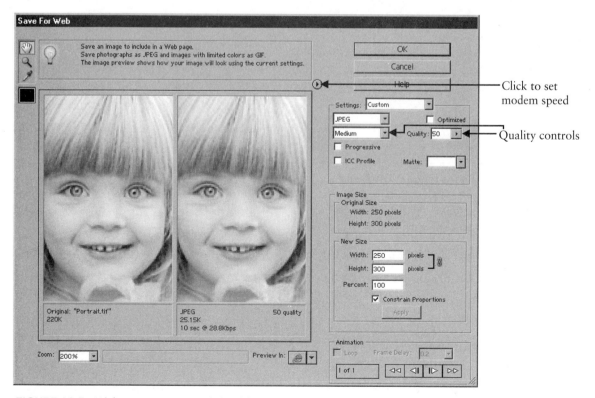

FIGURE 10.5   Web optimization tools enable you to preview the effect of different amounts of JPEG compression.

If you don't have a web optimization tool, you can use the standard File | Save As command to create your JPEG copy. When the Save As dialog box appears, select JPEG as the file format and enter a file name that distinguishes the image from the original. In some cases, you'll find JPEG options right in the dialog box; in other programs, such as Elements, clicking the Save button opens a second dialog box that contains these options. Figure 10.6 shows the JPEG Options dialog box from Photoshop Elements.

>> TROUBLESHOOTER

Selecting the Preview check box in the Photoshop Elements JPEG Options dialog box does not enable you to preview the effect of your settings in the image window, as it does in other dialog boxes. The Preview function simply turns on the estimated file size/download time display at the bottom of the dialog box.

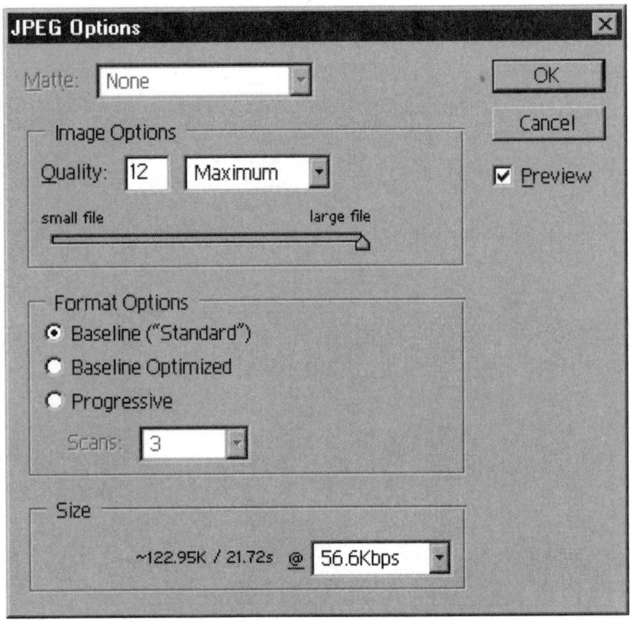

FIGURE 10.6 When you use the regular File | Save As command, the JPEG options may be presented in a separate dialog box, as shown here, after you click the Save button.

Regardless of what path you take to save your file, you'll encounter the same basic file options. The next five sections explain each option.

Quality

This option is key to both file size and picture quality. It controls how much JPEG compression is applied. As discussed earlier, higher compression means smaller files but reduced image quality.

To give you an idea of the quality/file size tradeoff you need to make, the three JPEG portraits on Page 32 of the color insert provide an approximation of the screen appearance of an image at three different Quality settings. Starting with the uncompressed TIFF version of this portrait on Color Page 6, I first reduced the pixel count to 250×300 and made three JPEG copies of the image. For the first copy, I used the Minimum Quality setting, which applies maximum compression. For the second copy, I set the Quality to Medium; for the third, Maximum.

As you can see, the Maximum Quality setting produces acceptable image quality. You'll also get a significant reduction of file size even with this amount of compression. My original 250×300-pixel TIFF image had a file size of 222K, for example, and the Maximum Quality setting trimmed the JPEG version to 113K.

How low you can go with the Quality setting depends on your picture. Some photos survive heavy compression more than others, so you need to experiment. However, the Minimum Quality setting almost always turns the photo into the same kind of blocky mess you see in the Minimum example on Color Page 32. This destruction doesn't apply just to color images, either, as illustrated by the black-and-white photos in Figure 10.7.

Before compression, 103K

Maximum Quality, 66K

Medium Quality, 24K

Minimum Quality, 9K

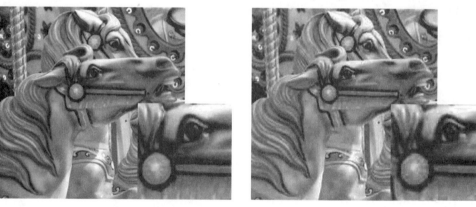

FIGURE 10.7   Too much JPEG compression destroys photo quality.

Also, the controls related to JPEG quality vary from program to program. In Photoshop Elements, which is the program I used to create the portrait examples, you can choose a general Quality category—Maximum, High, Medium, and Low—or specify a precise Quality value. (For some reason, the values range from 0 to 12 if you save your file via the Save As dialog box but from 0 to 100 if you use the Save For Web tool. A setting of 12 in the Save As dialog box translates to 100 in Save For Web.)

Baseline Standard, Baseline Optimized, and Progressive

These options determine how your image data is pumped through the Internet pipeline:

- **Baseline Standard**   For the best compatibility with older web browsers, choose this option. (If you're working with the Photoshop Elements Save For Web utility, you select the option by turning off the Optimized and Progressive check boxes.)

- **Baseline Optimized**   This option applies a special compression algorithm that is designed to produce better picture quality at smaller file sizes than Baseline Standard. Not all web browsers support Optimized JPEG images, though, so I don't use this setting.

- **Progressive**   When a web page contains a progressive JPEG, a faint representation of the picture appears as soon as the first bit of data is received, and then the image is completed in progressive passes. Images saved without the feature don't appear until all picture data is received.

  On one hand, progressive images enable site visitors to see whether the photo is of interest more quickly. However, the option actually adds to file download time and causes problems with some older browsers. So again, I say, skip it.

Modem Speed

When you save a file in the JPEG format, most programs display the approximate download time at a selected modem speed so that you can judge whether you've compressed the file enough. I suggest that you set the modem speed used to calculate the download estimate to 28.8Kbps (kilobytes per second). True, many people have faster connections, but just as many viewers live in areas where slower speeds are the norm. (If you're using the Photoshop Elements Save For Web utility, refer to Figure 10.5 to find the button you click to set the modem speed.)

Embed ICC Profiles

As discussed in Chapter 9, ICC profiles contain data that's used to achieve better color consistency between camera, monitor, and printer. If your photo software supports ICC profiles, you can embed the profile in the image file. Don't do so unless you've implemented a color management system (CMS) and are sharing the image with others who have done the same. Embedding the profile increases file size, and profiles are ignored unless the viewer also has a CMS.

>> TROUBLESHOOTER

If you need to create a screen version of an image that you've converted to the CMYK color model for printing on a commercial press, convert the image back to the RGB color model before saving it as a JPEG file. Some browsers can't cope with JPEGs made from CMYK files. See Chapter 8 for more information about CMYK, RGB, and color models.

Matte

This feature was designed to give JPEG users one of the benefits formerly reserved for GIF fans: leaving part of the picture transparent, so that the subject appears to float on the web page instead of being constrained to a square frame. JPEG can't preserve transparent areas, but if your web page has a solid color background, you can create faux transparency.

When an image contains transparent pixels, those pixels are filled with solid color when you save in the JPEG format. The Matte option enables you to specify that fill color. By default, the pixels go white, as illustrated in the left cable picture in Figure 10.8. Match the Matte color to the color of your web page background, and you have your floating picture, as illustrated by the second cable image. Of course, you can just as easily fill the transparent areas with the background color before saving the file if you prefer. Note that if your web page has a patterned background, rather than a solid color background, the effect doesn't work.

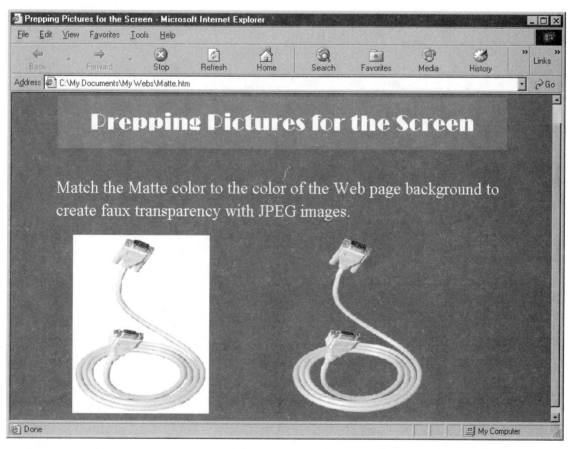

FIGURE 10.8 If your web page has a solid color background, match the JPEG Matte color to the background to create the illusion of a free-floating subject.

256-Color Grayscales: GIF or JPEG?

Chapter 8 discusses some of the many ways to turn a full-color digital photo into a black-and-white picture. One method is to convert the photo to the Grayscale color mode, which combines the red, green, and blue color channels into one, leaving you with an image that contains just 256 colors (black, white, and shades of gray).

For reasons discussed in Chapter 8, I don't use this method for important black-and-white conversions because it doesn't offer the best control over the conversion. In addition, most printers do better with RGB images than Grayscale pictures. But Grayscale mode does have an advantage over RGB in terms of web use: With only one channel and 256 colors, Grayscale images have a much smaller file size than RGB photos.

If you read the earlier section that discussed the GIF file format, you may remember that GIF also is limited to 256 colors, which may have you wondering whether GIF is a good match for grayscale pictures. The answer is, yes, it can be. But depending on the picture, JPEG may still offer a better balance of file size and picture quality.

When you save to the GIF format, you can specify how many image colors you want to retain, saving anywhere from 2 to 256 colors. At the full 256, a GIF image may be larger than a JPEG file, even if you apply minimum compression to that JPEG file. To achieve a smaller-than-JPEG file size, you may need to strip the photo to so few colors that you see *posterization*, as illustrated by Figure 10.9. These examples illustrate the screen appearance of an image that's approximately 300 pixels square. The left image, which I saved at a Medium JPEG Quality setting, has a file size of 19K. To create a GIF image of the same size, I had to reduce the picture to 16 colors. As you can see from the inset areas, this created significant posterization in some areas of the picture.

Medium Quality JPEG, 19K

16-color GIF, 21K

FIGURE 10.9 To reduce the GIF image to the same file size as a Medium Quality JPEG, I had to take the picture down to 16 colors, creating posterization.

The only way to know for sure whether GIF or JPEG offers a better solution is to experiment. I suspect, however, that you'll prefer the results that you get with JPEG more often than not.

Exploring New Ways to Share Photos

You're no doubt familiar with the three most common screen uses for digital photos: posting them on a web page, attaching them to e-mail messages, and adding them to a multimedia presentation. But you may not be aware of the following electronic avenues for sharing and enjoying your pictures.

Online Photo Albums

You can create and store online photo albums for free though sites such as Ofoto (*www.Ofoto.com*) and Shutterfly (*www.shutterfly.com*). These sites provide the software you need to upload your photo files and arrange them into albums. After creating an album, you can send e-mails inviting other people to view the pictures and order prints from the site. You can limit access to your photos only to those people, which is a nice security feature.

Although you don't pay anything to post albums, I urge you to buy pictures every now and then to help keep the free photo-sharing option viable for the companies that provide the service.

> **» TROUBLESHOOTER**
>
> Don't mistake an online photo-sharing site as a storage bin for your image files. If the web site goes out of business or has technical problems, you could lose all your pictures. Maintain your photo archive on your own system, CDs, or other storage media. (See Chapter 1 for archiving advice.)

Web-Based Image Galleries

Many professional photographers run full-fledged web sites, providing potential clients with a chance to browse online galleries of their work. But you don't need to go to the time or expense of putting up your own web site to create a simple image gallery.

Most Internet service providers (ISPs) offer customers a starter-sized chunk of storage space to use for a personal home page, and that's usually enough for a small image gallery. (Check the ISP's web site for information about size limits and instructions for uploading your gallery.)

Don't worry if you don't know about HTML (Hypertext Markup Language, the language used for documents on the web) or any other aspect of web design, either, because most photo editors and some image-cataloging programs offer a wizard that puts together the gallery for you. Figure 10.10 shows the Photoshop Elements version of this tool, which you open by choosing File | Create Web Gallery.

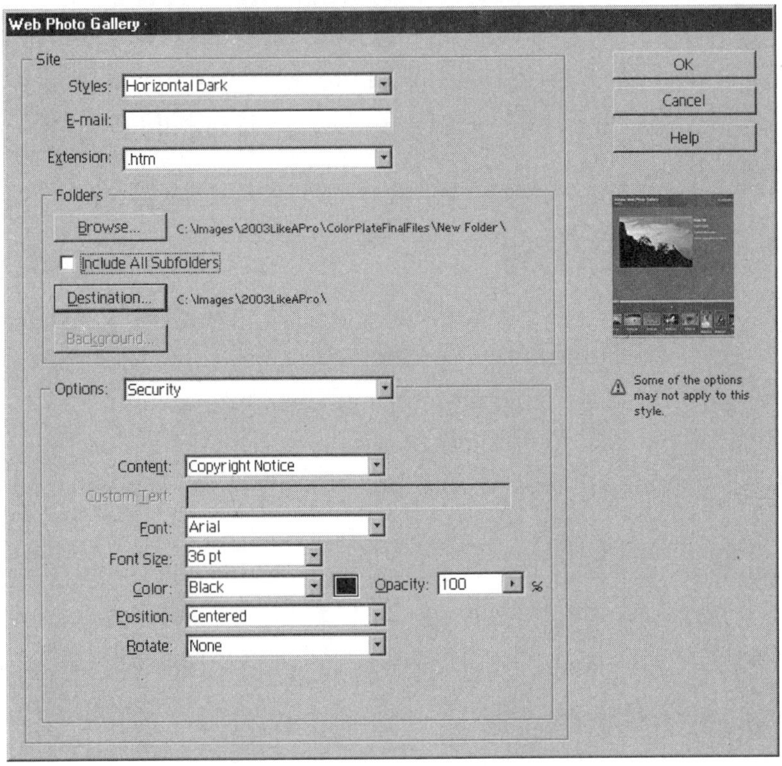

FIGURE 10.10 Like many photo editors, Photoshop Elements offers a wizard that automates the process of creating a simple web image gallery.

Figure 10.11 offers a look at a gallery page that I created using the wizard. As is the tradition with online galleries, you click one of the thumbnail previews to display a picture at a larger size.

Multimedia Slide Shows

Check your photo editor or image-cataloging program to see whether it offers a wizard for creating a multimedia slide show. After putting together a show, you can copy it to a CD for on-computer viewing or to DVD for folks who have a DVD player. (Make sure that your DVD burner uses a format that the player can read.)

If your current software doesn't offer this feature, several companies offer stand-alone multimedia programs. Figure 10.12 shows one such program from SimpleStar (*www .simplestar.com*). Called PhotoShow, this $30 program offers a beginner-level interface but provides enough features to create a nice show complete with music and special effects.

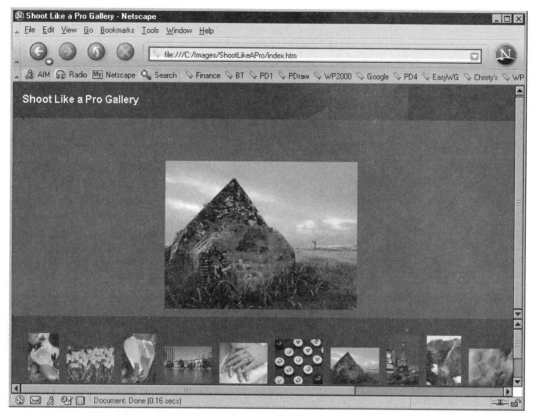

FIGURE 10.11   In this gallery, clicking on a thumbnail image displays the image at a larger size.

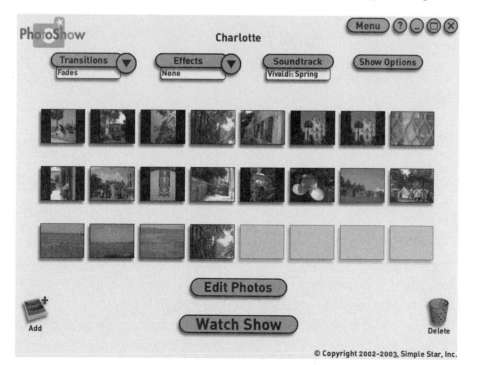

FIGURE 10.12   Programs such as SimpleStar PhotoShow help you create a multimedia slide show featuring your digital photos.

Camera to TV Displays

A number of companies offer devices that enable you to display images from your camera memory card on a TV. Of course, if your camera has a video-out port, you can do the same thing by plugging your camera directly into the TV's AV jacks, but a dedicated photo player eliminates the need to keep hooking and unhooking the camera.

Player devices usually offer slots for multiple types of memory cards, come with a remote control, and can automatically rotate images to the correct orientation. Among products to investigate are PhotoZen, from SimpleTech (*www.simpletech.com*) and eFilm Picturevision, from Delkin Devices (*www.delkin.com*). Both products sell for about $80.

CooL TooLs

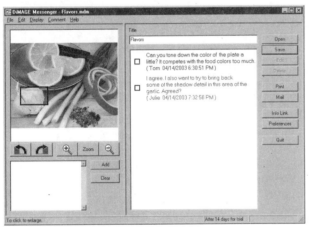

Minolta Corporation (*www.minolta.com*) offers a nifty product for people who need to pass digital photos along a chain of colleagues or clients for review. Called DiMAGE Messenger, this $30 program makes it easy to share thoughts about an image and even mark the area of the photo that you're referencing. After adding your input to the Messenger file, you pass it along to the next person via e-mail.

PART IV
Appendixes

A

Glossary

aperture   An adjustable iris in a camera lens that controls how much light passes through the lens to the image sensor. Aperture sizes are stated in f-stop numbers and written as f/2.8, f/4, and so on. A smaller f-stop number indicates a larger opening and greater light transmission, for a brighter exposure. Aperture also affects depth of field (focus zone); the larger the aperture, the shorter the depth of field.

aperture-priority autoexposure (AE)   A variation on full autoexposure mode. The photographer specifies the aperture setting, and the camera selects the appropriate shutter speed to expose the image properly. On a camera dial, may be abbreviated with the initials *Av* or *A*. *See also* programmed autoexposure (AE), shutter-priority autoexposure (AE).

artifact   A term describing color defects caused by too much file compression. See also compression.

aspect ratio   The ratio between image width and height. Digital cameras commonly produce images with an aspect ratio of 4:3; 35mm film negatives produce pictures with a 3:2 aspect ratio.

autoexposure (AE)   A feature that automatically selects the proper aperture size and shutter speed needed to produce a good exposure. On most cameras, pushing the shutter button halfway down tells the camera to analyze the light and set the exposure. Sometimes called programmed autoexposure. *See also* aperture-priority autoexposure (AE), programmed autoexposure (AE), shutter-priority autoexposure (AE).

autofocus (AF)   A mechanism that focuses the camera lens automatically; usually, focus is set along with exposure when you push the shutter button down halfway.

barn doors   Hinged doors found on some studio lights; moving the doors affects the angle and spread of the light.

BMP   One of several data file formats for digital images; officially stands for the Windows Bitmap format. Used mostly for images that will be included in help systems, screen savers, and other elements of the Windows operating system.

bracketing   A practice that involves taking the same shot three or more times, varying the camera settings for each picture to produce slightly different exposure results; provides a safety net when shooting a subject in a tricky lighting situation.

bulb exposure   A manual shutter-speed option found on some advanced cameras; keeps the shutter open until you press the shutter button a second time. Used mostly for nighttime photography.

burst mode   A camera mode that records multiple images with a single press of the shutter button and then stores all the pictures to the camera memory at the same time. Often limited to low-resolution image capture.

CCD, CMOS   Acronyms for two types of chips used in digital camera image sensors. CCD is short for charge-coupled device (the most common chip); CMOS refers to a complementary metal-oxide semiconductor.

center-weighted metering   An exposure metering mode that measures the amount of light throughout the frame but gives more influence to the center of the scene.

clone tool   Found in most photo editing programs, a retouching tool that enables you to copy good areas of an image to paste over flaws.

CMY   A color model that uses cyan, magenta, and yellow as its primary colors. Some inexpensive printers are based on this model; they typically aren't able to reproduce blacks well. *See also* CMYK.

CMYK   A color model, or system of producing colors, in which cyan, magenta, yellow, and black (called the key color) are the primary colors. Most printers are based on this color model. *See also* CMY.

color engine   The component of a color-management system that translates color information as an image file travels between different devices (camera, scanner, monitor, printer). *See also* color management system.

color management system (CMS)   A system designed to ensure better color consistency as a picture moves from camera or scanner to computer to printer. Utilizes color profiles, which describe the color capabilities of each device in the chain, and a color engine, which translates color data between devices.

color mode, color model   Interchangeable terms referring to a system of defining colors. Digital cameras, scanners, and monitors are based on the RGB (red, green, blue) color model; most printers are based on the CMYK (cyan, magenta, yellow, black) model. *See also* CMYK, CMY, and RGB.

color profile   A data file that describes the color capabilities of a digital camera, scanner, printer, or display device (such as a computer monitor). Used in a color-management system to help ensure better color matching between screen and print images.

color temperature   Indicates the temperature of a light source as measured on the Kelvin scale. As the temperature rises, the color of the light changes. At the low end of the Kelvin scale, light emits a reddish cast; at the high end, it emits a blue cast.

CompactFlash   A type of removable memory card used in some digital cameras.

compression   A process that eliminates data from an image file to reduce the file size. Can be either lossless, which does not sacrifice any important image data and so retains high picture quality, or lossy, which is less discriminating and leads to image degradation. The type of compression depends on the file format used to save the data; digital cameras typically store images in the JPEG format, which applies lossy compression. *See also* JPEG, TIFF.

contrast   The range of brightness values in a photograph. A high-contrast image has a broad range of brightness values, from deep shadows to bright highlights. In a low-contrast image, little difference exists between the darkest and brightest areas.

crop   To trim away the perimeter of an image, usually with a crop tool in a photo editor.

cross-platform   Computer software or hardware that works with more than one operating system; usually refers to a product that can be used on both Windows-based PCs and Macintosh computers.

depth of field (DOF)   The range of distance in a picture that is in sharp focus. When depth of field is short, only objects close to the subject appear sharply focused. With large depth of field, most objects in the picture are in focus. Depth of field is affected by focal length and aperture.

digital zoom   A digital camera feature with a misleading name; it does not actually zoom the lens but instead crops away the perimeter of the image and enlarges the remaining area.

downsampling   Eliminating pixels from a digital image file. *See also* resampling, upsampling.

dpi   Dots per inch. A measure of how many dots of color a printer can output per each linear inch. Don't confuse dpi with ppi, which indicates the number of image pixels per inch.

DPOF   Digital Print Order Format. Enables you to use your camera menus to add printing instructions to your picture files. Printers that support DPOF read that information and print the photos according to your instructions.

driver   Software that your computer needs to communicate with your camera, printer, and other devices.

dye-sub   Short for dye-sublimation, a printing technology in which dye is transferred from a plastic ribbon or film to photo paper. Dye-sub printers produce excellent picture quality but cannot print on plain paper.

edge   A digital imaging term referring to the border between two areas that differ in color, brightness, or both.

equivalent focal length   A way to express the focal length of a digital camera lens by comparing results with a lens on a 35mm film camera. Sometimes abbreviated as efl.

EV compensation   Exposure value compensation. A control found on most digital cameras that enables you to increase or decrease the exposure setting chosen by the camera's autoexposure mechanism. Raising the EV setting produces a brighter exposure, and a lower value darkens the exposure.

EXIF metadata   Information about the camera, date, and capture settings that some digital cameras record in a part of the image file. This data is written in a format known as EXIF (Exchangeable Image File Format) and can be viewed in image browsers and other programs that support EXIF.

Flash EV compensation   A control that enables you to increase or decrease the flash power that the camera thinks is necessary to produce a good exposure. Similar to EV compensation except that it affects flash output.

f-number, f-stop   Interchangeable terms that refer to the size of the aperture (lens opening). A low f-number translates to a large opening, which allows more light through the camera lens. A high f-number indicates a small aperture. Values are stated in the following format: f/2, f/2.8, f/4, and so on. Each step up the f-stop scale lets in half as much light as the previous setting.

focal length   The distance between the optical center of the lens and the recording element (the film negative or digital-camera image sensor). Focal length affects angle of view, depth of field, and the size and distance at which subjects appear in the frame. *See also* equivalent focal length.

gamut   The range of colors that a device can reproduce.

GIF   Graphics Interchange Format. One of two popular file formats for web graphics; it's not appropriate for most photographs because it preserves only 256 colors.

grayscale   Another way to describe a black-and-white photograph; an image that contains only black, white, and shades of gray.

Grayscale mode   The Grayscale color mode, which limits an image to 256 colors (black, white, and shades of gray).

histogram   A graph that charts the range of brightness values in an image.

hot light   A general term used to describe a light that emits a constant light source (as opposed to a flash, which emits a quick burst of light).

hot shoe   A bracket found on some cameras for attaching an external flash head.

inkjet   A printing technology used by the majority of home and office photo printers; pictures are reproduced using tiny drops of ink that are sprayed onto the page.

interpolation   The process of adding pixels to a digital image file; usually results in degraded picture quality. Also known as resampling and upsampling.

ISO rating   International Standards Organization rating. A number that indicates the light sensitivity of film or a digital camera image sensor. The higher the ISO number, the more sensitive the film.

jaggies   Photo slang for the stair-stepped appearance of curved and diagonal lines in low-resolution pictures that are printed at a large size.

JPEG   A file format developed by the Joint Photographic Experts Group. JPEG is the standard file format used by digital cameras to store images and is also the best format to use for web pictures and other screen images. The format applies lossy compression, which reduces file size but also degrades photo quality because it eliminates picture data. *See also* lossy compression.

JPEG 2000   An updated version of JPEG; too new to be fully supported by all web browsers.

Kelvin scale   A scale used to measure the color temperature of light.

Kelvin temperature   Also known as color temperature, the temperature at which a black body emits the same color as a particular light source.

LCD   Liquid crystal display. The type of display technology used in most digital camera monitors.

lossless compression   A process that reduces file size by eliminating only redundant data. Certain file formats, including TIFF, apply lossless compression. This type of compression does not affect image quality but doesn't shrink file size significantly.

lossy compression   A compression process that produces large reductions in image file size but at the expense of picture quality. The JPEG format applies this type of compression. When you store pictures on most digital cameras or save a JPEG file in a photo editor, you can control the amount of compression. The greater the amount of compression, the more picture data is dumped, and the greater the quality loss.

matrix metering   One of several types of exposure metering systems found in a camera; in this mode, the camera bases exposure on light throughout the entire frame. Also known as multizone metering and pattern metering.

megapixel   One million pixels; a term used to describe the resolution capabilities of a digital camera.

Memory Stick   The type of memory card used in Sony digital cameras and other Sony devices.

metadata   Extra information about camera capture settings that is stored along with the image file. *See also* EXIF metadata.

metering mode   Refers to the area of the frame that the camera considers when analyzing exposure. *See also* center-weighted metering, matrix metering, and spot metering.

moiré   A visual defect that occurs when the linear pattern of the chips in a digital camera's image sensor is out of alignment with a pattern in a fabric being photographed. Appears as wavy lines, color halos, or both.

multizone metering   *See* matrix metering.

native format   The proprietary file format used by a photo editing program (and other types of programs). For example, the PSD format in Adobe Photoshop Elements and Adobe Photoshop is a native format.

neutral density (ND) filter   A filter that reduces the amount of light that enters the camera lens, enabling the photographer to use a slower shutter speed or larger aperture in bright light.

nodal point   The optical center of a camera lens. When creating a panoramic image, the camera needs to rotate around the nodal point to produce correct perspective in a stitched photo.

noise   A digital-photo defect that looks like sprinkles of random color; often occurs in images taken at a high ISO setting.

optical zoom   A traditional zoom lens (as opposed to a digital zoom).

output resolution   A value established in a photo editor prior to printing; sets the number of pixels per linear inch (ppi). A good quality print typically requires a minimum output resolution of 200 ppi.

panorama   An image that contains several separate pictures that have been joined in a photo-stitching program to show a wider view than can be captured in a single frame.

pattern metering   *See* matrix metering.

PICT   An image file format used primarily to create system resources (help screens, screen savers, and the like) for a Macintosh computer.

pixel   Picture element. The colored squares that are used to create digital images; can be compared to the tiles in a mosaic.

plug-in   A software add-on that works in conjunction with a larger program; after installing a plug-in, you can access its features from inside the larger program.

PNG   Portable Network Graphics. An up-and-coming file format for web images; it's not yet suitable for most purposes because of limited browser support.

posterization   A color-blocking effect that appears when an image file has been reduced to too few colors.

ppi   Pixels per inch. The value used to indicate output resolution.

programmed autoexposure (AE)   Same as autoexposure; both shutter speed and aperture are set by the camera. *See also* aperture-priority autoexposure (AE), shutter-priority autoexposure (AE).

RAW   An image file format available on some high-resolution digital cameras; stores the picture file in its "raw" state—that is, without applying any of the image-processing that's normally done to improve the appearance of a picture. RAW files can't be opened directly in most photo editing programs.

reflector   A light-reflecting panel that's used to bounce light from one source in a second direction.

resampling   Adding or deleting pixels from a digital picture file; adding pixels is sometimes called upsampling, and eliminating pixels is called downsampling.

resolution   A term used to describe the capabilities of various imaging devices, including cameras, monitors, printers, and scanners.

RGB   The main color model for digital images; devices based on this model produce colors by mixing red, green, and blue light.

screen pixels   The pixels used by a computer monitor, television, or digital projector to display images and text.

screen resolution   The number of horizontal and vertical screen pixels; computer users can set their monitors to several different resolution settings (640×480, 800×600, and so on).

Secure Digital card   One type of memory card used in a digital camera.

shutter   A device behind the camera lens that opens and closes to allow light to strike the imaging sensor in a digital camera (or the negative in a film camera).

shutter-priority autoexposure (AE)   An autoexposure mode that gives the user control over the shutter speed; the camera selects the appropriate f-stop (aperture size) to produce a good exposure at the chosen shutter speed. *See also* aperture-priority autoexposure (AE), autoexposure (AE).

shutter speed   The length of time that the shutter remains open, usually measured in fractions of a seconds. Together with the aperture and ISO, determines image exposure.

slave flash   An accessory flash that fires automatically in response to the light from the main flash.

slow-sync flash   A special flash mode that allows longer shutter speeds than regular flash mode; at night, it makes backgrounds appear brighter.

SLR   A single-lens reflex camera; these models feature interchangeable lenses and other features not found on point-and-shoot cameras.

SmartMedia card   A type of camera memory card used in some digital cameras.

spot metering   A metering mode that bases exposure on the light at the center of the frame only.

TIFF   Tagged Image File Format. An image file format used primarily to store images destined for the printed page; can apply lossless compression, which doesn't degrade picture quality like the lossy compression applied by the JPEG format. Not suitable for web images and other screen purposes.

TTL   Through-the-lens. Used to describe viewfinders that show you exactly what the lens sees; also describes exposure metering mechanisms that measure light coming through the lens. Non-TTL viewfinders and metering mechanisms look out on the scene from a window offset from the lens.

TWAIN driver   Software that enables you to access your digital camera files or scanner from inside some image browsers and photo editors.

Unsharp Mask filter   A sharpening tool found in intermediate and advanced photo editors; sounds more complicated to use than it really is.

upsampling   Adding pixels to an existing digital image file. *See also* resampling, downsampling.

USB   Universal Serial Bus. Now the most common technology for connecting cameras and other devices to a computer.

VR   Virtual reality. Refers to immersive images that enable you to spin the display to see a subject from a variety of perspectives.

white balancing   A feature found in all digital cameras; compensates for the varying colors of light to ensure accurate color renditions.

xD-Picture Card   A type of memory card used in some digital cameras.

B

Online Resources for Digital Photographers

PRODUCTS	DESCRIPTION
PHOTOGRAPHY ACCESSORIES	
Bogen Photo (www.bogenphoto.com)	Tripods and other accessories
Cloud Dome (www.clouddome.com)	Domes for shooting reflective objects
Cokin (www.cokin.com)	Filters and close-up lenses
Delkin Devices (www.delkin.com)	Portable image storage, memory cards, card readers, and more
Hoodman (www.hoodmanusa.com)	LCD shades and cleaning cloths
Hoya (www.thkphoto.com)	Filters and other lens accessories
Ilford (www.ilford.com)	Artistic papers for photo printers
Kaidan (www.kaidan.com)	Panorama equipment
Kenko (www.thkphoto.com)	Filters and other lens accessories
Legion Paper (www.legionpaper.com)	Artistic papers for photo printers
Lowel (www.lowel.com)	Studio lighting and accessories
Luminos (www.luminos.com)	Specialty inks and papers for inkjet printers
Manfrotto(www.manfrotto.com)	Tripods and panoramic heads
Media Street (www.mediastreet.com)	Specialty inksets for inkjet printers
Metz (www.bogenphoto.com)	Flash products
Monaco Systems (www.monacosystems.com)	Coloromiters and other color-management tools
Peace River Studios (www.peaceriverstudios.com)	Panoramic tripod heads and tools
Photoflex (www.photoflex.com)	Reflectors and other lighting accessories
Pictorico (www.pictorico.com)	Artistic papers for photo printers
SanDisk (www.sandisk.com)	Memory cards, card readers, and more
SimpleTech (www.simpletech.com)	Portable image viewers, memory cards, card readers, and more
Smith-Victor (www.smithvictor.com)	Desktop lighting kits and more
SRElectronics (www.srelectronics.com)	Digi-Slave accessory flash units
Sunpak (www.sunpak.com)	Flash products
Tiffen (www.tiffen.com)	Filters and close-up lenses
Visual Departures (www.visualdepartures.com)	Reflectors and other lighting products
Wacom Technology (www.wacom.com)	Drawing tablets
Westcott (www.fjwestcott.com)	Reflectors, light tents, and other lighting supplies

PRODUCTS	DESCRIPTION
SOFTWARE	
ACD Systems (www.acdsystems.com)	ACDSee and other imaging software
Adobe Systems (www.adobe.com)	Photoshop Elements, Photoshop, Photoshop Album, and other imaging software
Apple (www.apple.com)	QuickTime VR viewer
Applied Science Fiction (www.asf.com)	Digital GEM and other image-correction software
Cerious Software (www.thumbsplus.com)	ThumbsPlus
ColorVision (www.colorvision.com)	Color management tools
Corel Corporation (www.corel.com)	Corel PHOTO-PAINT and other graphics programs
IseeMedia (www.iseemedia.com)	Photovista and other imaging programs
Jasc Software (www.jasc.com)	Paint Shop Pro
Minolta (www.minolta.com)	DiMAGE Messenger
Monaco Systems (www.monacosystems.com)	Monaco EZColor and other color-management tools
nik multimedia (www.nikmultimedia.com)	Color Efex Pro!, Dfine, and other plug-ins
Panorama Factory (www.panoramafactory.com)	Panorama Factory
Simple Star (www.simplestar.com)	PhotoShow and other imaging tools
Ulead Systems (www.ulead.com)	Ulead PhotoImpact, PhotoExplorer, and other imaging tools
MISCELLANEOUS SITES REFERENCED IN THIS BOOK	
Ofoto (www.ofoto.com)	Online photo sharing and printing
Shutterfly (www.shutterfly.com)	Online photo sharing and printing
Web Photo School (www.webphotoschool.com)	Online lessons in lighting techniques
Wilhelm Imaging (www.wilhelm-imaging.com)	Print-life studies and information

Additional Resources

To expand your technical knowledge and find more creative inspiration, also visit these web sites. You can find hardware and software reviews, how-to articles, forums in which you can chat with other photographers, and plain old creative inspiration.

WEB SITE	DESCRIPTION
www.dpreview.com	Hardware and software reviews and buying guides, plus discussion forums
www.imaging-resource.com	Some of the most detailed camera and equipment reviews you'll find anywhere, along with the latest digital photography news
www.edigitalphoto.com	The online edition of the magazine *eDigital Photo*
www.outdoorphotographer.com	The online edition of *Outdoor Photographer* (which has great information for *indoor* photographers as well)
www.pcphoto.com	The online version of *PCPhoto*, a magazine geared to digital-imaging novices
www.photographic.com	The online edition of *Peterson's Photographic*, a well-known film publication that now covers digital imaging as well
www.shutterbug.net	The online edition of *Shutterbug*, a popular publication that offers a balance of film and digital coverage

Index

INTERNATIONAL CONTACT INFORMATION

AUSTRALIA
McGraw-Hill Book Company Australia Pty. Ltd.
TEL +61-2-9900-1800
FAX +61-2-9878-8881
http://www.mcgraw-hill.com.au
books-it_sydney@mcgraw-hill.com

CANADA
McGraw-Hill Ryerson Ltd.
TEL +905-430-5000
FAX +905-430-5020
http://www.mcgraw-hill.ca

GREECE, MIDDLE EAST, & AFRICA (Excluding South Africa)
McGraw-Hill Hellas
TEL +30-210-6560-990
TEL +30-210-6560-993
TEL +30-210-6560-994
FAX +30-210-6545-525

MEXICO (Also serving Latin America)
McGraw-Hill Interamericana Editores S.A. de C.V.
TEL +525-117-1583
FAX +525-117-1589
http://www.mcgraw-hill.com.mx
fernando_castellanos@mcgraw-hill.com

SINGAPORE (Serving Asia)
McGraw-Hill Book Company
TEL +65-6863-1580
FAX +65-6862-3354
http://www.mcgraw-hill.com.sg
mghasia@mcgraw-hill.com

SOUTH AFRICA
McGraw-Hill South Africa
TEL +27-11-622-7512
FAX +27-11-622-9045
robyn_swanepoel@mcgraw-hill.com

SPAIN
McGraw-Hill/Interamericana de España, S.A.U.
TEL +34-91-180-3000
FAX +34-91-372-8513
http://www.mcgraw-hill.es
professional@mcgraw-hill.es

UNITED KINGDOM, NORTHERN, EASTERN, & CENTRAL EUROPE
McGraw-Hill Education Europe
TEL +44-1-628-502500
FAX +44-1-628-770224
http://www.mcgraw-hill.co.uk
computing_europe@mcgraw-hill.com

ALL OTHER INQUIRIES Contact:
McGraw-Hill/Osborne
TEL +1-510-420-7700
FAX +1-510-420-7703
http://www.osborne.com
omg_international@mcgraw-hill.com

Sound Off!

Visit us at **www.osborne.com/bookregistration** and let us know what you thought of this book. While you're online you'll have the opportunity to register for newsletters and special offers from McGraw-Hill/Osborne Media.

We want to hear from you!

Sneak Peek

Visit us today at **www.betabooks.com** and see what's coming from McGraw-Hill/Osborne Media tomorrow!

Based on the successful software paradigm, Bet@Books™ allows computing professionals to view partial and sometimes complete text versions of selected titles online. Bet@Books™ viewing is free, invites comments and feedback, and allows you to "test drive" books in progress on the subjects that interest you the most.